William D. Wilson

The Foundations of Religious Belief

the methods of natural theology vindicated against modern objections

William D. Wilson

The Foundations of Religious Belief
the methods of natural theology vindicated against modern objections

ISBN/EAN: 9783337262778

Printed in Europe, USA, Canada, Australia, Japan

Cover: Foto ©Lupo / pixelio.de

More available books at **www.hansebooks.com**

The Bishop Paddock Lectures, 1883

THE FOUNDATIONS

OF

RELIGIOUS BELIEF

*THE METHODS OF NATURAL THEOLOGY
VINDICATED AGAINST MODERN
OBJECTIONS*

BY

Rev. W. D. WILSON, D. D.

PRESBYTER IN THE DIOCESE OF CENTRAL NEW YORK, AND PROFESSOR IN
CORNELL UNIVERSITY

NEW YORK
D. APPLETON AND COMPANY
1, 3, AND 5 BOND STREET
1883

THE BISHOP PADDOCK LECTURES.

In the summer of the year 1880, GEORGE A. JARVIS of Brooklyn, N. Y., moved by his sense of the great good which might thereby accrue to the cause of CHRIST and to the Church, of which he was an ever grateful member, gave to the General Theological Seminary of the Protestant Episcopal Church certain securities exceeding in value eleven thousand dollars for the foundation and maintenance of a Lectureship in said Seminary.

Out of love to a former Pastor and enduring friend, the Rt. Rev. Benjamin Henry Paddock, D.D., Bishop of Massachusetts, he named his Foundation "THE BISHOP PADDOCK LECTURESHIP."

The deed of trust declares that:

"*The subjects* of the Lectures shall be such as appertain to the defence of the religion of JESUS CHRIST, as revealed in the *Holy Bible* and illustrated in the *Book of Common Prayer* against the varying errors of the day, whether materialistic, rationalistic, or professedly religious, and also to its defence and confirmation in respect of such central truths as the *Trinity*, the *Atonement*, *Justification* and the *Inspiration of the Word of God* and of such central facts as the *Church's Divine Order and Sacraments*, her historical *Reformation* and her rights and powers as a pure and National Church. *And* other subjects may be chosen if unanimously approved by the Board of Appointment as being both timely and also within the true intent of this Lectureship."

Under the appointment of the Board created by the Trust, viz., the Dean of the General Theological Seminary and the Bishops respectively of Massachusetts, Connecticut, and Long Island, the Rev. William D. Wilson, D.D., LL.D., L.H.D., Professor of Moral and Intellectual Philosophy, Cornell University, delivered the Lectures for the year 1883, contained in this volume.

PREFACE.

The request to deliver these Lectures took me entirely by surprise, and was not accompanied by any intimation of the subject on which it was expected that I would lecture, any farther than as the subject is prescribed in the Deed of Trust which creates the Lectureship.

In selecting my specific subject I was guided by a consideration of what my past experience and studies had, in my own judgment, best qualified me to undertake, rather than by any estimate I could have made of what is most needed just now, or what would be likely to produce the most immediate good results. *Non omnes omnia possumus.*

I was confirmed in the selection of the subject which, for these reasons, I had made, by the two following considerations:

1. There can be, in my estimation, no satisfactory or successful presentation of the Evidences of Christianity that does not assume the truths of Natural Theology and the legitimacy of the Methods by which they are obtained.

2. There is no objection that is urged, or that can be urged, against the doctrines of Natural Theology, that may not be and is not in fact urged with far greater force and appearance of reason against the doctrines of Christianity as taught by Revelation.

In selecting my topics for discussion I have endeavored to include in my list all those that are current in the popular thought of the day, or are seen in its literature and the predominant tone of conversation; and to trace them back, if not to their original source, yet at least to some name that has given them prestige and influence.

It will be observed that I have given to the subject of Evolution a large share of attention. This could hardly have been otherwise, since that is, in many respects, the great question of the age. It occupies, under one form or another, the largest part of the Second and the Sixth Lectures in this course. And I think that it will be seen that that theory, in any form in which the facts and reasoning from them justify us in holding it, only makes the argument for the existence and attributes of GOD stronger and more precise and explicit than it was before.

In the pursuit of my subject it has been my good fortune to find no occasion to controvert with any one of the authors from whose general views I dissent, any *fact* that either he or I can regard as of fundamental or controlling importance, or to assert any conclusion, as derived from these facts, which I have not been able to express in words selected from their own writings.

And yet I think that not even the most staunch advocate of Revelation and a Supernatural Religion will find any occasion to complain that I have not maintained all the ground he can ask for his cause so far as it is included in the domain of Natural Theology.

It is proper to add that in delivering the Lectures I omitted the Fourth, the last part of the Third and the first of the Fifth, as being so abstruse and tedious to those who are not metaphysically inclined, that I could not have heart to inflict that part of my discussion upon those whose duty it was to attend; and yet they form such an essential part of the line of argument, that I could not omit them entirely. The reader, if he chooses to do so, can omit these parts of the Lectures as he looks through the volume, now that it is published.

Perhaps I ought also to state that in consequence of the length of the Lectures, I was obliged to omit some parts and to condense other parts of the Lectures I delivered when I gave them before the students in the General Seminary.

W. D. W.

Ithaca, June, 1883.

CONTENTS.

LECTURE I.

THE SUBJECT STATED AND THE TWO METHODS DESCRIBED.

Introduction, Subject Stated	3
Reasons for Choosing it	6
I. The Objective Method	14
Paley's Illustration	18
II. The Subjective Method	20
The Law of Co-ordination	22
Plato's Theory of Ideas	33
Mediæval Philosophers	38
Descartes' *a priori* Argument	43
Modern Idealistic Theories	47

LECTURE II.

PHYSICAL OBJECTIONS; THEORIES OF EVOLUTION AND CAUSATION.

The Objections Stated	50
I. The Claims of Evolution	56
The Idea of Creation	62
1. Evolution implies a Supreme Being	63
2. The Nature of Matter makes a Personal Agent necessary	65
3. The beginning of Life implies something more than Matter	77
II. Theories of Causation	
1. The Equivalence of Causes and Effects	86
2. Causation implies a First Cause	92
3. Characteristics of a First Cause	100

LECTURE III.

METAPHYSICAL OBJECTIONS; THEORIES OF KNOWLEDGE.

The Objections to be Considered 107
I. Proof of the Reality of Mind.......................... 108
   1. Physiological Proof................................ 116
   2. Psychological Proof................................ 125
   3. What we learn of Mind from Consciousness 133
II. Limits to the Certainty of Knowledge.................. 137
   1. The Extent of Knowledge by Sensation 141
   2. The Relativity of Knowledge 144
   3. The Extent of Certainty............................ 152

LECTURE IV.

LOGICAL OBJECTIONS AND THEORIES OF REASONING.

The Influences of Training on Opinion 161
I. Logical Objections.................................... 167
   1. Objections to the Form of Reasoning................ 170
   2. Difficulties that arise from the Use of Words......... 172
II. Kant's Objections..................................... 186
   1. Bearing of his Theory of Perception................. 187
   2. His Limitation of Certainty......................... 188
   3. His Antinomies..................................... 190
   4. The General Result................................. 205

LECTURE V.

THE ATTRIBUTES AND PERSONALITY OF GOD.

I. The Influence of Language upon Thought............... 216
   Abstractions and Fictions............................ 218
   Three Classes of Realities........................... 238
   The Existence of God from this Point of View 249
II. Objections to the Personality of God.................... 255
   The Essence of Personality........................... 259
   God a Person.. 262
   All Conceptions of Him inadequate 264

LECTURE VI.

MIRACLES AND INSPIRATION.

Revelation Miraculous in its Nature 273
  I. The Essential Character of Miracles 275
    1. The Miracle of Creation or Beginning 282
    2. Miracle of the Beginning of Life 284
    3. Miracle of the Origin of Species 294
    4. Miracle at the Origin of Man 310
  II. Inspiration; its Nature 320
    1. Difficulty of Discriminating 325
    2. Time and Results as a Test 329

LECTURE VII.

PROVIDENCE AND MORAL GOVERNMENT.

Moral Government shown chiefly in Human History 334
  1. Examples from History 337
  2. The Objections of Pessimists 344
  3. Pain as a Means of Good 350
  4. Necessary Laws and Conditions 358
  5. Man's Relation to these Laws 365
  6. The Use made of Wicked Men 372
  7. Suffering as a Means of Holiness 376
  8. Christ and Christianity the Solution 381

LECTURE I.

THE SUBJECT STATED; REASONS FOR CHOOSING IT; THE TWO METHODS DESCRIBED.

HEB. II, 6.—*For he that cometh to God must believe that He is and that He is a rewarder of them that diligently seek Him.*

THE METHODS OF NATURAL THEOLOGY VINDICATED.

THE METHODS DESCRIBED.

Two avenues open out from the human self towards the ultimate and highest Being, Whom we acknowledge and worship as God. Both of these are ways of knowledge; and each of them may be pursued with the strictest conformity to scientific methods and with the most entire certainty in the results.

It is my purpose, in these Lectures, to point out and to vindicate, as best I can, these two methods, which, taken together, may be called the Methods of Natural Theology.

For my ability to do so, and for my fitness for the office and work to which I have been called, those who appointed me to this Lectureship must be held responsible; for the earnestness and fidelity with which I discharge the duty thus devolved upon me, I alone and by myself am responsible.

If we glance backward over the half century that is past we see great changes in the attitude of the world towards the Christian Religion. Then PALEY'S *Natural Theology* and BUTLER'S *Analogy* were in general use, and in the highest esteem. They were considered, each in its place and way, as presenting unanswerable arguments in favor of the propositions which they attempted to prove: the one, the existence of a God of infinite wisdom, power and goodness as manifested in Nature; and the other maintained that the Religion of Christ, as revealed in the Holy Scriptures, and taught in the Christian Church, is in harmony with human reason and the constitution and course of Nature.

Before the work of Paley, however, there had appeared the work of Dr. SAMUEL CLARKE, which had been delivered as the Boyle Lecture for 1704, on *The Being and Attributes of God*, differing from those of Paley and Butler, in that it proceeded from a different starting point and pursued a much more metaphysical method.

But all these books, and many others like them, have fallen into disrepute and neglect. And there seems to be a growing impression that this line of argumentation is worth but very little, if anything, towards laying a foundation for religious belief and culture.

Since these works were written new facts have been discovered and new theories adopted in science. And it is claimed that metaphysical principles which were then generally held, or allowed to pass unquestioned, are now no longer held by anybody; and these facts and principles, it is claimed, constituted the very foundation and basis of those arguments—and that, the foundation being removed, the superstructure must fall.

Now it is no part of my purpose to enter upon any warfare with modern science. I have no occasion to dispute its facts, or to disparage its importance. On the other hand, I think that there are but few persons who appreciate these facts and principles more highly than I do. Next to Religion, Science is the greatest benefactor of mankind. And if man has no soul, and is, as many contend, only a being of time—destined to perish with the brutes and like a brute—science is worth more to him than even Religion. And the preference can be given to Christianity, in my estimation, only because the soul can be saved by faith, through Christ, without Science or much knowledge of the affairs of this world.

It is, therefore, my purpose in these Lectures rather to show that whatever may have been taken, by the advance in modern science, from the foundation of those old arguments was but hay and stubble and sand, and that it has been replaced by something that is more substantial and enduring—as enduring as eternal truth itself; and that whatever new facts have been discovered in the physical sciences, and whatever new truths may have been reached in metaphysics, only tend to make the argument stronger, and to give to the conclusion more of point and precision as well as greater certainty.

I have spoken of the general subject of these Lectures as a statement and vindication of the Methods of Natural Theology. In this I assume that *Natural* Theology is the basis of a *Supernatural* Theology, and that what we can learn in this way of the character and attributes of God, constitutes a groundwork which we can accept, and on which we can erect, as a superstructure, the doctrines of the Revelation that has been communicated to us in a supernatural way by God Himself.

And I take up this subject the more gladly because, so far as I know, there is no objection, or ground of objection, to any doctrine of Natural Theology that may not be, and is not in fact, urged with as great if not with greater force against the doctrines of the Christian Religion. Whatever undermines the basis will in the end subvert the superstructure. If there are objections that are fatal to *Natural* Theology they will doubtless prove much more fatal to a reception of the teachings of Revelation. No one, as I believe, can be persuaded to accept Christianity as a Revelation from God, having authority over conscience and will, who has any serious doubts about any of the doctrines of Natural Theology.

There is a passage in the Epistle to the Hebrews that seems to me to inculcate this view of the general subject. I refer to those earnest and profound words which occur near the beginning of the eleventh chapter. Transposing their order a little, they read as follows: "For he that cometh to God must believe that He is, and that He is a rewarder of them that diligently seek Him. But without faith it is impossible to please Him."

This latter clause of the text needs no comment. Mere outward service cannot be acceptable to God, or in any way pleasing to Him; for we are abundantly assured that if there is any one thing that He hates above all others, it is hypocrisy and mere pretense of service when the heart is far from Him.

But does the Apostle mean to teach us also that, in order to accept a revelation as a supernatural religion, we must first, and as a prerequisite, believe in the existence of God and of His Moral Government? If so, then it must be, of course, on the basis of a natural theology—of some insight of that invisible power and godhead, which, as the Apostle says, is manifest in the phenomena of nature, or what, in another view, we may call an instinct implanted in our very nature, which must and will, from the very nature of the case, be developed into dogmas and dogmatic form by the operation of the mind in the years of thought and reflection.

Now, whether this is precisely what the Apostle intended to say in these words, I shall neither assume nor attempt to prove in this place. But I do most earnestly believe it myself, and shall assume it as one of the starting points in these Lectures.

To state my proposition otherwise and more briefly and distinctly, I believe there is in every human soul a natural insight of things divine; or, in the words of a Greek philosopher, ἡ κοινή τοῦ Θεοῦ νόησις,[1] and that this belief can be justified, elaborated and vindicated by most unanswerable arguments, drawn from the facts and phenomena of the external world and from the nature of mind and of knowledge itself.[2]

---

[1] Diog. Laert., B. X. c. I. § 122.

[2] Max Müller says, *Science of Language, Second Series*, p. 477, "It was one of the first articles in the primitive faith of mankind, that, in one sense or another, they had a father in heaven," for whom, "neither the language of the Vedic Rishis, nor that of any other poets or prophets had yet suggested a fitting name," p. 536.

In regard to Egypt, as a sample of the other civilized nations of antiquity, China, India, Mesopotomia, etc., I cite from Rawlinson, *The Religions of the Ancient World*. He says, p. 43, of the better

For the great mass of mankind, the uneducated and the unsophisticated—" the rank and file of humanity "—we appeal to this instinct, the feelings and the wants of men, and we show them how Christianity, in its doctrines and its discipline, in its helps and its hopes, meets their wants, satisfies their hearts, and gives them what nothing on earth, nothing else that comes within the range of their thoughts and conceptions, can give them, or even so much as confidently promise them.

But there are those who cannot be reached in this way; they will not be satisfied with this sort of appeal. Somehow or another doubts and questionings arise in their minds, and they are disposed to regard

---

minds, that they "understood clearly that the many gods of the popular mythology were mere names, *personified attributes* of the one true Deity, or parts of the nature which He had created, considered as informed and inspired by Him."

And on p. 43 he says, "The better educated Egyptian had a firmer grasp of the truths of natural religion. Below the popular mythology there lay concealed from general view, but open to the educated classes a theological system which was not far removed from pure natural theology."

It would be easy to show the same state of things with regard to the Religions of China, India, Persia, and in fact all the earlier nations which rose into existence as leaders of civilization in primeval times. And the question arises as both interesting and suggestive—was this the result of an early revelation, the lingering twilight of an earlier and brighter day—or was it the result of discoveries by the methods of Natural Theology? In either case, it adds interest and strength to our argument.

these instinctive wants and feelings as only a weakness of their nature, and to look upon the religion which would supply them as merely a delusion—a cunningly devised imposture which women and children may do well to accept, and which unscrupulous priestcraft may use for its own ends, but from which men of scientific attainments and those with a philosophical turn of mind had better keep themselves aloof.

The position and importance of these men, however, when considered from our point of view, cannot be estimated by their numbers merely. They claim to be the most intellectual men—men who are in advance of all others, in advance of their age; the men who ought to speak, who ought to be heard; the men with whom wisdom will die; or if it will not die *with* them, it has yet made *in* them an advance beyond which nothing but unimportant details by way of confirmation can be reasonably expected; the men who now hold what all men will in a few generations come to hold as the truth and the accepted views of all mankind.

The claim is indeed a pretentious one, and it is seductive as well. No one in this age likes to be thought deficient. However humble and ignorant he may be, he has a natural ambition to be thought, if not wise himself, yet at least capable of appreciating wisdom, even the highest wisdom he can anywhere get a glimpse of. Thousands will follow the leading of one self-confident man without the slightest appreciation of his fundamental principles, or any foresight of their consequences, if only he can succeed in raising a glamour of applause in his favor. And this is often much helped by the assumption of a confident manner, by a pomposity of style, or by an obscurity—a seductive obscurity—of diction that goes far to conceal whatever of real meaning, whether of truth or of falsehood, there may be in what is said. This result is often helped on also, and in many cases it is most effectually helped on, by some pandering to passions that ought to be kept in check, or by some promise of liberty there where what is called liberty can prove to be only licentiousness.

When, for example, Sir William Hamilton says, with all the confidence of assured truth, that "all knowledge is only relative," that " we know nothing of things themselves," and that " in any attempt to prove the existence of the Absolute " our " syllogism would collect in the conclusion what is not distributed in the premises," or when Kant says, " there are four pairs of antinomies on which all that we may claim or pretend to know depends, and yet that these antinomies involve irreconcilable contradictions," thousands and tens of thousands who have no adequate conception of what these profound philosophers really meant by these oracular declarations, and who for the most part do not care to know, and are perhaps rather glad, on the whole, that they do not know, take them as a declaration of release from all obligation to know or to believe in anything beyond the necessities and the pleasures of the passing hour. Or when some disciple of Darwin, out-Darwining Darwin himself, proclaims the theory of evolution as explaining all things here below, without the intervention or agency of God, or when Huxley declares in magisterial and defiant tones that this doctrine of evolution is as well established as the Copernican theory of the solar system,[1] multitudes who know but little or nothing of science, as they ought to know, take courage, and go on in the ways of irreligion and unbelief, in the ways of sin and transgression, that lead down to eternal death.

[1] I quote from memory from Huxley's Address in America in 1876, as reported at the time in the New York *Tribune*. He has greatly modified his expressions of confidence in the certainty of evolution, as well as in the adequacy of its solution of the problems of the universe since that time.

In his *Address before the Department of Anthropology* in Dublin, August, 1878, as published in Appleton's *Popular Science Monthly* for Oct., 1878, p. 674, he says in regard to this very question of evolution: "It is a difficult question, and one for which a complete answer may possibly be looked for in the next century. . . In what sense I cannot tell you. I have my own notion about it, but the question for the future is the attainment, by scientific processes and methods, of a solution of that question."

We must, I think, distinctly recognize and admit, moreover, the fact of "an evil heart of unbelief" in man, which prevails to some extent in all men in their natural condition, though it is more powerful in some than in others, and which inclines them to accept and urge anything that may be available, as an excuse or pretense for rejecting a religion that imposes restraints upon their liberty of choice and action, even when they know that without such restraint freedom would result, in the case of the great multitude, in what all men would regard as evil.

Were it not for this natural tendency in man to evade restraints which are acknowledged, indeed, to be wholesome, I doubt if many, or indeed any, of the objections I am about to consider would have ever been seriously felt or much urged against Religion, whether Natural or Revealed.

It seems to me, therefore, very appropriate, and the best service I can render, under the circumstances, to do what I can to dispel the illusion that these doctrines and theories of metaphysicians and physicists have created. And if the subject is, as I suppose it to be, one which, from its very nature, cannot be brought within the comprehension of all, or made attractive to the masses that gather "to hear and read some new thing," I think that I cannot be accused of having judged amiss, when we consider that I am addressing those who are to be themselves the teachers of the masses, and who will encounter in their life-work almost, if not quite, daily, one or more of those whose minds and hearts are affected by the forms of agnosticism and unbelief to which I have alluded.

As a preparation for a fuller and more detailed consideration of the objections that have been urged against these methods, I will devote the remainder of this Lecture to a statement and illustration of the two methods.

I. We begin our acquisition of knowledge by the observation of objects and events in the world around us. These objects are, for the most part, visible and tangible. Many of them also move about in space, and others are seen to change in their properties and appearance. To those that move about we ascribe life and spontaneity of action. For those that change, without moving, we soon find an antecedent or cause of the change, in something which is out of themselves, and which existed before the change began.

And thus, early in life and with but little reflection comparatively, "the idea of causation," as it is called, is fixed in our minds as one of its ruling and controlling principles.

Naturally enough we accept the axiom that every event or change has had a cause. And for the changes and motions of *living* beings we are content, for the time, to refer to the self or soul within, as a spontaneously acting agent. But for mere inorganic matter, whether in masses, molecules or atoms, we assume an inertia that compels us to look for something else, something out of themselves, as the cause of their motion and their changes.

This line of thought soon leads us back, naturally, and as I think necessarily, to a Beginning and a Beginner; a first Cause, Who was before all things, is over all things, and in all things, and is Himself uncaused. Further thought leads us to ascribe to this Being personality, with intelligence, moral purpose and spontaneity of action.

Recent investigations into the early history of mankind have shown that the first inhabitants of our earth were more impressible than we are. They were filled with what Max Müller has described as a kind of unconscious monotheism.[1] They saw God, or rather they felt him to be present in all things.[2]

---

[1] *Origin and Growth of Religion*, Lect. VI.

[2] The recent investigations into the earlier history of mankind and into their pre-historic notions and beliefs have been instructive in many ways. They bring to light facts that are inconsistent with, and totally antagonistic to, the modern theory of the evolution of man from the lower animals.

Thus RENOUF, *Religion of Ancient Egypt*, says, p. 130: "To take for granted that what the savages now are, perhaps after milleniums of degradation, all other people must have been, and that modes of

As yet they had no name for this unseen, everywhere present and ever active Agent. They said, as we do, "*it* dawns," "*it* rains," "*it* thunders." But soon came a time when they began to inquire who gives light in the morning? Who is it that sends the rain and speaks in the thunder? Who makes the plants to grow and clothes the earth with verdure?[1]

The pursuit of an answer to these questions, as Max Müller and others have shown, early led to the conversion of that simple unconscious monotheism—which was a pantheism as well—into a polytheism, with a consequent mythology and idol-worship.

These early inquiries and speculations it is likely, as Hearne has well suggested,[2] were set on foot quite as much, if not indeed much more, and much rather, especially among the Aryans, to satisfy a scientific instinct and want, than to gratify any religious propensity which those unsophisticated children of the

---

thought through which they are now passing have been passed through by others, is a most unscientific assumption, and you will seldom meet with it in any essay or book *without also finding proof that the writer did not know how to deal with historical evidence.*" He says of Egypt, p. 84: "Of a state of barbarism or case of patriarchal life anterior to the monumental period, there is no historical vestige."

[1] See especially MÜLLER'S "Comparative Mythology," *Chips from a German Workshop*, Vol. II. pp. 1-142.

[2] *The Aryan Household*, p. 286, etc. following.

earth's early day may have had. For no more then than now did men believe, or can they believe, in a mere materialism as explaining all the phenomena of the visible universe. In that day they invented a Zeus, a Ceres, and a Neptune, whom they regarded as the sufficient causes and explanation of the various phenomena of nature that were observed by them in the earth, the air and the seas, and those who were religiously inclined worshiped these fancies of the scientists as gods.

In these latter days we shall find, as I think, that men have been doing much the same thing, and find what they are disposed to regard as the adequate causes of the phenomena of nature, without, however, the same religious feelings towards them.

But to return: the Method of Natural Theology, which was at first scarcely more than an instinct, or, as I shall prefer to call it, an act of unconscious insight, has been carefully elaborated into a protracted argumentation in these latter days. Nor is the line of argument exclusively modern. Socrates[1] and Plato[2] urged it with great force in their day.

[1] XENOPHON, *Memorab.*, B. IV., c. iii. Here occurs that argument, so often used since, from the eye lashes, and the conformation of the eye brows, the one to protect the eye from dust and the other to protect it from the violence of blows.

[2] PLATO, *Repub.*, B. X., c. i., and *De Leg*. X. § 11. In this latter place he assumes as admitted that "the gods" know, see and

But within the last century the line of argument has been urged by such men as Paley, Chalmers, Whewell, and Lord Brougham, and in the Bridgewater Treatises, until all well educated persons are familiar with its general outline and character.

We may as well state this method of argument by the use of Paley's illustration. I see a watch before me. By means which I need not now discuss or describe, I know that it has not existed always. Whatever may be said of the particles of the metals used in it, brass and steel and gold, or of the molecules in the glass of the crystal, the watch, as the piece of mechanism that it is, has not existed always. Hence it had a maker, and its construction and movements show that the watchmaker was a being of intelligence and purpose, and possessed of power or physical force sufficient to work the raw materials of metal and mineral into their present shape.

Now note: I here claim that from the watch, considered as an effect, I infer the watchmaker, and I infer not only his existence, the mere fact *that he is*, but also much of his character, or of *what* he is. I see that he must have been an intelligent personal agent with something of bodily strength.

hear all things," and then proceeds to argue that from their essential activity they can no more be indifferent to or inactive in the affairs of men than from their knowledge they can be ignorant of them. His argument is a good answer to many of the objections we meet with in these days.

But what else do I know of him? Confining myself merely to the relation of cause and effect, but little else; perhaps nothing else. But on inquiry I should find, most likely, that there were several men engaged in the work of making the watch. I might also, if that were important to my purpose, learn much more about them—find their names and ascertain much that is interesting of their personal appearance and of their history.

By the method of reasoning from effect to cause, however, I could neither ascertain nor find grounds to believe much in answer to such inquiries. I could not, or at least I need not, know that there was more than one such being. But what is more to our purpose, I should not know, and I could not know, by this process, that he was not himself eternal, or that he had had a parentage and a line of ancestry reaching far back in the line of cause and effect into the darkness of the irrecoverable past.

But availing myself of my general knowledge on the subject I *assume* that this man had, like all the other men that I have ever known, ancestors reaching back in the line of genealogy to the first human pair; and thus I encounter the question of their origin and its Cause.

Or, starting from any other objects my eyes can see, or my hand can touch, I might pass along a line of objects in the same method of reasoning from effects to their causes until I should come to the same result. *Omnia exeunt in Deum.* Everywhere do we find Him as the First Cause, and the only adequate explanation of the existence of the things we see or know around us.

It would be most natural to proceed at once from this point to consider the objections to this method. They fall under two forms of objection when considered in reference to their surface appearance, the theory of Evolution and some recent doctrines concerning Causation. But I have decided rather to go on and state and illustrate the other the subjective or the *a priori* method, before taking up the consideration of those objections; and this, because the two methods are so connected that many of the objections to the one are damaging if not fatal to the other as well, unless they can be successfully answered.

II. All reflecting persons begin at an early day in their lives to look within themselves and to see there thoughts and feelings that come and go in a mysterious manner; and they naturally think that where there is thought there must be a thinker. *Cogito ergo sum* is but a natural expression of a natural instinct.

This may indeed be but a step in the matter of cause and effect. But there is another phenomenon in our consciousness that brings this idea, or this law, into a greater prominence, and gives to it its position as the corner-stone and first principle of all knowledge of everything and anything besides mere thought itself.

We see the motions of our limbs, our hands and our feet, and we are conscious of the effort we make to move them; that is, we are conscious of *ourselves as causes* of their motions. This consciousness becomes more conspicuous when we have occasion to move something that is heavy, or which, for any cause, resists our effort. We thus learn that there is something that is not ourselves in the world around us which is also an active and an efficient cause.

We soon come to the conclusion that whatever is recognized or in any way known as *an effect*, must have had a cause, the existence and reality of which is known in and by the very act by which we know the immediate object of our knowledge to be an effect.

But cause and effect are in a series. Before the effect there must have been the cause; and this, if not the First Cause, must have been an effect also, and so have had a cause; and so on, in a retrogression, until we come to a First Cause, which *as* the First Cause must be the Cause of all things, and so—in the only sense in which we can understand or predicate the word—the Creator of all things.

Another line of reflection and argumentation, starting still from within and adhering to the interior method, leads to the same result.

We soon find that all knowledge is by means of co-ordination. There must be a co-ordination of two objects in all possible acts of cognition that take place in time and are performed by a finite and imperfect being.

In the case of the blind man, all persons are familiar with the fact that he has no idea of light, or of the colors that we discriminate in ordinary daylight. But on a little reflection we find that it is just as certain that he has no idea of darkness either, and can attach no more meaning to that word, although he is immersed in the most profound darkness all the while, than he can to the words light, red, blue or white. But open his eyes and enable him to see, and he very soon comes to understand the meaning of both words, darkness and light, and all the varied terms that denote the colors of objects that are seen in the light. But until this experience, and without it, he had no idea of either of the co-ordinates, light and darkness, nor yet of any of the subordinates of either; or of the different colors which objects seen in the light appear to have.

Much the same may be said of the deaf man, with regard to the two co-ordinates silence and sound, and to the co-ordination of the one—silence, with any of the subordinates of the other, as a loud sound, a shrill sound, a whisper, a murmur, a strain of music or a peal of bells.

Now this law and this fact of co-ordination runs through all known human knowledge, and applies to, and controls, every act of cognition that takes place in time. It applies, therefore, to all the words and terms that we may use in any language with which to express our thoughts and beliefs. Hence, all things that are known or thought of go in pairs; the one implies the other, so that without both, or the thought of both, we could have no idea or knowledge of either.

It is said that no savage tribe has ever been found with a name for their social condition—savagery. But people who have become civilized have a name for both conditions—civilization and savagery.

Thus, by this law of co-ordination, the cognition or thought of any thing as an effect implies the thought or cognition of something as cause; and so the very idea of cause implies an effect, just as the word and idea of child implies that of parent. And the two are co-ordinates as objects of cognition and of thought. We might know a human being, indeed, without knowing that it was either parent or child. But we could not know it to be either the one or the other without knowing that there are now existing, or have been existing at some time in the past, the two; and one of them as certainly as the other.

The *a priori* demonstration of this law is very abstruse and difficult of comprehension, although, as I think, it is irrefragable and overwhelmingly conclusive. But I shall not attempt to present it here. I have aimed rather to state the law and to illustrate it with such examples as will make it easily intelligible.

After having expressed myself so confidently with regard to the universality and the certainty of this law, it is but fair that I should give notice that there are certain cautions to be observed in its application to words that may have been used, which, however, I have not time to discuss in this place. One of these only will I mention. In order to be a basis of proof of the existence of anything the two co-ordinates must have some property that is not common to both, otherwise one of them may be merely another name for the same thing or for some fiction, like that of a centaur, for example, which has no property that is not found in some real object, and hence the idea may be a pure creation of fancy.

Now let us apply this law to a few of the questions that are before us.

In every act of perception there are the two, the self that perceives and the object perceived. Whether I see this paper, or hear the voice of a friend, both the paper and the friend must exist, as realities, as truly as myself, or no such act of perception could take place. Hence the co-ordinates of self on the one hand, and the objects in the outward world, the not-me of the philosophers, on the other.

So again I am conscious of myself as acting *spontaneously*, or, as we often say for brevity's sake, I am conscious of spontaneity. If this is so, there must be something—and we must have had knowledge of it somewhere and somehow—that is not spontaneous, a something that acts under the law of inertia which is the co-ordinate of spontaneity; and this we hold to be the case with all the mere material objects in the world of inorganic matter.

This fact is important in its bearing on the question of free-will, so often discussed among philosophers, and so important in its bearing on many of the subordinate points of Natural Theology. There must be freedom and free-will somewhere or there would be no thought or conception of it, and no question about it in the minds of men; and no name or word for it in any of the languages that are understood or spoken by any of the inhabitants of the earth.

I cite as a further illustration of this law of co-ordination, Herbert Spencer's criticism of the argument which Sir William Hamilton and Dean Mansel had elaborated and urged to show that, on purely logical and metaphysical grounds, we have, and can have, no proof of the existence and attributes of God.

Sir William Hamilton had maintained that all our knowledge is "relative"; that we know nothing of things themselves, or " in themselves," as he prefers to express it, and that our idea of God, whether we regard Him as "the Absolute," "the Infinite," or "the Unconditioned," is only "negative," and of such a nature as neither to imply any proof of His existence or afford any knowledge of His attributes. But Spencer replies and insists, with his peculiar clearness of expression and force of reasoning, that the very existence of "the finite" implies the existence of "the Infinite"; the very existence of any thing "limited" and "conditioned" implies the reality of something that is "unconditioned" and "absolute." He admits, indeed, that this Something may not be, and in fact is not, an object of *immediate* knowledge, whether by consciousness or sense-perception. But he insists upon its existence, and its reality, as implied in the very nature and laws of thought.

Spencer recognizes the fundamental distinction of all things into two classes—*phenomena* which *appear* to and are cognizable by the senses and *noumena*, denoting by this latter word such things as are known to us only by insight and a process of reasoning, apprehended, as Plato had said, by reason and insight, but not by sight.

This distinction between phenomena and noumenia—things seen and things unseen—was sharply drawn by Plato. He speaks of things to which we are led by the insight of reason, and not by the seeing of the eyes, νοήσειν, ἀλλ' οὐκ ὄμμασιν.[1]

At a later date St. Paul recognizes the distinction and gives to it the sanction and weight of his great authority when he says,[2] speaking of God, that "the invisible things of Him, the ἀόρατα, things which the eyes of the body cannot see, are nevertheless νοούμενα, "noumena, made apparent, that is phenomenal, by the things that are seen by the bodily eyes, even His eternal power and godhead."

But Spencer is very emphatic; and although his language contains words and expressions that I do not altogether like, and should not use, yet I cannot

[1] PLATO, *Repub.*, B. VII, c. x., xi., 529 B. And a little further on he indicates the same contrast in still other words, speaking of things as ἃ δὴ λόγῳ καὶ διανοίᾳ ληπτά ὄψει δ' οὔ, received or accepted by reason and insight but not by the sight of the eyes.
[2] Rom. I., 20.

forbear quoting it. After a long review and criticism of Sir William's doctrine, and the fuller exposition of it given by Dean Mansel in his *Limits of Religious Thought*, he proceeds to say:[1] "Observe in the first place, that any one of the arguments by which the relativity of our knowledge is demonstrated distinctly postulates the positive existence of something beyond the relative. To say that we cannot know the Absolute [God] is by implication to affirm that there *is* an Absolute [God]. In the very denial of our power to learn *what* the Absolute [God] is, there lies hidden the assumption *that* it [He] is; and the making of this assumption proves that the Absolute [God] has been present to the mind, not as a nothing, but as a something. Similarly, with every step in the reasoning by which this doctrine is upheld. The Noumenon, everywhere named as the antithesis [co-ordinate as I would call it] of the Phenomenon, is throughout necessarily thought of as an actuality. It is rigorously impossible to conceive that our knowledge is a knowledge of Appearances only, without, at the same time, conceiving a Reality of which they are appearances [or manifestations] . . . Strike out from the argument the terms Unconditioned, Infinite, Absolute, with their equivalents, and in place of them write nega-

[1] *First Principles*, Pt. I., § 26.

tion of conceivability or absence of the conditions under which consciousness [cognition] is possible, and you find that the argument becomes nonsense. Truly to realize in thought any one of the propositions of which the argument consists, the Unconditioned [God] must be represented as positive and not negative. How, then, can it be a legitimate conclusion from the argument that our consciousness [cognition] of it is negative? An argument, the very construction of which assigns to a certain term a certain meaning, but which ends in showing that this term has no such meaning, is simply an elaborate suicide. Clearly, then, the very demonstration that a *definite* consciousness [cognition] of the Absolute [God] is impossible to us, unavoidably presupposes an *indefinite* consciousness [cognition] of it."

This is strong, and it seems to me unanswerable. I have taken the liberty to bracket in, in several places, words which will explain his meaning in my own terms. In this I do his thought no injustice.

If Spencer intended to use the word "phenomena" in the strict Kantian sense, the word "noumena" must be understood to include all substantial realities of whatever kind—everything, in fact, except the thoughts which we have of the things. This, however, is doubtful. But, in any view, his language must be understood to include the existence of God; and his argument is just or conclusive, and as much to my present purpose as though he had had no other object in mind. But be this as it may, the language constantly used by Hamilton and Mansel leave no room to doubt that they did intend to denote the Supreme Being, the Christian's God, by the words they used in the argument to which Spencer replies.

This, however, is not the only way, nor the only instance in which Spencer has recognized and acknowledged the existence of God as a First and Universal Cause. He says,[1] "We are obliged to regard every phenomena as a manifestation of some Power by which we are acted upon; phenomena being, so far as we can ascertain, unlimited in their diffusion, we are obliged to regard this Power as omnipresent." Again,[2] "He [the philosopher] like any other man may properly consider himself as one of the myriad agencies through whom the Unknown cause acts."

A more distinct recognition and admission of a First Cause, now and ever, everywhere and universally acting, not only in the phenomena of nature, but in the thoughts and feelings of our own minds, could hardly be made.

---

[1] *First Principles*, Pt. I., § 27, p. 99.
[2] *First Principles*, Pt. I., § 34, p. 123.

This, however, is not the first or only instance in which Spencer, under the guidance of his clear insight and sound logic, marches up squarely to, and sees a truth face to face, acknowledges it, and then turns away, and speaks and acts as though he had never seen it. Nay, he even virtually denies that he has seen it, by consigning it and its object to the region of the Unknown and Unknowable.

But surely that, or He, of whom so much can be said is not unknowable nor altogether "unknown." It would seem rather that, though incomprehensible, He is about the best known of all things.[1]

It is worthy of note, it seems to me, as a piece of grim irony, this attempt of Spencer to refute such men as Hamilton and Mansel, in a matter of this kind. They were both Christian believers and earnest Christian men. He is professedly an agnostic, and has admitted that agnosticism is practically atheism.[2] "The knowledge that is within us is the only knowledge that can be of service to us," are his words. And yet we have the strange spectacle of Spencer, the confessed agnostic, trying to convince

---

[1] If Spencer would only change his phraseology and substitute for "unknowable" the good honest English word "incomprehensible," we could readily agree with him, and he would moreover express much more adequately what is really the legitimate conclusion from his premises.

[2] § 25, p. 86.

these professing Christians, on purely philosophical grounds, that God is not an abstraction or a mere negation, but is rather a most positive Reality, a reality without which nothing else can be real, and declaring that all their arguments are absurd and "elaborately suicidal."

And Kant has argued in one of his world-famous *Antinomies*, of which I shall have occasion to say something more in a subsequent Lecture, that the existence of God is so involved in the very laws and conditions of thought that it is about the only thing that we cannot deny without involving ourselves in a contradiction of terms. And yet neither of these philosophers—neither Kant nor Spencer—accepted as a part of their philosophy the doctrine which they had so earnestly asserted, and had defended with so much ingenuity.

I have already said that this law of co-ordination requires some caution in its application. It applies only to the origination of what we may call simple or elementary ideas. Thus I regard the color redness as such an elementary property. Hence I suppose that one who, although he had seen objects of any other color, had seen nothing that is red, could not imagine, or even so much as dream of, one that is red. But suppose he had seen some objects that are red and others that are blue, I presume he could originate the idea of purple without actual cognition of any purple object.

This law applies only to the *origination* of knowledge—the original act of cognition, and hence it can have no application to the Divine Mind, as there was no beginning to His knowledge.

But let us return to the consideration of the *a priori* method. It is about as old as the other, although it has not always been presented in quite the same form. It is implied and used by Plato. It was made necessary, in fact, by his theory of ideas as the elementary parts of knowledge. As these ideas do not originate in the human mind, but are retained as the result of a past experience in some former state of existence, they imply both the pre-existence and the future immortality of the soul.

His doctrine of ideas implied their eternal existence; and also, and of necessity, the eternal existence of the Logos, God Himself, as the ground of their possibility, while they were the patterns or archetypes by which He created all things out of the matter, which, without Him and the ideas, had no properties and no specific forms or modes of existence.

As the Platonic theories and speculations so extensively underlie and give explanation to most or all the arguments in the subjective method, I will go a little more fully into a statement of them.

The first passage I shall cite is found at the beginning of the tenth Book of the *Republic*. Plato is there giving a very elementary explanation of what he means by *ideas*. He says of the artisan who is making household furniture, that in order to make tables, bedsteads, etc., he must have in his mind an idea, a pattern, or paradigm of the bed or table to guide him in his works; otherwise, though he may hew and hack and waste lumber, he will not make any one definite or useful thing. He then proceeds to do what Plato never loses an opportunity for doing. He alludes to the creation, and says that in the same way as the human cabinet maker must have an idea of the table, etc., in his mind before he does his work, and while he is doing it, so the great Artificer and Creator of the Universe must have had in His mind ideas or patterns of all the things that are in it before he made this universe.

The next passage I shall cite is from the *Meno*. Plato is here trying to prove that ideas are innate and not acquired from observations and experience. He—or rather Socrates—calls a boy before him and asks him a question with regard to the area of a rectangle. The boy at first answers wrong. Socrates proceeds to ask question after question until he gets the right answer. He then turns to his companions and says to them, "You see I have *told* him nothing and yet he answers right now; the idea was in his mind and all I had to do was to draw it out."

Then follow some remarks with regard to "education." It consists as Plato teaches in *drawing out*—not the mind as we say—but in drawing out the *ideas* which are already there—innate in the mind.

He then goes on to teach that all ideas are in the Divine mind, constitute its very essence, were always there and were communicated to us—*put into our minds*—in some pre-existing state of being, and at the time of our birth we forgot them; that what we call education should rather be regarded as reminiscence, recollection, ἀνάμνησις. And in the *Phædo*, Plato used the same line of argument to prove the future life and the immortality of the soul.

In the *Timæus*, chapters xxvii and following, we have an account of the creation. He assumes that there is a certain pre-existing matter, τὸ ὄν for which Aristotle introduced the word ὕλη or matter, ὕλη ὑποκειμένη, underlying matter, and which came at a later day, especially by the Stoics, to be called ὕλη ἄποιος, or material substance without properties or specific kinds or character.

Now in this we must carefully notice the fact that Plato's theory of ideas makes them to be *things in the mind*. They are not mere *states of the mind*, as warmth is a state of the body, but they are *things in the mind*, as the heart and lungs are in the body, or the blood is in the veins. These ideas Plato regarded as the proper object of study in order that we may obtain "true knowledge"—ἐπιστήμη—or general principles and absolute truths, as distinct from the mere first impressions—δόξα—as he calls them, which the mere unreflecting mind gets from observation of external things.

But in his discussion of the relation of these "ideas" to creation, Plato has two points to be considered. The first is that which I have already alluded to, namely, that they were the patterns, ideals, or paradigms after which, or in accordance with which, the Creator formed all the things that are made.

The other point is more obscure. In the *Parmenides*,[1] and again in the *Cratylus*,[2] and in the *Timæus*,[3] as well as other places, Plato discusses the relation of these ideas to external things and to the acts of creation, whereby the primeval, formless matter came to be, by the Divine agency, what we see it to be in the material objects around us.

[1] § 10. [2] § 119. [3] §§ 25, 26.

In these discussions Plato assumes, as before, that *ideas are things*. If we regard them as *only in the mind*, they are ideas, and ideas only. But if we consider them as external to the mind, they are *the properties of the objects* which we see around us in nature. Thus "whiteness" considered as in the mind is only an idea; considered as an objective reality, it is a property of the objects around us that we call white, the paper, the snow, and whatever else appears to us to be white. So, too, take the word humanity: as a thought *within us*, it is an idea; as a property without, it is a characteristic of man—a property that is common to all men. And Plato explains the process of creation in the passages above cited, and speaks of it as *imparting*,[1] as the actual transference of, these ideas of the Divine mind to mere substantial matter, thus making of it the various objects and the different kinds of matter in the universe. He imparted the idea of whiteness to some, and they became white; hardness to others, and they became hard; the properties of iron to some, and it became iron; and so of all the other kinds of matter. He gave animality to some, and

---

[1] This relation or transference of ideas is denoted by such words as μεταλαμβάνειν, μετέχειν, μέθεξις, παρουσία κοινωνία, etc. I am indebted to a Note in ZELLER's *Hist. Greek Phil.*, vol. Plato, p. 335, for this list of words.

they became animals; humanity to others, and they became human beings, men and women.

And so, too, among the Philosophers of the Middle Ages. Whenever any one of them had occasion to imply or expressly state any of the grounds of believing in the existence of God as a doctrine of Natural Theology, they pursued a line of argument similar to the one we are now considering. I have space and time to mention only a few.

Thus John Scott Erigena, born in the beginning of the 9th century, and died 877 A. D. He insists very strenuously that the very name or idea of God implies his existence. In his view God can be no mere *phenomenon*, not a thing or being that can be seen by the bodily organs. He is nevertheless really *noumenon*, seen by the insight of reason, and is "manifest" everywhere and in all things; seen, as Plato had said, νοήσειν, ἀλλ' οὐκ ὄμμασιν, by the insight of reason and not by the bodily eyes, so that all *phenomena* or objects are but the manifestation of some *noumenal* Power whose presence is seen throughout creation.

Plato's theory of ideas was, with him, the foundation of the argument. In that view God and ideas alone have essential or substantial existence. God is the First Cause of all things, and they are "primordial causes" [*causæ primordiales*] in Him. God is in His essence incognizable, both for men and for angels. Nevertheless His being and attributes are seen and manifest in visible things. They are His manifestation. His wisdom is seen in their order, and His life in their motion and change. All predicates may be affirmed of Him which have not in their nature an opposite such as to imply limitation, and so, imperfection. Hence God may be called truth, goodness, light, justice, and many other things, figuratively, or symbolically. But strictly speaking and literally He can be called Being, *essentia*, ουσία, alone. Hence in the view of Erigena, the nature of God is, in fact, superessential, ὑπερούσια, above the ten categories of Aristotle and cannot be expressed or represented in either of them.

God created ideas. They were first in the order of creation. And hence they were called primordial causes, or in the terms of Plato paradigms and patterns. These ideas make up the Divine Wisdom. When imparted to matter and made manifest, that is, visible and tangible, they become and constitute the objects which make up the external or material world.

Anselm, Archbishop of Canterbury and a great scholar, was born about two centuries after Erigena, A. D. 1033. He seems to have taken a most comprehensive view of things. His fundamental axiom that all knowledge exists on faith, *credo ut intelligam*, has a broader application than is generally conceded to it. By faith in our senses we begin to know and understand the phenomena of the external world. In like manner by faith in the teachings of the Church, we believe the Creed, and then proceed to consider and understand the articles of the Christian Faith. But, as in the former case, no one feels at liberty or thinks it wise to deny the reality of the external world around us, because he cannot understand and comprehend all its mysteries; so, on the other hand, no one may reject the Christian Faith because he finds many things in its facts and doctrines that are beyond his comprehension, *non a fide recedere si intelligere non valet.*

Anselm thought the observation of external phenomena naturally turned the thoughts in upon themselves, and thus, in his view, we find the thought or idea of a Supreme Being. He then proceeds, by way of analysis, to argue that the very idea of this Being in our minds implies His reality and existence somewhere, out of our minds. "One is convinced, therefore," says he, "that there must be somewhere, either in the mind or out of it, a Being than Whom there can be no greater, because when he hears these words he understands their meaning, and whatever is understood is in the mind." But certainly that Being than Whom there can be no greater, cannot exist in the mind *alone* (*in intellectu solo*). It may add a little to the right comprehension and the rhetorical effect of this argument to consider that St. Anselm is speaking with reference to "the fool" (*insipiens*) whom David had represented as saying, "in his heart, there is no God."

St. Aquinas, born A. D. 1225, about two hundred years after Anselm, and about four hundred after Scott Erigena, was perhaps the greatest man in all the Middle Ages, taking into account both theological attainment and philosophical acumen. The discussions of the preceding centuries between the Realists and the Nominalists had had their effect on him. He yielded certain points which may be regarded as in some sense concessions to the Nominalists, and he came in consequence much more nearly to a common sense view of things than the earlier Realists had done. He reversed the order of Anselm, and held that knowledge is in fact the basis of faith. He called the beginning of knowledge the *præambula fidei*, the morning walks of faith. We must know something, in his opinion, before we can begin to exercise faith.

I think, however, that in this he meant merely to recognize the obvious fact that we begin to exercise our minds by the observation of the objects in the external world by sense-perception, before we begin to reflect much on their origin and cause, or on the existence of God. In doing this we have faith in our faculties, and in our theological speculations we need do only the same thing.

However, this is not very important for our present purpose. St. Thomas fully recognized and appreciated the external or synthetic method. He believed that from the first step in knowledge, which consists in the act of perceiving objects individually and one by one, and seeing the relation of cause and effect here and there in separate instances, we naturally, and by a sort of unreasoning instinct, proceed by generalization and synthesis, until we reach the idea of a First Cause and a *summum genus*, which includes all being; or, as I should prefer to say, in deference to modern usages, a genus which includes and in some way comprehends all the individual objects that exist, or can exist anywhere.

Thus St. Thomas held that the existence of God cannot be regarded as a self-evident truth, although it is a truth which may be proved; and the grounds of this demonstration are to be sought in what is more and better known, and very much in accordance with the *a posteriori* methods of more recent times.

This mode of proof consists, in his estimation, of two elements. (1) Assuming, as Aristotle had done, the inertia of all material objects considered as mere matter, there must be something that is not inert, a first Mover, whose existence is implied in all motion. And (2) St. Thomas held that in any recession along the line of effect and cause we must come at last to a First Cause, before Whom there was no other. But when he had arrived, by his exterior or synthetic method, at the idea of God, he adopts the interior and analytic method of developing the idea, with as much confidence, and he develops it with as much energy and clearness, as any of the philosophers we know of, and as confidently, too, as though he knew of no other method.

I cannot do justice to this part of my subject although I have already lingered long upon it, without mentioning one more great name—a name which is, in some respects, better worth mention than any we have had before us. I mean Renè Descartes.

Descartes was born in A. D. 1596. Inferior to no one of his predecessors in acuteness of penetration, or in logical precision of expression, he surpassed them all in the comprehensive grasp of his subject, and he had the advantage of them all by the three and a half centuries of controversy upon this and kindred subjects, that had passed away since the time of St. Thomas.

He considered all knowledge, all thought in fact, as made up of primary and elementary parts, just as the visible universe is made up of the individual objects which we see and feel, suns and stars, mountains and streams, rocks and trees, plants and animals, from the largest cosmic mass to the smallest grain of sand or molecule of water. These parts he called ideas; and taken together, they make up the sum total of our knowledge. They are our thoughts of objects—all objects, whether seen or unseen, real or imaginary.

These ideas he referred to three classes: (1) Innate, *nées avec moi*; (2) Adventitious, *étrangeres et venir de dehors;* (3) Factitious, *faites et inventées par moi même.*[1]

The "adventitious" ideas he supposed to be made within the mind, either by the mind itself, or by external objects acting through the organs of sense; and hence they represent real but material objects.

The "factitious" ideas are, in his estimation, pure creations of fancy; they may or they may not represent objects that exist in reality.

He considered the innate ideas as the result of the action of God within the mind. Hence they were a sort of revelation, or inspiration, and the best proof he could have of the existence of God.

---

[1] *Meditation*, III., Cousin's edition, vol. i., p. 268.

Factitious ideas are of necessity complex ideas, and can be made up of only such simple ideas as are found in one or the other of the other two classes, and they must be either innate or adventitious ideas. In the one case they represent eternal realities; in the other the properties of material objects; although the combination may be entirely arbitrary and represent no really existing thing anywhere, as a centaur, and hippogriff, and the thousand and one monsters of heathen mythology, or Christian superstition.

Now among these "innate ideas," as he regards them and calls them, Descartes finds the idea of God, Who appears in this connection as the Perfect and the Infinite one.

The points of the argument in Descartes' argumentation may be stated as three in number.

1st. The idea of God is a perfect idea, or the idea of perfection; and he does not appear to make any distinction between a perfect idea and the idea of perfection. But, as he argues, I am imperfect, hence I cannot have originated the idea of God, Who is, from the necessities of His nature, a perfect Being.

2d. The very idea of perfection is seen, on analysis, to imply the existence and reality of that which is perfect; as without existence or being the idea would lack at least one element of perfection or completeness. What is not and does not exist, cannot be perfect, since an object can be perfect only in the mode of its existence.

3d. In the third place, Descartes presupposes and applies the doctrine of co-ordination, used with so much force, as we have seen, by Herbert Spencer in his answer to Hamilton and Mansel.

In this brief historic review it is impossible to do so much as name the many men who have rendered admirable service in this line of argument. Before coming, in conclusion, to one or two that are now living, I must not omit to mention at least the name of one more honored man—that of Dr. Samuel Clarke. His Boyle Lecture on *the Being and Attributes of God* mark an era in this controversy. Contemporary with Berkeley and Butler, his work was in an important sense a preliminary to Butler's *Analogy*, and a correction to Berkeley's excessive idealism—an idealism which amounted well nigh to a form of pantheism. He held, as Descartes had done, that the Perfect Being must be a Reality, since existence is more and better, for anything that is good, than non-existence. Without His existence we must believe in a series either without beginning, which is absurd, or without anything to begin it, which also would be absurd. It would also suppose finite things without anything infinite; dependent things without anything to depend upon; or compel us to believe in an infinite space and time without anything to occupy them—any objects existing in space, or any events that had occurred in time. And he held, as we do, that the attributes of this Being, aside from His necessary and eternal existence, must be inferred from His works.

The theories of sense-perception, introduced by Malebranche, Berkeley, and Fichte, have prepared the way for another modification of this internal or subjective method. I have not seen this line of argumentation presented anywhere with more clearness, force of reasoning, and ingenuity of statement and illustration, than in the recent work on *Natural Theology*, by Dr. Bascom,[1] President of the University of Wisconsin. And I quote him the more gladly because I shall have occasion very soon to cite him for another purpose, and in regard to a matter in which I shall have occasion to dissent from his view and criticise his admission.

In this view, mind is essentially the creator of matter; and matter and material things can hardly, if at all, be said to have any existence, substantial or phenomenal, except while the creative act continues. With Berkeley it was a favorite and a funda-

---

[1] BASCOM'S *Natural Theology*, Chap. iii., § 7 and following.

mental saying, with regard to material things, *esse est percipi*, to be is to be perceived.

In an extreme presentation of this theory, it is held that each human mind, for itself, creates the material objects which it supposes it sees in the world around it. But, in a more moderate form, it holds that this individual energy is insufficient to account for the phenomena which are observed by so many millions of beings, and under such endlessly varied conditions and circumstances. Hence it is held that there must be an eternal Mind, everywhere present, and everywhere active, Whose activity is essentially creative. It is represented to be, in some most important particulars, analogous to the activity of our own minds in producing—creating—our thoughts; they are while it acts, and they cease to be with the cessation of its activity.

One argument for this view is derived from the nature of matter, and the impossibility of supposing it to have any independent substantial existence.

Another argument, and one that is presented with great force and ingenuity by President Bascom, is derived from the mind's control over the body and material things. They are inert, but we can move and control them pretty much at will. This influence rises to its highest manifestation in those cases where we become insensible to pain even, in consequence of the intense occupation and absorption of the mind with matters of its own. In such cases, bones are broken and flesh extensively lacerated, with no consciousness of pain; the mind proves itself to be thoroughly master of the body, as much so as though it were its creator, and the body were itself but a "*visualized*" thought.

It would be easy for me to add many more to this list of names in our effort to describe something of this interior, analytic, or *a priori* method of Natural Theology, but time and space alike forbid.

I note in conclusion two things that are specially worthy to be considered and remembered.

1st. The two methods, though starting by different routes, come together and run into each other before they reach their final result. Or perhaps I had better say that the two, each of them, imply something of the other, and neither of them is quite complete in itself without the other.

2d. The second remark is that a method that has been so long in use, confided in and depended upon by so many of the profoundest, keenest, and most comprehensive intellects that have blessed humanity with their lives and their thoughts, may not be lightly regarded or set aside as worthy of no further consideration.

I might add to these remarks that this historic

review, brief and imperfect as it has necessarily been, has shown what could have been shown much more fully if that had been my object, namely, that the truths of Natural Theology are really the first in the natural order, the basis on which to erect the superstructure of a supernatural theology, the *præambula*, the very "morning walks" of religion, to use again St. Thomas Aquinas's expression. Doubtless millions may believe and be saved without any such knowledge or mental exercise. But for those whom we are educating in our schools and colleges, those whom we are encouraging to enter the paths of science and of scientific pursuits, those with whom we have to deal as men who have been taught to think for themselves, and even for those who, with no good right to do so, claim to be able "to think for themselves," and to be free and independent in their thoughts, something more is necessary. They cannot be expected to take, and will not take, opinions and doctrines on mere trust. Least of all will they take the Articles of the Christian Faith, or of any other faith or philosophy that calls for self-denial and submission to the will of another, unless the grounds and first principles of that faith can be cleared from all reasonable doubt, not even though that other be Infinite Goodness itself.

LECTURE II.

PHYSICAL OBJECTIONS; NATURE OF MATTER; THEORIES OF EVOLUTION AND CAUSATION.

ROM. I, 20. For the invisible things of Him, from the creation of the world are manifest . . . even His eternal power and godhead.

PHYSICAL OBJECTIONS.

In the preceding Lecture I stated the two Methods that are open to the student of Natural Theology, and endeavored to illustrate them so far as may be necessary for a due appreciation of the criticisms I have to make on the objections that are urged against them.

These objections are of two kinds: those that refer more especially to the *a posteriori*, or objective, method, and those that are more particularly aimed at the *a priori*, or subjective, method. I begin with the former class.

1. The *a posteriori* or objective line of argument has been based largely on the principle of causation.

But to this it has been objected (1) that we know nothing about the relations of cause and effect; (2) that the modern doctrine of "the equivalence of effects and their causes" precludes the idea of any personal agency, whether by way of creation or subsequent miraculous intervention; (3) that in the recession from observed effects to their causes we nowhere find a veritable First Cause; that, stop wherever we will, we stop arbitrarily, and with as much demand for our supposed, or assumed, First Cause as for any one of the objects or events in the series which we had regarded as an effect.

2. Then, in the second place, much stress has been laid upon the argument from design and the evidences of what we regard as design in nature.

But it is objected that what we call design is a mere assumption on our part; that we have no right to call it design until we have proved that there is a Being capable of designing. The objection may be thus stated: Suppose I am standing on the sea-shore, desirous of a shell of a peculiar kind. If a friend brings it to me, I may reasonably suppose that he has some *design* to gratify my wants. But if a wave of the sea should cast it up at my feet, I could not suppose that either the wind or the waves had consciousness of my want, or any purpose or design in the matter; although the shell comes to relieve my want in the one case as in the other.

3. But again. It has been argued that the probabilities are untold millions against such an order as we see in nature without a Designing Mind. To this the objector assents. But he adds, it is not a question of probabilities *now;* it is now an accom-

plished fact. Take the case of a dice, and the probability *beforehand* of any particular side falling uppermost—say the ace—is one to five against it; and no prudent man would risk anything needlessly with such an odds against him. But *after the dice has been cast* the case is altered; there was no reason why the ace should not have fallen uppermost—no reason against that way of falling any more than against any one of the other five faces falling uppermost; and consequently this fall no more proves design than any one of the others would have done.

So it is, say the objectors, with the order and course of nature. The present order is one of those that were possible, *but having occurred as a past fact*, it no more proves design than any other one of the untold millions of ways would have done if it had occurred.

4. Then finally comes the theory of Evolution, which assumes to explain all things in accordance with mere natural laws, and without any recognition of the existence and agency of God.

I proceed to consider the first and last named forms of objection—Evolution, and Theories of Causation—in the confident belief that whatever force the other two I have named may have been thought to possess, will disappear as we proceed with our discussion.

I. The theory of Evolution, by assuming the eternal existence of matter, will leave us no means of proving the act of creation, or the existence of God as a *Creator*. And, in the estimation of some of its advocates, it goes much further than this, and by accounting for and explaining all the facts and phenomena of the universe, precludes us from any means of proving the existence and agency of God as an Organizer and Moral Governor.

It is not my purpose to discuss the theory of Evolution as a whole; nor yet to deny it altogether. There are certain observed processes in nature which we may call Evolution or not, as we please. It is merely a question of words, and not worth many words at that. What I aim to show is that Evolution itself implies and *proves* the existence of God, and makes the argument for His existence stronger and the illustrations of His attributes clearer and more striking than they were before.

The term Evolution has gotten such a hold on scientific men, that I presume it will always remain in use, in one sense or another. But the word is only a name for a process; and the process, by itself and alone, is no adequate explanation of anything.

Herbert Spencer, if not the most able, is yet in many respects the most noteworthy of all the advocates of the doctrine of the evolution and development of all things now existing in the universe out of a formless chaos of matter, without Divine agency. And beside this position in relation to the theory, which he unquestionably occupies, he and his works are by far the best known, as well as the most complete exposition of the theory in all its bearings and relations that the readers of these Lectures are likely to have known.

In citing Herbert Spencer, however, as I shall freely do, I wish to have two things kept constantly in mind. The *first* is, that I shall cite and criticise —though citing from him—only those features or principles that are common to all theories and views of Evolution that do not recognize God as its agent and cause; and the *second* is, that, in citing from him admissions or concessions, I shall cite none that are not inevitable deductions from principles or assumptions that are essential to the theory in any of its atheistic forms or statements, by whomsoever it may have been expounded or advocated.

Spencer says:[1] "Respecting the origin of the universe, three verbally intelligible suppositions may be made. We may assert that it is self-existent; or that it is self-created, or that it is created by external agency." But without attempting to prove

---

[1] *First Principles*, Pt. I., § 11.

either of these propositions, he rightly, as I think, regards the second—self-created—as absurd, and accepts the first, which means, of course, that matter is uncreated and eternal.

If then this visible universe is uncreated and eternal, the mere fact of its existence is no proof of the existence of a Creator. And if Evolution by itself explains all that has occurred, or now exists in its diversified forms and objects, or in its changing phenomena, no proof can be found in nature of the interposition and agency of any Being outside of the universe, or different in character from the objects of which it is made up; and we are precluded from any argument in favor of the existence and attributes of God that might otherwise be drawn from either the objects, or the constitution and course of nature.

However, Herbert Spencer is not always quite consistent with himself in his adherence to this theory; and it is but fair to give him the credit for whatever he may have said that is of an opposite character and tendency. Thus he says (§ 27): "We are obliged to regard every phenomenon as a manifestation of some Power by which we are acted upon; phenomena being, so far as we can ascertain, unlimited in their diffusion, we are obliged to regard this Power as omnipresent; and criticism teaches us that this Power is wholly incomprehensible." And again, speaking of the philosopher, our author says (§ 34): "He must remember that while he is a descendant of the past, he is a parent of the future, and that his thoughts are his children born to him, which he may not carelessly let die. He, like any other man, may properly consider himself as one of the myriad agencies through whom works the Unknown Cause."

Now, here, in germ and principle, is all that I care to assert or prove in these Lectures. The *existence* and omnipresence of God as First Cause are admitted, nay, rather, asserted. And we have only to study "the phenomena" of nature in which he works and *manifests* Himself, to learn all that we can know by the objective method of Natural Theology, of His attributes and character; of His plans and purposes; of our origin and destiny; of our duties here, and of our hopes for a hereafter. And for anything more than can be obtained by this method by the careful study of the phenomena of nature and of the human soul and its thoughts, feelings, and aspirations, and by legitimate inference from the facts thus observed, we are prepared to look to, expect, accept and depend upon, a Revelation from God Himself.

But we have the admission of the existence of a God Whose agency in all things and all phenomena is conceded; and Whose omnipresence is not only distinctly recognized as obviously and necessarily implied in the phenomena which manifests His existence and presence.

This, however, is not the attitude which Spencer is generally understood to hold towards the doctrines of either Natural or Revealed Religion. Few of the scholars who read his books, and still fewer of the thousands who claim to be his disciples, and cite his authority, have ever, apparently, noted these admissions of his. And still fewer have comprehended their importance, or given them a place and position in what they regard as Spencer's philosophy.

I return, then, to the consideration of that doctrine with regard to the origin of matter and the theory of the evolution of all things from it, for which he is mostly known, and for the influence of which upon the minds and the thoughts of men—upon their lives here and their destiny hereafter—he is justly held responsible.

Now I am not going to dispute or deny Herbert Spencer's doctrine concerning what he calls the "self-existence" of matter, implying its eternal existence, or its existence without beginning or any act of creation. For it is a subject about which, aside from Revelation, I know nothing, and about which it may be a matter of doubt whether philosophy and

Natural Theology can ever prove anything either way, that will be finally accepted as satisfactory. It is a matter of which, as I am willing to admit, nothing can be known, aside from Revelation. And it may be fairly questioned whether what we thus gain from Revelation should not be called faith or belief, rather than knowledge.

And as to knowledge, of course we have had no personal observation or experience of any act of creation properly so called. The act itself may be, and, indeed, I think it is, incomprehensible to us in so much that no one can explain it, or tell precisely how it may have occurred. I freely acknowledge, that while I can *imagine*, while I can and *do* believe it to have occurred, I can form no such conception of it as would allow me to reason about it, whether to prove it had occurred, or to deny its possibility.[1]

---

[1] I think it worthy of note in this connection that none of the ancient philosophers, none of the heathen philosophers, in fact, so far as I can remember, have had any doctrine of a *creation* of matter. All the old *religions* had a lingering tradition of some such act of creation, which had already become a mere travesty before their dogmas were reduced to writing. But in regard to the *Philosophies*, I cannot now recall one of them that did not assume the eternal existence and the uncreated nature of matter in some form and under some name or another.

Now, while the religions may be regarded as traditional—with an undercurrent of Natural Theology—the philosophies were almost, if not quite wholly, intuitional and rational; expressing such views of man and nature as insight and fancy might suggest. But

For these reasons I shall allow Spencer's assumption with regard to the "self-existence" of matter, whatever it may mean, to pass without challenge or contradiction.

And yet, in a certain sense, all that is necessary to a belief in the creation of matter out of nothing, occurs and may be seen in any day's experience. When we look into the clear sky of a summer's day, and see a small cloud appear where there was nothing visible a moment before, we have for the sight and for imagination all there is in an act of creation. Modern science has taught us, indeed, that here is only a case in which something that was not visible before, has become visible now; and *science* cannot explain how the thing happened. That is all. Science has raised a question—a perfectly legitimate question, indeed—that did not exist before. And it is a question which even science cannot answer. But this fact by no means proves the creation of something out of nothing, impossible.

John Stuart Mill[1] has recognized this fact. He says: "All that is necessary for imagining matter annihilated is presented in our daily experience. We see apparent annihilation whenever water dries up

even so, they were based on observation, and to some extent, at least, under the restraints of reason and common sense.

[1] *Examination of Sir William Hamilton's Philosophy*, vol. II, pp. 29, 30.

or fuel is consumed without visible residuum. The fact could not offer itself to our immediate perception in a more palpable shape if the annihilation were real."

What is thus true of annihilation is just as true of its opposite—creation. The visible appearance of a cloud of steam on a cold morning, just above the safety-valve of a steam-engine, is to our perception and imagination as much a case of "the creation of something out of nothing" as one could have had if he had stood by as an observer at the time of its creation.

To the adequacy of Evolution as an explanation of the phenomenon of the universe, I offer the following three objections, each of which seems to me to be fatal:

1. *If the present order of things had no beginning, Evolution must have produced a Supreme Being long before this time.*

If matter is eternal, and Evolution is the law or mode, Evolution must be as eternal as matter itself.

Eternity may, for our purpose, be assumed to be the same as unlimited time; for so the theory we are discussing assumes it to be, and so its advocates treat it in all their discussions and reasonings.

Now, in the infinity of time, and with no overruling Power to prevent it, all things that are possible, whether good or bad, and however good or bad, must have become real. Evolution has already, on their theory, produced man. Why not something higher than man? infinitely higher? even a Being of infinite power and goodness?

Surely no one will say that such a Being is impossible. Too many millions of men have believed in Him to allow that objection to have much influence now. Nay, the very name by which we indicate His existence, for this purpose, implies His possibility. We ask for what is merely the highest possible Being.

Has then Evolution produced such a Being? It won't do to say "not yet," for in the infinity of time there is all time, and time enough for all things, and for each thing, many times over.

Here, then, we have the dilemma. Either Evolution had a beginning, and so a Beginner, in which case we have the existence of God confessed, or it must have produced a Supreme Being long before this time. In the one case we have God as Creator, and in the other as a result. But in each case, and alike, a God over all and through all and in all, "in whom," in the words of the Apostle, "we live and move and have our being."

If, then, there was a beginning to Evolution there

was a Beginner, and His will is its law and limit. If there was no beginning it would have produced a Supreme Being long before this time, *so* long that we may say that He has existed from eternity; and this seems to me to be about the same as God "in the beginning."

2. I come now to my second point. *The present order of things had a beginning.*

Evolution is but a process. It has successive stages or steps, and must have had a first stage and a beginning.

The universe, in this aspect of it, consists of a series of events or stages. These events constitute a Series; beginning somewhere and tending to something. This is inseparable from the nature of the case.

Herbert Spencer speaks (§ 44) of a primary stage —a primitive condition—in which all matter was in a gaseous state, diffused to a maximum of diffusion, so as, in his own words, "to fill all space."[1] "The first advance," says he (§ 44), "towards consolidation resulted in a differentiation between the occupied space which the nebulous mass still filled and the unoccupied space which it previously filled." With this, as he goes on to state, there came a dif-

---

[1] It seems difficult to understand how anything that is *infinite*, as Spencer says that space is, can be considered as *full* of anything.

ference in density among the parts, with also a difference in temperature; and in due time and order, light, electricity, and all the other "forces," so called, made their appearance and began their career of activity.

Now, as the process of condensation goes on it must always tend to, and ultimately reach, the opposite extreme, or the minimum of expansion and diffusion. This Spencer sees and admits. As there was a time—a stage—in this progress when life began on the earth, so there must and will be a time when "this process must bring Evolution [itself] to a close in Universal Death" (§ 136). Nor is that all. Even the "forces," light, heat, etc., must become extinct, or retired to a state of inaction. But Spencer adds: "When pushing to its extreme the argument that Evolution must come to a close in complete equilibrium or rest, the reader suggests that for aught that appears to the contrary, the Universal Death thus implied will continue indefinitely, it is legitimate to point out how, on carrying the argument still farther, we are led to infer a subsequent universal life." "It would be unwise," however, he admits, "to accept this in any positive sense."

Since Spencer has admitted this result—a "universal death" and "a complete equilibrium or rest"—it would seem to spare us the labor and trouble

Physical Objections.

of showing its inevitable necessity. This, however, can easily be shown.

Spencer holds that these "modes of force," light, heat, etc. (he enumerates seven, light, heat, electricity, magnetism, affinity, and gravity), are all "alike transformable into each other" (§ 82). But if they can be transformed into each other, it is a fact which Mr. Spencer knows as well as anybody that they cannot always be got back into their original form. I am not aware that any means has yet been found for converting either gravity into heat or heat into gravity. But with regard to all the rest of them it is conceded, I believe, and proved by experiment, that they may be transformed or converted into heat. But when converted into heat, the heat becomes diffused by radiation, until all objects coming to be of the same temperature they cease to act on each other at all. The heat cannot be gotten back into its original form, and we have, as Spencer has called it, "a perfect equilibrium or rest," with no force causing further change, and Evolution itself is at an end.[1]

---

[1] It is hardly any part of my duty to assist these gentlemen to a more favorable, or at least a less objectionable, statement of their theory. But I can see no good reason for speaking of this extreme as an "equilibrium or rest," when "all force is latent." Accepting this theory of "the conservation and correlation of forces," I would suggest that they all—the whole seven of them—may have

The material forces in nature are of two kinds. The one act by impact, and produce motion in straight lines, with uniform velocity and with no recurrence to the same point or condition of existence. The others act constantly, and when combined with those of the first class, may produce motion in curve lines with recurrence to the same point or condition. As examples, we have the sun in its action on the planets; the earth on the pendulum that swings back and forth in space; the air that resists whatever would pass through it; the steam that keeps the piston moving back and forth in the cylinder. But in all these cases the force that acts constantly is outside of the moving mass—the sun, the air that resists the bodies that are passing through it, the earth that attracts the swinging pendulum, and the steam that moves the piston-rod.

Even in the phenomena of animal life, where we find animal sensibility, the law is the same. The

---

been "converted" into the one, heat, in the state of the greatest diffusion, which may be very intensely active, as *repulsion*, keeping the atoms apart in a gaseous form, and at the other extreme they may all be "converted" into attraction, and so keep the atoms in the closest condensation and unity. They, or it—the forces I mean—may be active as gravity, affinity and cohesion, or these forces may be, as some philosophers maintain that they are, only different forms of one force. But whether as one or as three, there is no reason that I can see why they should not be most intensely active in the state of the greatest condensation of the matter of the universe.

expansion and contraction of the chest in breathing would not occur but for the heart sending the blood to the lungs. Nor would the heart contract but for the constant action of the capillaries in sending the blood to the heart through the veins.

The only case in which we know of any recurrence to the same place or condition, without the action of some such outside force, is found in the actions of man. But here we have a soul, a personal agent or force acting within the man, the moving mass, which is the body itself.

The forces of nature can always be represented by a "variable" in an analytic equation, and the rates of motion or change which they produce can be expressed by a coefficient in a differential equation.[1] In this respect they are unlike the will-power

---

[1] In order that there may be maxima or minima, nodes, cyclic or cycloidal returns to the same place or condition, there must be two variables. These variables represent forces so situated, *ontologically*, that the one may be active and producing its results, while the other is inactive, or kept in equilibrium so as to produce no result or change; for at these points the differential coefficient of one of the variables must become zero, in its passage from a positive to a negative value, or the reverse. Thus in the common cycloid generated by a point in the wheel of a carriage, as it passes along the road, while x, denoting the *abscissa*, distances in space and time, is constantly increasing, y, denoting the *ordinates*, is alternately becoming zero or $2R$, the diameter of the wheel, and at each of these points dy becomes, for the instant zero, or nothing. So with evolution. When dy is nothing or the "forces" spoken of are at their "equilibrium" or "rest," the Force or Power represented by x must be

in man, and the emotional power or force in animals. Hence, with regard to the forces that are at work in inanimate nature, we can always, by means of the mathematical formulæ, ascertain the bounds and limits to the possibilities of which they are capable. With a constant variable we have only straight lines with no maxima or minima, no return to the same points or over the same track; while with the variable coefficients which represent the constantly acting forces combined with the constant, we can have such nodes or cyclic recurrences.

But for the material universe itself, there can be no such *outside* mass to carry it through these extremes. The only alternative, therefore, is that there is a Moving Mind in the universe, as in the body of man. He can go back and forth from point to point and state to state *at will*. So it is with God in this material universe.

I do not know that it is necessary to assume or prove that matter has ever actually been in either of these extreme conditions. And yet, without the intervention of some personal Agent to prevent it, I do not see how it could have been otherwise. We do know, however, that for many millions of

---

active in order to carry the mass through its extremes, or maxima and minima points, as truly as the horse that draws the carriage and keeps the wheel turning on its axletree.

years now past it has been going and changing from a state of greater heat and diffusion to one of greater cold and condensation. And this process is still going on, as recent attainments both in geology and astronomy abundantly prove.[1]

At these cosmological extremes, therefore, the atoms of matter must either change their nature and become spontaneously active, or there must be the intervention of some Force or Agent of a nature entirely different from theirs. At these points of extreme diffusion and extreme condensation, where there is, as Spencer calls it, a "complete equilibrium or rest," either these atoms must become *spontane-*

---

[1] The reality of such extremes is not wholly a matter of speculation; nor is the time when they occur wholly beyond computation. Professor TAIT, *Recent Advances in Physical Science*, Lect. VII., gives three computations. (1) One based on the loss of internal heat as about ten millions of years since the earth was cool enough for plants to grow on its surface. (2) One based on the retardation of the earth's revolutions by the tidal influences of the moon, which reduces the period to something less than ten millions of years. (3) The length of time that the sun, from its radiation, can have "kept the earth in a state fit for the habitation of animals and vegetables." This "tends to about the same result." Professor YOUNG, (work on *The Sun*, p. 276), computing by a somewhat different process, gives us a 4th result, which is about sixteen millions of years. And then WALLACE, in his *Island Life*, Part I., c. x., by a purely geological computation, reaches a result somewhat larger—say about twenty or twenty-five millions of years, giving an average in all, of about fifteen millions of years of time since the earth became sufficiently cooled and consolidated for the beginning of animal and vegetable life.

ously active and start into action *of themselves*—action both mechanical and chemical—or there must be some spontaneously acting Being or Agent to start them out of their equilibrium of perfect rest and inactivity. It is not a question of moving on *through* time and space, but it is the question of the beginning of motion and action *in* time and space, by atoms of matter which nowhere else, and at no other time, have shown themselves capable of originating such kinds of action.

Our author thinks that he is provided against this emergency, for he has prepared himself, or rather his theory, with what becomes at this point an "outside agency," to use his own expression. He has Force, or one force that becomes diversified into the seven already named, light, heat, etc., and they help him, as he thinks, through this "dead point" in nature, to use an expression familiar to engineers and machinists.

But do you see where we are? These modern scientists are in the same difficulty as their early Aryan congeners of whom I have already spoken. Seeing that there must be something beside the visible objects in nature, they invented a Jupiter to "compel" the clouds and send down the rain; a Neptune to control the seas and look after the tides; an Æolus to restrain the winds; and a Ceres to cause the earth to bring forth its fruit in due season.

This view of the matter seems to have occurred to Tylor also, for he says:[1] "The scientific conceptions current in my own school-boy days, of heat and electricity as invisible fluids passing in and out of solid bodies, are ideas which reproduce, with extreme closeness, the special doctrines of fetichism."

If now men may *invent* causes rather than *discover* them, no effective argument can be derived from any of the phenomena of nature to prove the existence of God, or any other proposition that the objector does not choose to admit; for in any case and in reference to any phenomenon or class of phenomena, he has but to invent a cause, call it up from the vast "unknowable" that these men talk so much about, and make it what the case demands; clothe it with all the attributes that may be necessary to make it adequate to the observed effects, and all is done that the demands of science call for. There is no need of a Personal Creator, and it may be triumphantly claimed that there is no proof of His existence or of the manifestation of his attributes anywhere.

But never mind. Even so there is a confession of the existence of something besides matter, something that is immaterial in its nature and that can act, and act on matter, too, when matter in all its

[1] *Primitive Culture*, vol. i, p. 147.

forms, whether mass or molecule, is at rest—"in the perfect equilibrium of rest."

I have not taken much notice in this discussion of the theory which is a favorite with many persons just now, which holds that "force," like matter, is eternal, and incapable of either increase or diminution. This is a "good working hypothesis" for most purposes of the physical sciences. But it is not held, and cannot be held, as I understand the matter, except as we recognize two distinct and opposite conditions of force, the "kinetic" and the "latent" or "potential," as they are called. The following has been given as an illustration. If I throw a ball upwards into the air it has a force while moving up which is a product of the weight into the velocity. But at its highest point, its maximum or extreme of elevation, it is at rest for a moment, and has in consequence no force, although in the process of descending it regains all that it had in starting. But it is held that the force is not lost during its ascent, it only passes over from being kinetic to being latent or only potential.

In the case of the ball, it is the attraction of the earth that starts it back again after it had reached its greatest elevation, and awakes the force out of its "latency" and rouses it to a kinetic mood again. But in the case of the material universe there is no such outside mass to act upon it. It can be only a Personal Agent, with will-power or psychical force —in short a Spiritual Being—that can start the dead matter into life and action again after its force has become latent and inoperative, and has for all practical purposes ceased to be a force at all.

We reach the conclusion, therefore, that mere inanimate matter with such properties and forces as it now has is not adequate to the explanation of the phenomena of the universe by the mode of Evolution or any other mode without the intervention of a personal Cause and Creator.

Aristotle[1] came to the same conclusion from a study of the phenomena of motion. He held that matter ὕλη is mere capacity, capable of being moved and put into motion. And he argues that it is possible that that which is only moved or capable of being moved has no necessary existence, and may be supposed not to exist. But he adds: "It is therefore necessary that there should be a first Principle or Being Whose very nature is energy, and the cause of motion."

The late Professor Benjamin Peirce, of Harvard University, in his great work on *Analytic Mechanics*, which is doubtless the profoundest mathematical work that has ever been produced in this country,

---

[1] *Metaphysics*, B. xi, c. vi.

begins and ends his volume with the declaration that motion in matter implies a Cause and Agent that is immaterial and personal. "Motion is an essential element in all physical phenomena; and its introduction into the universe of matter was necessarily the preliminary act of creation." And in concluding his work he says: "But it is time to return to nature and learn from her actual solutions the recondite analysis of the more obscure problems of celestial and physical mechanics. In these researches there is one lesson which cannot escape the profound observer. Every portion of the material universe is pervaded by the same laws of mechanical action, which are incorporated into the very constitution of the human mind. The solution of the problem of this universal presence of such a spiritual element is obvious and necessary. There is one God and Science is the knowledge of Him."

Unless we deny to matter that inertia which is assumed as its fundamental property and character in all our physical sciences, whether chemical or mechanical, and ascribe to it life and the capacity for voluntary action, this conclusion seems to be inevitable.

Here, then, we have what seems to me to be a demonstration of the existence of a being Who acts spontaneously, of His own will and motion, and

Whose works must, in the words of St. Paul, show forth the invisible things of Him—even His eternal power and godhead, the attributes that make up the essentials of a personal character.

3. I have one point more for consideration: *Evolution without God does not account for all the phenomena since the beginning*.

I do not propose, as I have said, to discuss Evolution in all its phases and assumptions. It is enough for my purpose to show that it does not destroy or even weaken the force of the argument for the existence of God. It may be a divine method with such limits as scientific investigation has already or may hereafter fix to it as a legitimate part of scientific truth.

Nor again, do I intend to urge against it in this place,[1] the objection, so forcibly urged by Wallace, Mivart, Quatrefages, Virchow, Elam, and many others, that in fact no case of the actual evolution of one species from a stock belonging to another in any proper scientific classification, has ever been *seen* or actually *proved* to have taken place. I believe this line of objection is well chosen and fatal to any theory of Evolution, which does not regard it as a part, and only a part, of the divine method, or

---

[1] For this part of the argument see the first part of Lecture VI.

that looks to Evolution alone as solving all the phenomena of the universe.

My line of objection is for the present of a very different character, and, as I believe, it affords a still more insuperable obstacle to the reception of that theory in any form that can operate as an objection to our belief in the existence of God and "in the operations of His hands," which we call Miracles, Inspiration, and Providence.

It is as well ascertained as any fact in science can be, that this earth through a long period of its early history was without any living thing, plant or animal, on its surface. At a time life began; and it is beyond dispute that it began in some of its lowest forms. Whether the first living thing on this earth were a simple cell, without yet a nucleus or cell-wall, or were an animal with an organization of parts and organs, and whether it belonged to the animal or the vegetable kingdom, is a matter of no importance to our present inquiry.

With this first living thing there was a new compound of the chemical elements, such as did not in fact exist before, and could not have existed at a much earlier period. It is an exceedingly unstable compound, which ignites and burns at a temperature somewhat above that of boiling water, and always at or below that of red heat. This compound is such that no chemist has yet been able to produce it in his laboratory. He cannot even tell under what circumstances it would occur or why he cannot produce it himself.

Was there then a Divine Agent? I only ask the question. The chemist will very likely say that there was in that act no violation or contravention of the well known laws of chemistry. Very likely; but the same may be said of *miracles* in general. They are not violations of the laws of nature; not departures from its ordinary courses, except in the one thing,—the intervention of a new Agent—the Miracle Worker Himself. He it is, and not the method or the result in itself considered, that makes the miracle.

But this is not all. Here was the beginning of a new process, a new order. We have now life, growth, development of parts and organs, with reproduction, decay and death. Nothing like it had occurred or been seen on earth before. No crystal —no mere mineral—undergoes these changes or performs these functions. The crystal had no parentage, produces no offspring, and will have no line of posterity. What it was, it is, and will be, with none of the phenomena or indications of life, and no life history in the records of its existence.

Professor Tyndall has stated the problem here

presented very sharply, in his way. "Two views," he says,[1] "thus offer themselves to us. Life was present potentially in matter when in the nebulous form, and was unfolded from it by the way of natural development, or it is a principle inserted into matter at a later date."

Putting this problem into plain English, without metaphysics or rhetorical embellishment, we have: either there were living beings on the earth at this early stage, or there is such a thing as life which is a substantial entity capable of a separate existence, which *came into* the earth at a later period, as some meteoric stone, or new chemical element, possibly an invisible gas, might have done.

But I can suggest a third alternative: there was a Creator who organized this dust of the earth and made what He had thus produced out of these organic elements, a living being; and gave to it the power of perpetuating itself and its species through all coming time.

Of the three "suppositions" which, in the words of Spencer, are "verbally intelligible," one is not to be held for an instant. There were no living things on earth when it was in its incandescent or nebulous condition; living things did not appear until long after that period had passed away.

---

[1] *Fragments of Science*, Appleton's Ed., 1872, p. 156.

Only two hypotheses then remain: the one is that there is a living God Who is the Creator of all living things, and Whose presence and agency were manifested in this new phenomenon, or there is such a thing as life, which is not a mere mode of existence, but a "substantiated reality" like the gases, oxygen, hydrogen, etc., which at the time came into the world, or which at the least entered at that time, and then for the first time, into new relations and began a new career of existence.

But even so, are we not doing as our early Aryan fathers did, creating a new god for our mythology? Are we not ascribing to "life" something of personality, the power of choice and spontaneity of action?

Anyhow, "life" did not begin without something more, and something besides and different from mere evolution; for if we accept what Tyndall declares to be the "scientific idea," evolution can be only the way in which molecules act upon each other.[1] This surely precludes all idea of "forces" to be denoted by such abstract terms as heat, light, etc., or, as Tyndall calls it, "the intervention of slave labor,"

---

[1] *Fragments of Science*, Appleton's edition, 1872, p. 114.
"The scientific idea is that the molecules act upon each other . . . that they attract each other at certain definite points or poles and in certain definite directions."

and reduces us to the dilemma, either the atoms of matter were endowed with intelligence and capable of plan and purpose, or there was a Personal God, Who planned and executed whatever we see, whether we call the phenomena a creation or an evolution.

There was also at the introduction of organic life the beginning of another new thing, which Dr. Elam has well and sharply pointed out.[1] "The organic force in vegetable tissue can decompose carbonic acid at ordinary temperatures into carbon and oxygen. Now this cannot be effected by the intensification of any one, or by any combination of the ordinary forces of the inorganic world." And we may add, no chemist can do it, or knows how it can be done in his laboratory. And yet it takes place daily in the vegetable world and in the growth of every plant in that world.

I am aware that there are those who would meet my argument with the claim of what is called "spontaneous generation," although, as I understand it, they do not claim that living beings have been produced out of inorganic matter by mere chemical processes. And the claim in any form is not allowed by the best authorities on the subject.

I know too, that there are chemists who, in the

---

[1] *Winds of Doctrine*, being an Examination into the modern theories of automatism and evolution, London, 1876, p. 89.

ardor of their enthusiasm for their favorite science, claim that the time will come and is in fact fast approaching—pretty nearly here—when the chemist can do all these things in his laboratory—put together in proper proportion, and in the right way, the elements that are essential to organic compounds, and produce the living being in his crucibles and under our very eyes.

Well, I do not care to discourage their enthusiastic hopes. He would be a rash man who should venture to set any limits to the progress of discovery and to say what may and what may not be attained in the future.

But it is just as much to my purpose, and the purpose of my argument, to say that whatever *you* may be able to do in the *future*, there was Somebody, millions of years ago, Who knew how to do these very things *then*, and did them, too, as the geological records of the past most incontestably prove. He knew how and did *then* with a certainty and a success that shows no defect or imperfection, no indication of a limit to His knowledge or His power, what you cannot do *now*, and do not even know why it cannot be done. Did the molecules of matter *make themselves* into living beings? Are they wiser than we are? Did they know more *then* than we do *now*? or was there a Personal Agent

Who showed Himself in this to be a First Cause and Creator?

I have confined myself here to the three objections to the theory of Evolution that are of the most general character. I shall have occasion to say something more which will be more specific in the sixth Lecture.

But I think we have seen enough to justify the proposition with which I started. The word evolution is only a term to denote a process, and the process in itself and alone is no adequate explanation of anything.

The mere evolutionist seems to me to reason very much as we might expect a very intelligent savage to do who might happen to be visiting, for the first time, a highly civilized country, and seeing all the comforts and conveniencies of life which our modern civilization has accumulated in our modern homes. He would be taken, of course, into our mines, our manufactories, and wherever else our industries are most successfully prosecuted; and he would see the machinery we use in all its complicated forms and in the performance of all its wonders. He would most likely conclude that it was machinery, and the use of machinery, that has constituted the superiority of our home life, and the splendors of our towns and cities, whatever, in fact, makes our homes superior to his. He would extol the glories of machinery and machine manufactures as the cause of what he had seen.

And he would be right as far as his theory goes. But he would be seen to have overlooked, or failed to discern, the fact that machinery, however perfect and complete in itself, can do nothing without a moving Power. There must be wind or steam or falling water to propel the machinery or it can do nothing.

So with nature. Call its manifold on-going processes evolution or whatever else you will, it is itself but a piece of machinery, and its evolutions and changes are but processes which imply a moving Power or First Cause.

But I must hasten to the consideration of the remaining objections that belong to this group—the objections to the *a posteriori* method.

II. The objections that are urged under this head come before us in two forms: the one is based on what is called "the equivalence of effects and their causes," and the other on the ground that there can be no First Cause except as we *arbitrarily* assume some one to be the first.

1. The first of these objections, though very fully elaborated by Sir William Hamilton, is so well stated

by President Bascom in the book already referred to,[1] that I will state it in his words. "This line of argument," he claims, involves "the exact equivalence of causes and effects." This law he regards as inexorable; and, as he says, "it carries with it the uniformity of nature as a congeries of causes. These causes remaining the same, can produce no other effects than those which now belong to them. But causes cannot change themselves within their own circle, for that change would be an effect without a cause. Still further, the notion of causation includes the unbroken continuity of causes and effects in their several series. Hence the correlation of forces— their indestructibility—is a corollary of the law of causation. . . . We are quite certain that no force, either in aid of our purposes or in opposition to them, will ever disappear, no matter how great a variety of forms it may assume. . . . . With this notion of causation . . . what argument can be constructed for the being of God? We answer, no argument that offers the least proof. The results reached are quite the reverse of those sought for. . . We may affirm that we are thus led up to a First Cause. The conclusion is wholly illegitimate for many reasons. If for convenience of expression we divide the ascent to a First Cause into distinct steps, the causes in

---

[1] *Natural Theology*, pp. 40-43.

each step will be the exact equivalents of those which precede it and those which follow it. No movement backward or forward alters the causes dealt with, either in quantity or quality. It discloses them as divided and combined in a great variety of ways, as assuming many new and striking appearances, but never as different either in nature or amount from what they have always been. An ascent, therefore, no matter how far, puts no change on the face of the facts, and brings us no nearer their ultimate explanation. If we stop at any point we stop arbitrarily. The causes we have chosen stand as causes in no different relations from those already passed over. Equally with them they are intermediates between previous and subsequent causes . . . the energies of the universe, like those of a torrent, come pouring out of the past, and simply spread out over the future as an open field."

This objection assumes in the first place the eternity of matter as self-existing, and does not regard it as a perpetual creation of the Divine Mind, which has already been suggested as the opinion of Dr. Bascom, and which, I will take occasion to add, seems to me the most plausible and the most probable hypothesis that we can entertain on the subject. But of this I have said all that I have time or occasion for, in the previous Lecture.

The second assumption made by those who urge this objection, is the eternity and indestructibility of force, or forces, as something distinct from and dual with matter.

I have already spoken of this doctrine with regard to "force" as having its value as a "working hypothesis." But in any other view it is liable to very serious objections. And even as a working hypothesis it must be taken with the doctrine that "force" has its two forms of existence—kinetic or active on the one hand, and latent and passive, or at least quiescent, on the other—when, for all practical purposes, it becomes no force at all. Hence I think we may safely dismiss that theory without farther consideration.

The laws of causation and the classes of causes are pretty well understood. Aristotle, with that wonderful sagacity that never forsook him, teaches and repeats in several places, that, to a complete scientific comprehension of any subject, there are four causes to be considered: (1) the material cause or the matter out of which anything is made; (2) the formal cause, which, in our modern sense of words, means the specific character, although in his day a formal cause was always an "idea" in the Platonic sense of the word, or a "form" in the later scholastic sense; (3) the efficient cause, or that which produces the object; and (4) the final cause. This, in reference to moral agents, is the purpose or aim which the agent had in mind in producing the object. But in a more general sense, and without implying personal agency at all, it would mean the uses of the object or possibly the effects which it, considered as a cause, produces.

Bacon[1] recognized these four classes of causes or heads as topics of investigation, and thought that the knowledge of the material and formal causes of things constituted the proper sphere of Natural Philosophy or Physical Science, and that an inquiry into the other two—efficient and final causes—belonged more properly to the department of the Metaphysical Sciences.

But with the careful study and use of the Inductive Method, and the conditions and laws of scientific investigation, it was found that each event had more than one cause acting at the time of its production, of which notice must be taken, and in like manner no one cause ever acted without contributing to the production of more than one effect. This led to the idea of an equivalence of the sum of the causes and the effects, as a fundamental principle of scientific investigation.

This doctrine of the equivalence of causes and ef-

---

[1] *Advancement of Learning*, B. III, c. iv.

fects led to a recognition of what is called "residual phenomena," which has been the basis of many of the most important discoveries in modern science. These principles of scientific investigation have been carefully studied and well stated by such men as Whewell,[1] Sir J. F. W. Herschel,[2] John Stuart Mill,[3] and Professor W. Stanley Jevons.[4]

But the law or principle has no application to the question before us. We are not now seeking for the full scientific comprehension of anything; but we are trying to find whether there was a First Cause of all things or not.

The two purposes are totally different, both in their aims and in the principles that should guide the inquiry. Hence mistakes or omissions that would be fatal in the one case, may be only the wise disembarrassment that would relieve us of what would prove only a useless and unnecessary encumbrance in the other.

I see an oak growing before me. It is small and has just started out of the ground. If I were intent on the pursuit of *scientific knowledge* only, I should

---

[1] WHEWELL, *Philosophy of the Inductive Sciences*, Pt. II, Book xiii.

[2] SIR JOHN F. W. HERSCHEL, *Preliminary Discourse on the Study of Natural Philosophy*.

[3] JOHN STUART MILL, *System of Logic*, B. III.

[4] W. STANLEY JEVONS, *The Principles of Science*, B. I, c. vii, B. II, c. xi, and B. IV.

begin with considering the conditions of the soil, the climate, and the moisture on which the germination of the acorn and the growth of the shrub had been dependent. But my object being quite other than mere natural science, I begin by seeking the cause in another direction, and perhaps in another sense of the word. I start with the acorn. I have no doubt it was produced by an oak tree; and this tree in turn grew from an acorn, and so on, until we come to the time when there was neither oak nor acorn on this earth; and I ask who or what then existed as the acting, creating Cause?

Or I may begin with the fact of sunlight, and ask about the sun. I know *now*, as thinkers in the past did not always know, that the sun has not always existed. Whatever may be said about the eternity of matter and the indestructibility and conservation of forces, I know—and nobody denies—that there was a time when there was no such combination of matter and forces as makes up the sun which we now have; and I ask, naturally and legitimately, what was before the sun? what was its cause? who was its creator?

In this line of investigation and inquiry occurs no question of the "equivalence of causes and effects," whatever that may mean. And I have no hesitation or difficulty in admitting, if that will at all relieve the difficulty, that I might pursue the investigation through many lines of causes and of causation, acting in different ways and with different senses for the word cause. But they would all converge at last in One, Who is supreme and the sum of all causes and causation, as from another point of view He is the sum and comprehension of all being.

From this point of view I can have no hesitation in admitting their doctrine of the "equivalence of causes and effects." It rather helps my argument, for the universe *without God* is the sum of the effects, and He, as First Cause, is the sum of causes; and by this law He must be adequate and equal to [the causation of] all the effects. I say equal to the causation of all, for this is obviously the only point of comparison or co-measurement that is possible in the case. And this "equivalence," or adequacy, gives us the attributes of goodness, wisdom and power, just to the extent to which they are manifested in nature—the works of creation around us or in the course of human history.

2. The other form of the objection is of a different character, and much more widely diffused among thinking men. In fact, there are but few, if any, who have not met with it. It is that the argumentation from effect to cause to prove a beginning and a First Cause of all things, is ineffectual because

it has no natural or logical stopping place. When we arrive at our so-called First Cause, the question may still be asked, as they allege, and asked as pertinently, and pursued with as much force, as before, who or what caused this, your so-called first cause; what was before Him?

This objection may be found in the writings of Sir William Hamilton and John Stuart Mill, to name no others. Dr. Bascom, in the work referred to, as will be seen in the quotation just given, yields to it, apparently, as though he thought it fatal to this line of reasoning.

It is much easier to show the logical fallacy on which this objection is founded than to do away with the evil effects it has produced far and wide upon the minds of men; the former being, as I think, comparatively easy, while the latter is a work of labor and tact and perseverance, which will often prove ineffectual after we have done all that it is in our power to do.

Now, the fundamental mistake of these men who either make, or are troubled by, this objection, is in supposing that we affirm that "every *thing* had a cause." Even so shrewd a philosopher as Sir William Hamilton makes this mistake, and John Stuart Mill, when commenting on Hamilton's words, repeats it without dissent or apparent consciousness of it. He says "the alleged impossibility of conceiving any phenomena of the universe to be uncaused, applies equally . . . to the First Cause itself."[1] And in his posthumous work[2] he says: "It would seem, therefore, that our experience instead of furnishing an argument for a First Cause is repugnant to it."

But the doctrine is not that every *thing* had a cause, but that every *effect* had a cause.

Whatever we know to be an effect we know, in the very act of knowing it to be an effect, to have had a cause; and we believe in the reality and nature of the cause just to the extent that we believe in the reality of the effect and know it to be an effect.

If, now, there is anything which we know by any means whatever, *without knowing it to be an effect*, we know it, *to that extent*, and *so long as we know it in that way only*, as a first cause.

And this is, in substance, my answer to their objection. *Effects* only have causes, and causes, *as such*, do not call for or demand belief in their causes.

When the French astronomer Leverrier discovered the perturbations of the planet Herschel, he knew them to be an effect, and that there was for them a

---

[1] *Examination*, etc., Vol. II, p. 37.

[2] *Three Essays on Religion*, p. 142 and following, MILL repeats his objection *even after he has admitted that there are first causes* in the strict and proper sense of the word.

cause, which at the time and for the time was a first cause. He *knew* it only as producing the observed effect. He *supposed* it to be a mass of matter as yet undiscovered in the heavens, and the telescope soon made it an object of immediate observation. Then it was classed among the other cosmical masses that are regarded by the common consent of mankind as effects, or created things.

Mill, in his *Posthumous Essays on Theism* (p. 143 and following), has recognized and admitted this doctrine. The example he gives is water. We know this, like every other chemical compound, to be an effect, the result of the union of chemical elements that could not have been so united in the earliest stages of the material universe, or at any rate, at the beginning of the present evolution in mundane affairs. In view of the newly discovered doctrine of the *Corelation and Conservation of Force*, he sees his way, apparently, to the admission of first causes, without the acknowledgment of a Personal First Cause of all things. These elements, as the oxygen and hydrogen of water, he says, are not known to have had any beginning to their existence, and may hence properly be regarded as first causes.

Now, in this order of retrogression from any given or assumed effect, we must, of necessity, come somewhere at some time to an object which we know only as a cause, and as *the* cause of the last object, which we have known in any such way, or by any such means, that we know it to be an effect. Hence, at this point and with this object, we may stop and study this, as yet unobserved object which we know only as cause, as the French astronomer did, and learn what we can of the nature and mode of its existence, its modes of action, and its ways of manifestation.

And if there is anywhere a cause that is or was before an effect, then there must be somewhere a Cause before Which there was no cause and no act of causation. Any possible concatenation of cause and effect, and any law of causation or of causal sequence, involves this result as an absolute necessity; so that if there be no First Cause, there is nothing that can be called an effect anywhere; no consecution of cause and effect; no law of causation.

Now it is quite true, as Mill claims, that so far as the sixty-four or five chemical elements are concerned, we see nothing in them to imply that they are created effects—that they are not eternal as God Himself. But we do know that there was a time in this material universe when they were not united or acting upon each other as they now do in forming and perpetuating the mineralogical compounds of which this earth is made up. Hence, as I have argued, the necessity of something besides them, something of a nature different from theirs—something capable of spontaneous activity, and possessed of infinite wisdom and power to set them into activity, and begin the present order of things; thus the existence of God, if not as the Creator of all things visible and invisible, is proved in the capacity of First Cause and Organizer of what we now see in the world or the universe in the process of evolution.

The solution of the difficulty, so far as Mill is concerned, is in the fact that he uses the word cause in two senses. In the passage just quoted it is evident from the context that he means by causes not the "substantial objects," oxygen, etc., but only the acts of uniting, and in this sense he is doubtless correct; for we cannot conceive of any union without some "object" or "substantial reality," to use his own words, to be united, and something or somebody acting as cause to unite them. But Mill uses the word "cause" to denote both the act of uniting and the agent that produces the union; thus perpetrating the fallacy in diction which in logic, we call technically, *ambiguous middle*.

Now this Being is, from the very nature of the case, like the chemical elements in this at least: there is nothing in His nature or in what we know of Him to suggest that He is an effect, or requires a cause for His existence.

But unlike them He must, from the nature of the case, be *spontaneously* active. He can have no periods of "absolute rest," or if He has, He must be able *sua sponte*, by His own will and from Himself alone, to start into action, to begin anew a state of activity. He must be in this respect, at least, totally unlike all material objects, atoms, molecules, or masses, and like nothing that we know of but the human mind itself.

These causes and effects constitute a series like the successive stages of evolution. If, however, one objects, as Comte, Lewes and "the positivists" do, that we know nothing of causation, and have no right to affirm it in any case, or speak of anything as a cause, I reply that we have no need to do so for the purposes of our argument. We may treat these phenomena as mere *events* in the order and sequence of time and the result will be the same.

Every series must have five elements: a first term a, a rate of change d, a number of terms n, a last term l, and a sum of all the terms s. Now with any three of these the others may be found. But let the algebraist try and see what he can do with any of the formulæ if a, the first term, is thrown out and becomes not the mathematical zero as in the series 0, 1, 2, 3, 4, but ontologically nothing—so that there is no first term. In that case there can be no second term, no succession, and no number of terms, no sums of terms, and in fact no series.

The same will be the result if he assumes that the number of terms as well as the last term and the sums of the terms is infinity. He can do nothing with the symbol of infinity in his formulæ in place of *l* or *n* or *s*. He can neither add nor substract it. He can neither multiply nor divide by it. It indicates to him, in fact, as surely as the absence of a first term, that there is no series.

This applies, of course, only to *actual* series. Series may be theoretically infinite—that is, they may be of such a nature that there was actually and in fact no term before which there might not have been another; and no one so late that there may not yet be another in the same series, although that other has not yet come into being. But this is not and cannot be the case with any actual series of any ontological facts or events.

But as I have said, it is much easier to expose the fallacy logically, than to do away with the injurious impression it has made on the minds of those in whom it has gained a lodgment. Like many another deeply-rooted and long-cherished error, it clings very tightly to its hold upon us. It is like a case of momentum in which we begin to move on in any direction rapidly, and seeing no occasion to stop at any particular point, we either keep on at the original pace or we come to a stop with such violence as to cause unpleasant results.

We live in the midst of things that are transient and temporary. We are so much accustomed to think of them all as effects—that we cannot easily realize, however undeniably we can prove—that there is or can be anything that is cause, without being effect or the product of anything.

Mill bases our belief in causation and expectation of a cause where we see a result on habit formed by long continued " association of ideas." I base it on insight into the nature of the observed object or event. On his theory when we arrive at the First Cause the force of habit leads us to inquire for its cause, and the inquiry is as pertinent and well grounded as at any previous step. But on my theory, whenever we have reached a conception of that in which we can see no evidence of previous causation—no indications of its being an effect—the mind is satisfied, and will see, on a moment's reflection the unwisdom and the unreasonableness of asking for its cause. If in all our scrutiny into its nature as a cause we find nothing to suggest its transitoriness, its production in time, there is nothing in the case to either suggest, or to justify, the question as to its cause.

We have seen from another line of argument that we must stop somewhere. I think we see now where we must stop and the reason why we must stop there in our search for a First Cause of all things.

The belief in the existence of God is, I have no doubt, with the great majority of mankind a matter of mere instinct, or of sentiment, or it may be the result of early training. But yet we nowhere see Him as we see ourselves in consciousness, or as we see the objects around us, by the organs of sense-perception. Hence the necessity for reasonings like what we have been pursuing.

But what we can hope to produce in this way needs to become something more than a matter of intellect. It needs to become a matter of the heart and of the life, as vital and as influential too, in the control of our actions and our thoughts, our plans and our purposes, as the consciousness of our own existence or our sense of liability to pains and pleasures, that controls us in the affairs of our daily lives.

This I say will be for many the natural, and perhaps for some persons the only possible course. But for the great mass of mankind no questions regarding the existence and attributes of God ever arise; the idea, the instinct in their hearts is there, and the earnest appeals of the preacher, the sadder experiences of life, call it out and into activity in a way that they know not and for the most part do not care to know. They believe, and believing, they obey, and following on they are transformed in their lives and in the spirit of their minds, until they come to know, through the enlightening influences of the Holy Spirit, that the things that have been told them are indeed true and of God.

Hence I hold as cleared and vindicated from all reasonable objections that the method of reasoning from effects to cause and to a First Cause, from the things that we see to the unseen God and Creator of all, is perfectly legitimate and irrefragable.

The conclusion, therefore, seems inevitable:

1. If there is any relation of cause and effect, or any sequence of causes and effects, there must be a First Cause whose character and attributes are manifested in His works.

2. Or, without assuming any relation of cause and effect, if there is so much as a sequence of *events* one after another in the order of time, there must have been a *first event*. If this event was the act of a spiritual agent then he was a person and acted spontaneously. If it was only a motion or action in mere matter, there must have been, nevertheless, a Personal Agent to cause that action. This the law of inertia necessitates, and in either case God is proved to have existed before all things.

Then to the objections to the method of Natural Theology, which doubters urge on the ground of the theory of Evolution, I answer:

1st. We are in the midst of a process of development from the lower up towards the higher, and we have not yet (in your view) got beyond or higher than the production of man. But certainly it is possible that there should be many orders of beings higher than man, even a One Who is Supreme, and exclusive of all others of the same order because He is Supreme. These higher orders, even the Highest, being possible, must exist as products of Evolution unless there is some One who is above Evolution, controlling its productions and guiding its course.

2d. Evolution itself is not and cannot be an eternal process without beginning or end. The present evolution, in the midst of which our lot is cast, had a beginning and will come to an end; and both beginning and end are "dead points" through which, and out from which, there is no possible escape without the agency of some Being, Who is distinct in His existence, and different in His character, in many important respects, from any of the material substances or forces of which the objects in the visible universe are constituted.

3d. There have been occasions all along in the

earth's life-history when something has occurred, which, although not necessarily implying any change in the laws of nature or any violation of them, did, nevertheless, imply and prove the intervention of an Agent different in kind and in modes of operation, from any and all of the material forces, whether chemical or mechanical, that are known to the physical sciences, or are recognized in our speculations concerning the origin and causes of the phenomena of nature.

I claim, therefore, that, so far as Evolution is concerned, or the advocates of Evolution can have anything to say to the contrary, we have a right, in accordance with our natural instincts, and the common sense and the common sentiments of mankind, to regard these phenomena of nature as manifestations of thought and purpose and as thus proving the existence of Him Whom we, as Christians, acknowledge, worship and adore as God, Who is over all blessed forever.

LECTURE III.

METAPHYSICAL OBJECTIONS; COMTE'S, AND SPENCER'S THEORIES OF KNOWLEDGE.

MATT. VI, 23. If the light that is within you be darkness, how great is that darkness!

METAPHYSICAL OBJECTIONS.

In the last Lecture I grouped together and considered the more obvious objections to the objective or *a posteriori* Method of Natural Theology.

But underneath these objections, as the soil on which they grow, and from which they derive their nutriment and support, there are other doctrines of a different character, which we shall now have occasion to consider. They lie at the foundation and starting point of the *a priori* method indeed; but they are equally subversive of the objective or *a posteriori* method, unless they can be shown to be without any sufficient foundation.

The objections which we have to consider under this general division of our subject are four in number.

1st. The first is that there is no soul or immortal part in man; or if there is, we have no means of knowing it, or knowing anything about it.

2d. The second is that all our knowledge is only relativity, and mere personal opinions or impressions.

3d. The third is that any line or means of argument by which we would seek to prove the existence of God, or attain a knowledge of His attributes, involves a fallacy in form which must be fatal to any certainty in the conclusion.

4th. And finally, we have the doctrine that all knowledge, or pretended knowledge, is based on mere assumptions, or at least upon contradictions, which are of such a nature that we may as well and as successfully maintain any one of them as its opposite, and its opposite as well as itself.

Surely here is a good array of challenges, or objections, to any claim that we may make to any *knowledge*, or even so much as well-founded opinion, on any of the subjects that are the most deeply interesting or the most vitally important to man.

The first and second I will consider in this Lecture; the other two will remain to form the subject of the next Lecture in the course.

I. Natural Theology begins with either assuming as admitted, or claiming to prove as a result, that man is or has a spiritual soul—living in a material body—that the soul has an " inner light," or a " light within," by which it knows something of itself, and its destiny, something of the God Who made it, and to Whom it is subject, both in this life and in the life to come.

Our Lord spoke of "a light within us," and compared it to the eye. As by the eye we see and know external things, so by the "light within" we see and know spiritual things.

This "light that is within us" we know and call by various names. A slight inversion of the words gives the familiar form of "inner light." It corresponds, in many respects, to what Theologians and Christians very generally call "faith," when the word is considered as denoting a subjective act, faculty, or mental process, rather than an objective system of doctrines that are believed and held by an act of faith.

But for the purposes of philosophy it is known rather by such words as "reason," "intuition," or "insight"—"the insight of reason." It is sometimes called $\lambda\acute{o}\gamma os$ and sometimes $\nu\acute{o}\eta\sigma\iota s$ by the Greek philosophers. It is thus related to the *Noumena* which St. Paul, and after him, Herbert Spencer, contrast with *phenomena*, or things that are seen by the eyes.

In its moral relations, this "light that is within" us is known as conscience; and the two, Conscience and Reason, in the absence of any special Revelation, constitute the best, and, in fact, the only, guide we can have to duty and happiness in this world; as well as our only encouragement to hope for anything better hereafter.

But there are those who deny this inner light altogether.

Thus Comte says:[1] "It pretends to accomplish the discovery of the laws of the human mind by contemplating it in itself. Such an attempt cannot succeed at this time of day." And again (p. 461): "As for this fundamental principle of *interior* observation, it would certainly be superfluous to add anything to what I have already said about the absurdity of the supposition of a man seeing himself think." This he thinks takes away "the last phase (or ground) of theology" (p. 11).

Herbert Spencer adopts the same view, and urges it against Sir William Hamilton and Dean Mansel. "The cognition of self, properly so called," he says (§ 20), "is absolutely negatived by the laws of thought; ... the mental act in which self is known implies, like every other mental act, a perceiving subject and a perceived object. If, then, the object perceived is self, what is the subject that perceives? Or if it is the true self that thinks, what other self can it be that is thought of? ... So that the personality of which each is conscious, and of which the existence is to each a fact beyond all others the most certain, is yet a thing which cannot truly be known

---

[1] *Positive Philosophy*, vol. I., p. 11 and p. 461. I quote from Martineau's translation.

at all; knowledge of it is forbidden by the very nature of thought."

Now, connect with the foregoing that other fundamental principle of these men, "the knowledge within our reach is the only knowledge that can be of service to us,"[1] and we have agnosticism complete and fully justified, so far as any knowledge of self, or of our souls is concerned.

This, as you will notice, is beginning early, and laying the foundations broad and deep. If we cannot trust consciousness, and if we know nothing about the self or the soul, except what we can learn by consciousness, we cannot be quite sure whether we have souls or not. Nor can we be any more sure whether there is anything in the mind, or out of it, that manifests to reason the existence and attributes of God.

The inference which both Comte and Spencer draw from their premises is that we must *begin* with the study of the body, and especially the brain; and stop there also, unless we can in some way prove the reality of mind, and justify an appeal to consciousness by a purely physical or physiological method, beginning with the body.

We do not, however, get the full force of the objection without looking a little further. In August,

---

[1] SPENCER'S *First Principles*, § 20.

1874, was delivered Huxley's famous address, in which he attempted to prove that animals are mere "automata," mere machines, without mind or soul.[1]

In this argument, Huxley, taking advantage of the present attainments of science with regard to what is called "the reflex action" of the nerve centres, claims that we can account for all that animals do in the whole course of their lives, by the reflex action of these three nerve centres—the spinal cord, the sensorium, and the hemispheres of the brain.

This reflex action implies neither thought, nor consciousness, nor volition. It is purely physical in its nature. It is, so far as this one point is concerned, precisely what we call *re*action in mechanics. I throw a ball on the floor; the floor reacts and sends the ball back to my hands. In the same way any excitation that is capable of producing a sensation in the nerve centres, is conveyed up the afferent nerves to one or another of these centres, and is returned by it along the efferent nerves, and produces a contraction of the muscles, and some motion of body or limb ensues.

In this way, as Huxley argues, we can account for all the phenomena of animal instinct and activity.

---

[1] Appleton's *Popular Science Monthly*, Oct. 1874. The address has since been published, with some changes, in Huxley's later Vol., *Science and Culture*, p. 206-522.

And he extends his doctrine to man also; and claims that this theory explains and accounts for all that appears in the life of man that is commonly regarded as implying mind or soul.

But we answer to Huxley: Your theory may be true in regard to animals, and probably it is; certainly we cannot disprove it. But with regard to man it is far otherwise. Besides the reflex actions that you speak of, we *know* that we have another class of acts, which are of an entirely different character. It is quite true that an electric current, for example, will produce a contraction of the muscles of the arm as an excito-motor result; but I can contract the muscles and jerk the arm in precisely the same way without any excitation from the electric apparatus. It is true that I draw back my head and close my eyes when I see something approaching that may do me harm, and that I do this involuntarily, and as a sensori-motor action. But I can jerk my head and close my eyes, in precisely the same way, when there is no such occasion for it. It is quite true that you can make me laugh in spite of myself by your wit and drollery; but then, I can imitate that laughter, so far as mere outward appearance is any indication, when I feel like anything but laughter. And herein I have abundant proof of something in my own experience that is more than mere reflex action; something that implies thought and consciousness and volition; something that implies a mind that can act originally and spontaneously; and not only by way of mere reflex-action or *re*action, as do all the masses of mere matter.

But how do we know this? asks Huxley and the agnostics. I answer: I know it by my consciousness of what takes place within, and they will express surprise, perhaps, that I am so far "behind the times" as not to know that consciousness is not recognized as a guide, is no authority; that Comte long ago said that it was absurd to depend upon consciousness for anything, and that no such "attempt can succeed at this time of day." And Herbert Spencer, he may insist, has even proved it absurd, twenty-five years ago at least. "The cognition of self, properly so called, ... is absolutely negatived by the laws of thought," implies in fact a contradiction in terms.

The first point presented in the citation from Comte occurs in the midst of an effort to show that, in order to be successful in our inquiries, we must always begin with the study of the body, and of the brain in particular, and that we must confine ourselves to this method at least until we can prove by it that there is something more than brain, something besides matter in the general make-up and constitution of man.

This idea of considering man as a whole, and studying the brain and its functions as a preparation for the study of the mind, had been begun before the days of Comte,[1] and has been pursued with results that are quite far beyond anything that he knew, and very unlike anything that he could have foreseen or expected. It has given us a far more precise idea of what the body is, and what it can do, than we had before or could have had without, and has thus added great force to the proof that over and besides the body there must be a mind or soul in man, which is of an essentially different and entirely distinct nature from the body, and may possibly exist without it.

We accept, therefore, the challenge of Comte in this respect, without, however, entirely conceding its justice, and may well thank God for this new line of proof, which He, in His Providence, has brought to light just now, when apparently we stand in the greatest need of it.

Let us then distinctly understand the task that is before us. We have to prove first that there is a soul, an immaterial soul in man; and secondly, that consciousness, or conscience, is a legitimate means of knowledge concerning it.

---

[1] GALL began to publish his views as early as 1791, and he and SPURZHEIM began to lecture on the subject in the principal cities of Europe in 1805. Comte was not born till 1798.

1. I begin this argument by a line of proof to which these men certainly cannot object, and with the presentation of some facts which I believe are comparatively new to the scientific world. These facts I regard as peculiarly forcible, when addressed to that class of persons whom we have now chiefly in mind. They are the result of a series of experiments instituted at Cornell University for another purpose. They were conducted by men who did not believe in the reality of mind as anything else than a modification of matter, or a product of brain activity.[1]

In order to appreciate the argument, let me recall to your mind the fact that the "nerves," as they are called, which are distributed throughout the system, consist of exceedingly small fibres, encased in a white sheath or *neurilemma*. They are of two kinds: the one afferent, or centripetal, carrying up stimuli to the nerve centres; and efferent, or centrifugal, carrying out from those centres the stimuli that produce muscular contraction.

It is now well known and admitted by all scientific men, that anything which produces pain or other irritation in any of the tissues of the body, produces—acting through the afferent nerves—a reflex emo-

---

[1] A report of some of the experiments was published in the *American Journal of Science and Arts*, for June, 1878, pp. 413-422.

tion from the gray matter of the spinal cord. This becomes so strong in many cases as to result in involuntary or spasmodic contraction of the muscles and a corresponding motion of the limbs. It is also known and admitted, that any object external to the body may act on the encephalic nerve centres, through the organs of special sense, as the eye, the ear, etc., and produce reflex action of what is called the sensori-motor kind. But all these are purely physiological phenomena. We may be conscious of them when they occur, and are so, for the most part. But they can occur without our consciousness as well. They may occur after the brain proper has been entirely removed, and thus all possibility of consciousness and of voluntary action has been taken away.

But the brain, which is the organ of mind, obeys the same law in all of its reflex action, called ideo-motor, as is observed in the lower centres. It is important to notice this fact in connection with our present subject.

Let any one of us see or hear something that is exceedingly ludicrous or laughable, and the laugh comes involuntarily and beyond our power of self-restraint, even though—as will sometimes happen—very much out of place and unseemly. Or let one receive a sudden announcement of some sad calamity;

the outcry of grief, and the flow of tears will come unbidden, and persist beyond our powers of control. We cannot put them off—as we sometimes do our repentance—to "a more convenient season," or to some chosen opportunity. We do not and cannot take time to think about the matter, and delay our sadness and our mourning until we choose to give way to them. They come from a necessity over which we have no control.

The experiments to which I refer were established to ascertain the rate or velocity at which these stimuli pass along the nerves. Thus, if we apply an electric current to the hand, for example, the current passes up the afferent nerves to the gray matter in the spinal cord between the shoulders, and then passes back by the efferent nerves to the muscles of the lower arm, and a slight jerking motion of the hand and fore-arm ensues. Professor Garver found that the current passes at the rate of about ninety feet per second.

But he wished to try the experiment through a longer circuit. He proposed to give the signal by touching the toe of the left foot, and having the patient give the sign, as soon as he felt the touch in his foot, by a motion of the index finger of the right hand. But there is no continuous nerve leading from the foot to the hand; and he found that there

Metaphysical Objections. 119

was no constancy or uniformity in the time that elapsed between the signal and the sign that it was perceived. Here was a new and unexpected phenomenon.

To understand this, let us suppose a telegraph wire extending from New York to San Francisco, and a person wishing to ascertain, by means of it, the velocity of the electric current. If the wire should coil around an insulator there, and return to the operator in New York, being *a continuous wire*, the message would go and return in just twice the time that it would take for it to cross the continent. But if there were *no continuous wire*, so that the message must needs be taken off and re-written at San Francisco, the case would become quite different. Not only would some time be required for the re-writing, but the operator could *take his own time for it*. He could stop to think, "think twice," perhaps, and he could even refuse or neglect to return the message at all, if he should choose to do so.

Or take another case. It is well known that some metals, as copper, for example, will conduct electricity freely, while others, as platinum, will scarcely conduct it at all. If now a current of electricity passes over a copper wire into a piece of platinum, the platinum becomes very hot, or as we say, "converts the electricity into heat." Now suppose we had another wire that would conduct the *heat*, as the copper wire conducts the electricity. In that case the operator might send the electricity to the non-conducting platinum, and receive it back by the other wire, *as heat*, in a time exactly proportioned to the length of the two wires.

So with the nerve centres. Send up an excitation to the gray matter, by the afferent nerves, and it is converted into emotion, and sent back by the efferent nerves, producing muscular contraction, as in the case of the electric shock.

But in the case of Professor Garver's experiments, there was no "through line" from the left foot to the right hand, with a nerve centre in its course to convert the sensory excitement into an emotor impulse. The message had to be "taken off." He found that there was an "operator" in the case, who received the message and "took time to think," and took his own time to do it in, before giving, by his finger, the sign which would indicate that he felt the signal given to the left foot, as agreed upon.

Professor Garver says, in his report referred to, (p. 422): "It seems that when an individual is experimented upon, as in the given cases, he is conscious of being *surprised* by the signal, even when expecting it. And sometimes the surprise is such that he forgets to answer until he is conscious of considerable time elapsing. At times he has to 'think twice' before he moves his finger or stipulated muscle."

Here, then, is proof demonstrative and unanswerable, that there is something in the brain that acts in a totally different way and in accordance with a law that is totally different from that in which the nerve centres in the body act. Here is something that is capable of self-control; that can take time to think, can pause, and think twice before it acts, and then, act or not, as it determines to do; something that can resist and withstand impulses, and that can act, too, without any impulse that originates from any source except what is within itself.

It seems to me that we have here a genuine case of the application of the crucial experiment—the *experimentum crucis* of Bacon. The mind can act when it chooses to act, and take its own time for acting. It can start *of itself* from inactivity to action and change the intensity of its action at will; the brain cannot. Like every other piece of matter that we know anything about, it acts, or rather *re*acts, only when it is acted upon.

This is our method in all the physical sciences. The chemist, to suppose a case, has pursued his analysis until he has reduced the question of a metal, we will say, to either sodium or potassium. He applies the spectroscope and gets the well-known combination of the lines which indicates sodium, and distinguishes that metal from all other known substances. Or he applies some reagent, as chloride of platinum. If the metal is potassium it is precipitated, but if it be sodium no such result follows.

Or, in another case, in the examination of some rocky mineral, the chemist comes at last upon something that yields none of the characteristic marks of any one of the "elements" yet known to science, but has a well marked peculiarity of its own. He adopts the conclusion that he has made a discovery and found something new that is not yet described or named in his scientific books.

The brain itself, as we have just seen, is, in this respect, and when it is merely a case of brain action, no different from any other mass of matter—even of *in*organic matter.

Here, then, is something that does not act in accordance with *inertia*, which is a fundamental law and characteristic of matter. This something, therefore, is not matter, and we call it mind.

I regard this as wholly unanswerable from a purely physical point of view. We come here to a limit to the powers and possibilities of mere matter. While pursuing our investigations along a purely physiological line, we come upon something that is not physical in its nature and mode of action, and is not amenable to the laws of matter in any form. Where matter ends there mind begins to manifest itself, and becomes all the more unmistakably noticeable in its manifestations, because we had so carefully watched and studied the phenomena of the bodily or material organs.

There are one or two other classes of phenomena that serve to illustrate this argument.

After a day of labor, with the body in perfect health, we feel sleepy. Every molecule and tissue of the body is disposed to sleep, and all the physical and physiological conditions indicate sleep. But we know that we ought not to go to sleep; some duty calls for watchfulness, and we keep awake and watchful. Now here is the body, every part, particle and tissue of it, inclined in one direction, and this something within that we call ourselves, resists the body and controls the result. The mind is different from the body and controls it.

Again, the well-known case of Dr. Tanner. Here was an instance in which, by mere force of will, by mind controlling the body, he fasted and continued without taking food for forty days. Hunger is a physical emotion. Soon after eating the stomach becomes empty, and we are hungry. The unpleasant feeling extends until, in the condition of perfect health, every part and molecule of the body that is capable of feeling or of emotion at all, sympathizes and suffers with the organs of digestion. There is no part of the body, limb or tissue, to counteract the prevailing tendency. And yet for the full forty days he ate not. The mind, on the one side and alone, insisted, the body collectively, and all its parts separately acted together and unanimously on the other. It was body and mind in conflict, a deadly conflict, which if persisted in, as we know it might have been persisted in, would have ended soon in the death of the body.

Sometimes when one is on the whole sleepy or hungry, he may be kept from eating or sleeping by the counteracting influence of some organ or tissue that is in pain or diseased, and will not allow the rest to go to sleep. But in these cases there was nothing of the kind. It was the body as a whole, and acting in its entirety, on the one side, urging in one direction; and the mind, solitary and alone, acting against the body in the other; and the mind triumphed and prevailed.[1]

[1] When these Lectures were delivered, I skipped from this place to the second part of Lecture V, thinking that the second part of this Lecture, Lecture IV, and the first part of Lecture V, would prove too *metaphysical* for the taste and the patience of most hearers. Fearing that the same may be the case with the readers, I give them this timely and—as I think I may call it—friendly warning.

2. Having now fully met, as I think and claim, the demands of the materialists, to prove the existence of mind proceeding and arguing from a purely physical or physiological starting point, I proceed to consider the second part of this subject, and vindicate my right to use the subjective or psychological method, in which we can study the nature and phenomena of mind by means of consciousness or that "interior observation" which every one of us has it in his power to use, when it may suit his purposes to do so.

What we know of a thing in any case depends upon the means by which we know anything about it. I *see* this paper, and by that process I know it to be opaque and white. I feel it, and by the sense-organ of touch I know it to be cold and hard and smooth. By the physiological method alone, pretty much all that we can know of the mind, as we have seen, is that it exists, is a substantial reality—a real cause or agent, and not a mere product of brain activity. We find, also, that it acts spontaneously and under laws of its own, which are in most respects totally unlike the laws that obtain in physical nature. May we use consciousness as one of the means of studying further into the nature and modes of activity?

The men who object to this use of it do not object

altogether and wholly to the testimony of consciousness, and to every use we may be disposed to make of it. They object to it only as a means of studying the *soul*, its nature and possible destiny.

While insisting upon consciousness as a means of knowledge for *external objects*, Comte and Spencer, together with Huxley, Tyndall, and others, who object to our using it, or depending upon it, as a means of knowing *ourselves*, do use it, and depend upon it as a means of knowledge for other things.

And in fact it is a part of the philosophy or the agnosticism with which these names are connected, that *what* we know and *all* that we know or can know as absolutely true, is the facts and states of our own consciousness. And they are right, so far at least: for our sense-perception is no means of knowledge except as we are conscious of the acts of perception which are phenomena or states of our own minds.

Spencer admits, indeed, in the very passage I have quoted, that the existence of this self, which constitutes the personality in each one of us, is "a fact beyond all others the most certain." I might, indeed, stop here and take him at his word. But I greatly fear that if I should do so the poison that is in the statement would remain and do its work nevertheless, and notwithstanding the admission.

He, as Comte before him, speaks of the absurdity of any "interior observation" whereby the soul can know or study itself.

But Spencer, as usual, is more explicit, and gives us the clue to the true resolution of his difficulty. He accepts his fundamental doctrine of a co-ordination in all acts of cognition, and, with a haste which is rather inconsiderate, he runs to the application of it in this particular case. Says he (§ 20): "If the self—the mind or the soul—is the perceiving subject, what is the perceived object? a true cognition of self implies a state in which the knowing and the known are one—in which subject and object are identified." If he had said "indentical," the statement would have been less liable to misapprehension.

It will be observed that the major premise, the principle which Spencer assumes as the ground of his assertion, is that *in all cases* the "subject" and the "object" must be two distinct substantial realities.

But is this really the case? I say "I strike myself." Here, manifestly, the "subject" or agent and the "object" are one and the same thing. Again I say "I see myself walking." Here, also, the "subject" or agent and "object" are one and the same thing, unless we assume that the mind is one thing—the "subject" or agent that sees—and the body that is seen is another thing. But in that case we have an admission that mind and body are two different and distinct substances, which can act independently, the one of the other, and upon one another; and also, that we have some means of knowing each of them separately, and not the one through and by the other exclusively. Let us take good care not to allow these men to ignore the admission which they have thus made.

And we may add that in all languages, the fact of a "middle voice" and reflex forms for all transitive verbs, implies and is based upon the universal conviction that in some cases, at least, "subject" and "object" may be identical. The Greek middle voice, the Hebrew hithpael, the French *se*, the German *sich*, as well as the English *self*, that may be used as above after transitive verbs, are all proofs of this fact or law.

Hence, in this case, as so often elsewhere, Spencer's great haste in making generalizations has led him into a mistake, which may be easily pointed out and rendered forever afterwards entirely harmless.

The law of co-ordination here assumed by Spencer is undoubtedly fundamental and inexorable. There is, however, one case, or I should rather say, class of cases, in which the co-ordinate objects are not necessarily ontologically different. We have within the easy reach of all persons an illustration of what I mean. No one can ordinarily see his own eyes. But let him look in a mirror, and the apparent impossibility is accomplished. He sees his own eyes, or *the eye sees itself*, and is, in the exact words of Spencer, "both subject and object"—both "seeing and seen" in this intellectual operation.

It is quite true that in this case we see the eye by reflected light, by its own reflected image of itself. But it is true also that in consciousness, or that form of self-consciousness in which it is claimed that the soul can see itself and study its own nature and operations, we see it and study it by *reflection*, and by reflected light, so to call it. The mind turns its attention in upon itself, as truly as the mirror turns the light that goes out from the eye in upon the eye itself.[1]

And I will take occasion here to point out another of Spencer's mistakes. And I do so not because it is his merely, but rather because his is a

---

[1] I am inclined to think, however, that "the eye could not see itself" unless it had first seen something else; and that we could not see or think of ourselves *in consciousness*, unless we had previously cognized and distinctly thought of something that is not ourselves. But the pursuit of this subject would lead into an abstruse discussion which the subject does not call for, and which, as it seems to me, the occasion will not justify.

great name with the class of philosophers whom I have chiefly in mind at present, and every statement of his, whether admission or contention, is eagerly caught up and made the ground of confidence and of inference, all of which tend in the same direction as this advance towards utter unbelief and irreligion, which its advocates seem very intent upon accomplishing.

One of the points in Spencer's theory, which is indeed rather implied than expressly stated by him, is that the mind cannot be occupied with two thoughts or engaged in two acts at the same time. The objection may be stated in the form of a question as follows: "If the mind is engaged in any act of thinking, any act of perception, cognition, memory or volition, how can it be engaged also, and at the same time, in the act of perceiving itself, or thinking of itself, and of its own act of thinking of, or perceiving, something else?

The case of the eye will furnish an answer, so far at least as the demonstration of the fact is concerned, without perhaps explaining the way in which the apparently impossible act can occur.

While looking at my eyes in the glass, I can stand there, if need be, for several minutes, both looking at my eyes, seeing, and being conscious all the while that I am seeing them, and at the same time be thinking of their structure, their appearance, and being conscious, also and moreover, of the fact that I am thinking of their appearance and structure. Now here is most certainly a case that is within the reach of all that may be disposed to try it, and which, on trial, will be found to demonstrate the fact that somehow or other, explainable or inexplicable, there is a process of "interior observation" in which a man can "see himself think," and the mind becomes, in the language of Spencer "both subject and object," "the perceiving and the perceived," "the knowing and the known."

And in fact what is assumed here to be impossible is occurring all the while, and may be observed at any moment of our conscious wakefulness. We may be looking at and examining some external object, and yet be conscious, all the while, that we are thinking of something else as well, something that we will speak of to no one, and quite possibly something that no one, but ourselves and that God who sees and knows all things, suspects that we are thinking of.

I have already endeavored to give to the experiments of Professor Garver great prominence as a proof of the reality of a mind or soul in man, not, however, because I think it the only proof we have, nor yet because I regard it as being intrinsically stronger or more convincing than the other line of argument, which depends exclusively upon consciousness, but because I regard it as better adapted to our present purpose. It begins where our agnostics and the advocates of physical science claim that we ought to begin; it pursues the method they point out as the only legitimate one. But it comes to a conclusion which they did not expect nor desire, and one which, as I firmly believe, they cannot repudiate, and from which they can find no way of escape.

The other method is no less conclusive, and is in some respects more germane to the subject. It is as old as Descartes, and was first, so far as I know, formulated by him. He began the agnostic, or skeptic process, and rejected all opinions until he might have time to examine into their foundation and see exactly on what they depended. In this process he professed, and aimed, to go back or down until he should come to a proposition that he could not deny, or even so much as doubt. In this way he reached his famous proposition *cogito ergo sum*. He argues[1] that this inference of his existence did not depend on the differentia or peculiarities of the act of thinking, strictly understood; the conclusion from the act of doubting or denying was as legiti-

---

[1] *Discourse on Method*, Pt. IV, Cousin's ed., vol. i, p. 156 and following.

mate and as irresistible as that from thinking or affirming. "If I doubt," said he, "I cannot doubt that I am doubting; or if I deny, I cannot deny or doubt my act of denying; but from the one as from the other, and from the one as legitimately and as inevitably as from the other comes the inference of my own substantial existence. And there must be the two, subject and object, the me and the not-me, and the one as real and as substantial as the other."

Sense-perception and consciousness are alike, also, in this, that they must have an object, and a *substantial* object as well. We cannot see or hear except as there is something that is seen or heard. We cannot see *walking*, for example, but what we see is the man or animal that walks; walking is the process or mode, and the man or animal is the thing that is seen in that process or mode. As in the external world, there is no whiteness or hardness without something that is white and hard, so within, there is no perception, no thinking, feeling, or choosing, without something that perceives, thinks, feels and chooses.

We have, then, an "interior observation," by which we know directly and immediately the mind and what it is doing; an "interior observation" for the acts and phenomena of the mind within, as well as an exterior observation for the objects around us.

And just as we are liable, in our observation of the outward objects, to false perception and to mistakes with regard to the identity and the qualities of objects, to their nature and character, even when there is no occasion to doubt their reality; so on the other hand, much occurs within without our notice, we are liable to mistake the facts and acts of our consciousness, and are very liable to err in our analysis of them and in our inferences from them.

Thus it appears that in fact we have the means of a better and more immediate knowledge of our minds than we have of the objects in the external world. In the words of Huxley:[1] "The most elementary study of sensation justifies Descartes' position that we know more of mind than we do of body; that the immaterial world is a firmer reality than the material. For sensation is known immediately. So long as it persists it is a part of what we call our thinking selves, and its existence lies beyond the possibility of doubt. The knowledge of an objective or material cause of the sensation, on the other hand, is mediate; it is a belief, which in any given instance of sensation, may, by possibility, be devoid of foun-

---

[1] *Sensation and Sensiferous Organs*, in Appleton's Popular Science Monthly, May, 1879, p. 93. The same essay with modifications, in *Science and Culture*, p. 253. I quote from the Pop. Sc. Monthly.

dation. It may arise from the occurrence of appropriate molecular changes in the nerve or in the sensorium, by the operation of a cause distinct from the affection of the sense-organ by an external object. Such subjective sensations are as real as any others, and as distinctly suggest an external object, though the belief thus generated is a delusion." But of course the internal state, and so the mind in which it occurs, is no delusion, or, as Huxley says, "it lies beyond the possibility of doubt."

I quote Huxley the more gladly and in preference to other authorities, because he is commonly considered as belonging to the school of philosophers whose views I am criticising, and in most respects he does undoubtedly belong to that school.

This advance in Physical Science, from which the materialists expect and claim so much for their cause, helps us in more ways than one. I have referred to it as affording a means of demonstrating the existence of a mind or soul in man, which is a substantial reality and a spontaneously acting agent or cause.

I turn to some facts that have been established by the line of investigations and experiments for another matter which is of interest to us in our present undertaking.

The facts and laws with regard to reflex action

have enabled us to make a new classification of the motives and to see more clearly some of the laws of their influence upon our acts of choice.

We have three classes of motives: (1) the lower or the appetites that arise out of the condition of the body. (2) The affections which originate in some mental act or state. (3) The rational emotions, like those of conscience and religion. The appetites are impulsive in their natures—they grow more intense, like hunger, until they are gratified, and then cease to exist. No man is hungry after he has eaten all he wants.[1]

The affections, on the other hand, do not become extinct by exercise, they are more likely to become stronger; this is still more surely the case with the ethic emotions—the impulse to duty.

From these facts we derive two very important results.

The first is that we are capable of increasing the force or intensity of our effort, at will.

Suppose, for example, there is something on the floor that is offensive to me. I stoop down to pick it up and toss it out of the window. This I do with

---

[1] Or possibly some of our philosophers who are so much smitten with the doctrine of "the indestructibility of force" would prefer to say that the hunger has not ceased, it has only become "latent" for the time being.

the impression that it weighs but a few ounces. But I find it weighs several pounds. I "put to the more strength," until I accomplish the object. But, meanwhile, the motive occasioned by the offensiveness of the object has not increased or changed at all. The object is no more offensive than it was.

Now this increase of force or effort *at will* is what no mere mass of matter can do. And this is one of the facts of consciousness that serves to distinguish the mind from matter and to prove and illustrate the freedom of will.

The next fact is that we do often follow the weaker through the higher motive, acting in a direction contrary to the stronger, and lower. The appetites, as we have seen, are lower and more in the nature of passions than the affections or the dictates of conscience. But we often follow conscience in disregard of the appetites.

The case may be illustrated by a phenomenon in physical science. If I strike a ball and send it upwards, the blow is the greater force for the moment and the ball goes up; but gravity is stronger in the end, and the ball comes down at last. *We*, however, unlike the ball, can resist from the first, and go no one step in the direction of the appetite, which is the lower, and for the moment the stronger motive.

II. The next point that I have to consider is the

doctrine that we know nothing of things in themselves, and that all knowledge is only relative.

Passages from the writings of Sir William Hamilton are cited as authority for this doctrine, and in fact he is usually regarded as the originator of this view of the nature and foundations of human knowledge.

Herbert Spencer, however, adopts it, enlarges upon it, and makes it the subject of one entire chapter in his *First Principles* (Part I, c. iv). He says: "The reality existing behind all appearances is and ever must be unknown"; and not only cites Hamilton as saying that "with the exception of a few late Absolutists in Germany, this is the truth most harmoniously held by philosophers of every school," and Spencer himself says: "To this conclusion almost every thinker of note has subscribed."

1. The theory of perception and the question how we perceive the objects around us, has indeed occupied the attention of thoughtful men and philosophers from the times of Plato to our own day. During the Middle Ages there had grown up a notion of certain properties or essences of things, which may be considered as distinct from the things themselves. Descartes[1] gave this theory a lucid exposition when

---

[1] *Meditations: Meditation Second*, Cousin's Ed., Vol. I., p. 259. "And yet what do I see of this crowd of men as I look down from

he compared the properties to the clothes one may have on. By this one appears black or white, possibly a nobleman or a peasant. And as he would say, we never can see the man himself, but only the clothes he has on, so we never see the object, the "thing itself," but only the properties that surround it and cover it up so that we see it never, but only them.

Locke had said: "If these external objects be not united to our minds . . . and yet we perceive their original qualities in such of them as singly fall under our senses . . . it is evident that some singly imperceptible bodies must come from them to the eyes, and thereby convey to the brain some motion which produces those ideas which we have of them in us,"[1] as the means of perception of external objects.

These "imperceptible bodies" or particles—or something analogous to them—Kant regarded as the matter or material out of which our ideas of objects are made. But he also held that while the mind might be thus receiving the matter or "*contents*," as he calls it, of our ideas of things from the things themselves in the external world in this way, he

---

the window, but the hats and cloaks that might cover artificial machines, which only move themselves by springs? *qui ne se remueroient que par ressorts.*

[1] *Essay on Human Understanding*, B. II., c. viii., § 12.

held also that the mind itself was the active agent in their formation, and furnished the form or *schema*, so that it depends on the mind itself, rather than upon the external objects themselves, what sort of an idea we form of them. The idea thus formed he called the phenomena, *the appearance*, which the thing has in our minds. These "appearances of things," or our ideas of them, as he held, make up and limit our knowledge; the "things-in-themselves," *ding an sich*, as he called them, are mere matter of guess and conjecture; we *know* nothing about them.

But from his psychology there could be in the mind ideas or phenomena—that is, "appearances"—of such things only as we can perceive by the bodily senses, and hence we have in this sense of the word ideas of material objects only. I say in this, which is the English sense of the word idea; for Kant would scarcely call these mental acts ideas at all. He prefers to use the word to denote such objects as can have no visible representation, as time, space, etc.

It is but due to Kant, however, to add that he included the "things-in-themselves" among the "noumena," or objects of thought. He included the Supreme Being, or God, in the same class of objects. And it results from his philosophy, and passages can be cited from his writings to prove it, that he regarded the existence of God as being as certain and as rest-ing on the same kind and means of knowledge as the existence of the external world around us, or of any one of the objects within it. Neither the one nor the other could be regarded, in his opinion, as being *immediately* known, as phenomena, that is, as appearing to the mind, but only as noumenal—realities lying beyond and outside of consciousness.

Sir William Hamilton adopted the notion that was prevalent in his time, that in perception we do not see the objects themselves, but only their properties, the color, the form, etc., with which they are clothed and covered up. Hence, he, too, adopted the expression (*ding an sich*) thing in itself, which Kant's theory had made necessary and to which it had given a peculiar and very significant meaning. But in the case of Hamilton, I can see no necessity for such an expression. Nor can I see that it makes any difference with our method of argument, whether his theory of perception is true or not. I certainly think that it is not true. But all that we ask, all that we need or assume, as the basis of our argument, is the existence and reality of the objects around us as they are seen by us and as they appear to us.

But the very act of perception implies the reality of the object perceived. And so Hamilton taught. He insisted upon this view with great emphasis.[1] In

[1] *Philosophy of Common Sense*, Appleton's Ed. of "The Philoso-

this I agree with him, although I should not explain the matter as he does. He makes the perceived object a matter of consciousness. I think it is not.

But the act implies the object. We say, "I perceive the paper." If, now, the paper does not exist, is nothing, the proposition becomes "I perceive nothing," which is equivalent to "I do not perceive." The act of perception is not performed.

In this, perception differs from imagination and memory. In mental acts of these two kinds we think *of* the object without its presence, and possibly without its reality. But perception is one thing; false-perception, imagination, and memory are others, and perception differs from them in that it implies the reality of its object as they do not. And it results from the law of co-ordination that perception must be as real as an act of the mind, and as a matter of consciousness as either memory or imagination. If there were no real perception we should have no such idea and no such name, any more than the blind would have names for colors, or the deaf words denoting sounds.

Theories of perception have been vitiated, from Descartes down, by a theory of the relation of substance and properties; the theory makes the

---

phy of Sir William Hamilton," p. 31, also p. 173. Lectures on Metaphysics, Lects. XII., XIII., and XIV.

properties as substantial as the substances themselves. It supposes that the properties are things that lie upon and cover up the substance, as a man's hat and coat cover his body. Hence the doctrine is expressly declared as a fundamental principle that we do not perceive the objects themselves, but only their properties.

But the whiteness and hardness of this paper—though properties of the thing itself—are not things. They are not envelopes or coverings of the real substance. It does not *underlie* them. What we see is the substantial thing itself. It *is* white and hard; but the whiteness and the hardness we do not perceive, and in supposing that we do so, we make them to be substances and not mere properties, as we had professed to regard them.

These truths are so obvious that they need only to be stated to secure the assent of everybody. It is only when the mind is intent on something else, that this old mediæval error creeps in like a sort of *survival* and does its work on the course of our speculations, and leads us to a result, which is the same as though we had not ever rejected the dogma. We still speak of the sun's rising and setting, as though its motion was the cause of the alternations of night and day, although the scientific world have long since abandoned that view. Nevertheless, we all of us have to unlearn it with the beginning of our education.

2. The other point, "the relativity of our knowledge," is more serious.

It seems to me that we have here the old question of Plato's day revived. He contended sometimes that if there is such a thing as insight, νόησις, or διάνοια there must be ἐπιστήμη or true knowledge; at other times, as in the *Timæus* (§ 25), if there is any true knowledge ἐπιστήμη as opposed to mere impression and individual beliefs, δόξα, there must be not only νόησις or insight as a means of that knowledge, but also both νοούμενα or things that are known by insight, and νοητά, truths absolutely known concerning them.[1]

Or to put this contrast in its psychological, rather than its logical or ontological point of view, Plato, as we have seen, Lecture I., began by drawing a sharp distinction between the things that we know and are led to contemplate by "the eyes" and "the seeing of the eyes," ὄμμασιν καὶ ὄψει on the one hand, and by insight and reason, or reasoning on the other. And in the *Timæus*, § IX., XXI., XXV., and others, Plato combines the two, and speaks

---

[1] I introduce these words in the Greek because they have an etymological connection which gives them an argumentative force that cannot be well retained or exhibited in any mere translation.

of νόησις μετὰ λόγου, and then proceeds to say that in consequence there must be realities that are not seen by the eyes, ἀναίσθητα, but are known to insight alone, νοούμενα μόνον, which are unchangeable in their nature, ἀεὶ κατὰ ταὐτὰ ὄν, which are the same always, and for all rational or intelligent beings.

I think it is undoubtedly true that we have in what is generally called knowledge the two elements, one of absolute certainty and the other of mere relativity, mere personal opinion or impression. But the statement that all knowledge is merely relative, like most of the others which I have had occasion to criticise, has two or more meanings, in one of which at least it is usually quite true, and in the others it is clearly false.

If by the relativity of knowledge we mean to say or imply that knowledge is only of the relations of things *one to another*, we should hardly feel inclined to question the doctrine. Even in mathematics the truths that make up our knowledge, express relations, possible or real, of objects one to another.

Every proposition must have a subject and a predicate. These two terms are, for the most part, expressed or represented by names which denote the objects we are thinking and speaking about, and between which a relation is affirmed or denied. All the other words in the proposition, of whatever parts of speech, as verb, adjectives or adverbs, are used merely to denote the relations that exist, or that we wish to assert as existing, between those objects: "the earth *moves around* the sun," "the table *stands on* the floor," "the man *rides in* the carriage," etc. To this extent all knowledge is relative. And if this is what and all that is meant by the *relativity of knowledge*, nobody can dispute it.

But in another sense the statement is intended to assert that nothing is absolutely true; that all truths are only relative to us, and that any statement can be regarded as true only *in relation to us* individually.

This doctrine results from a too hasty generalization of some facts that had attracted the attention of some of the great philosophers of our century.

I see an object before me; it is red. But what is redness? Of course the object may change its color and cease to be red without losing its identity. Moreover, redness may not be precisely the same thing for two persons. But what is more important, there might be a change in my eyes, or in my brain, so that the object would appear to be of a color different from that which it now appears to have, with no change in the object itself. Hence redness is said to be relative, and the word to denote only a relation between me and the object.

Or let us take another example: the fluid that feels warm to our hand when it is cold, may feel cold to us when our hand is warm. The water on which the autumn leaf floats before the wind is as solid to the leaf as the rock-quarry on which stands the hut of the hunter, or as the pavement is to our feet as we go about our daily round of business or pleasure. And thus at first sight, and with only a hasty glance at a few examples, *all* knowledge does seem to be only relative, one thing for one person, and in one relation, and quite another for other persons and in other relations; nothing the same to all, or certain for anybody.

Now this is true of most of what we know of the *properties* of external objects, but is not true of all. Take form for example. The objects I see around me are of various forms, round, square, and irregular, and of great varieties of irregularity. But their form is absolute. No change in me, in my eyes or my brain, can cause them to be of a different form. With a change of position or of medium, they may indeed *seem* to have a form different from that which they now appear to me to have. But they are of the same form still, with no change *in the things themselves*. Their form is absolute, and the same for all beings that can see them.

So with their individuality or separateness. I see

two objects. They are distinct and separate. This is no idea that is relative to me. It is true that from defect in our organs of vision we sometimes see things "double"; but never, that I know of, do we see two things as one when we can see them distinctly at all. But however we may see them they are distinct and separate.

Now here we have the basis of most, if not of all of the sciences. In form we have the basis of geometry; in individuality, *after abstracting the properties*, we have the basis of arithmetic and the science of numbers; and *with the properties* we have the ground of that classification of objects with which science begins, and on which it ultimately depends.

It is especially worthy of note, also, that all the sciences that deal with objects in the concrete, as botany, zoölogy, mineralogy, geology, astronomy, etc., base their classifications chiefly on the form of objects rather than on any other of their properties, which are only accidental in an ontological point of view, since they may be different for different persons, and even for the same person under different circumstances, as in the case of the water just spoken of.

There is still another aspect of this doctrine of "the relativity of all knowledge," which deserves a passing notice. It is claimed that we can know a thing only as it is in relations with other things, but what it is absolutely or would be if it were in no such relations, we do not know.

It is indeed quite true that we know of nothing except as it is in relations. Nor do I think that this can be regarded as a very serious matter. Whatever exists, if indeed there is more than one thing existing, must exist in relations to other things. Some of these relations are accidental, and others are permanent and essential; and permanent because they are essential. This is the case with all the mathematical relations. It is the case also, though to a less extent, with those relations on which the classifications on which all scientific knowledge is based, on the one hand, and those natural classifications, on which all possible use of language depends, on the other.

What we want to know, then, is these very relations, and the knowledge of these relations is all the knowledge that can be of any use to us. In the midst of them we live here. In the midst of some of them at least, we must live, if we are to live at all, hereafter. Our relations to things of time and sense may indeed pass away. But we have relations of a higher kind that are eternal; as eternal as God and Heaven itself. These cannot pass away.

But speculations about the way in which things

would appear if they were not in relations to one another can have no practical or scientific value. For if the time has ever been, or shall ever come, when anything shall exist that is so absolute as to be in no relations with other things, there will be either nothing to be seen or nobody to see it.

I have already spoken of those who would deny or question the reality of the existence of substantial objects around us whose existence is independent of our thought and of our will. The skepticism or agnosticism of these men gives rise to another phase of what is sometimes called "the relativity of knowledge." If these objects exist only for us, in relation to us, and as we create them or conceive them to be, they are most surely only relative to us.

But by the necessities of co-ordination there must be two objects—the subject and object—the perceiving agent and the perceived object—in every act of perception or cognition. And this object cannot be mere matter in general, nor the outward world as a whole. It must be some one individual object, and the individual objects as they are seen one by one individually.

This results from the necessity for co-ordination.

But as a matter of psychology, as we have seen, perception is a distinct act, and different in its essential nature from either imagination or memory. It is an act of which we are conscious. Hence if any one should deny his consciousness of the act of perception, he would be virtually proclaiming himself consciously unconscious of something that he is conscious of, or unconsciously conscious of something that he knows nothing about; and in either case, much like the man that should vociferously proclaim himself speechless.

But it is claimed that these laws and conditions of knowledge depend upon classification, and that "the First Cause," "the Absolute," "the Infinite," cannot be *in any class*, cannot be "conditioned" and "related" to other things so that "the relativity of knowledge" excludes, at all events, the knowledge of God.[1] It is indeed perfectly true that whatever we cognize, we must cognize under the law of co-ordination; and whatever we think or speak about, we must think of and name under the laws of classification, and by referring to some class. Hence we think and speak of God as a Being—one among many—and we call Him, by way of distinction, the Supreme Being; or if these men prefer it, as the Infinite Being, the Absolute Being. We also think of Him as a cause, and call Him the First Cause. I can therefore see no force in their objection, al-

---

[1] HERBERT SPENCER'S *First Principles*, §.24, p. 81, and following.

though Herbert Spencer makes a great account of it in his chapter on the "*Relativity of Knowledge.*"

But what is meant by these men when they speak of "the relativity, the absolute relativity of all knowledge," is often only the *uncertainty* of knowledge. This I think is eminently the case with the first part of Spencer's argument just referred to. This is obvious on a slight inspection of § 23.

Now in all "knowledge" there is undoubtedly an element of uncertainty. Call it by this name and all men will understand what you mean; and all men who have had any cautious experience in dealing with human affairs, or in the pursuits of scientific truth, will appreciate and admit the truth of what we say. But "relativity" is another kind of a word. It is of vague import and very uncertain application.

If, however, we will make another, and, as I think, better analysis of the phenomena that Spencer discusses in the Section of his *First Principles* to which I have just referred, we shall come to a very different and a much more satisfactory result.

Knowledge may be considered as made up of two elements, "facts" and "principles."

Facts we may *know* for a certainty, but we never *comprehend* any one of them completely and thoroughly. I know the fact, for instance, that some years ago an apple seed was planted in a certain place in the soil. I know the fact that it grew to be a tree, blossomed in the spring and bore fruit in the autumn following. Now we may call this one fact or many—a series of facts—as we please. We *know* the facts as *certainly* as we know our own existence, as certainly as though we were omniscient. But we understand and comprehend it, or them, as we choose to regard them, but very imperfectly. There is much of uncertainty, something of relativity, and very likely some thing of error and mistake in what we think we know and call our knowledge with regard to it.

But in regard to *principles*, strictly so called, there is no such element of error, uncertainty, or relativity. Take as examples for illustration the axioms of geometry. They are said to be self-evident. But at all events we know them for a certainty and we *comprehend* them, too, perfectly—comprehend them as well—with profoundest reverence be it said—as Omniscience itself, does or can do.

Now such first principles or self-evident axioms underlie all branches of science and scientific knowledge, and are either expressly stated or tacitly assumed in every book that is written that is intended to teach anything—nay, in every statement that is made with the intention of asserting a truth. The physicist *assumes* that *inert* matter cannot start from rest to motion, or change its rate of motion, *of itself.* The chemist assumes that elements not in action on each other will not begin to act without something outside of them changing their relations to each other; and that he cannot, in any possible analysis or synthesis that he can make, either create or annihilate and destroy one atom of the matter that comes into his crucibles or in any way under the manipulations of his hands.

Now of these two elements, facts and first principles, all knowledge, properly so called, is made up. In what we call the inductive, or *a posteriori* sciences, the sciences that depend on observation, the element of facts enters the most largely and forms the largest as well as the most conspicuous part. But in the *pure* mathematics, the element of fact scarcely enters at all. The truths are obtained by demonstration from (1) the axioms and (2) definitions, exhibiting the *nature* of the things we reason about, entirely abstracted from their *accidents;* so that so long as our reasoning is without fault or fallacy, the conclusions are as certain and without intermixture of uncertainty or "relativity" as the axioms themselves.

We may then grant these agnostics their philosophy of "the relativity of knowledge," so far as facts show that it is only relative, and still have enough left for all the purposes of our argument. We have as much and all that these advocates of the physical or positive sciences have or can have for their own use. If we gain all the certainty they can have, or if they will concede to us as much certainty as they claim for themselves—their facts, their theories, and their speculations in their various stages and degrees—it is all we ask for our own purpose and use. All men believe or know that there are the two bodies in space, the sun and the planet Venus. Most men know or feel very sure that there will be another transit of Venus in June, A. D. 2004. Now if they could be made to feel as sure that there is a God Who has created us and all things in heaven and on earth, visible and invisible, and if they could be brought to feel as sure that there is a life to come and a day of judgment at the close of this life, as they do of the coming transit of Venus, it would be all that we could hope or desire as a doctrine of mere Natural Theology. It is, in fact, vastly more than we expect to be able to accomplish by our method.

But the facts are as sure, the foundation is as secure for us as it is for them.

The methods of the sciences are, in their essential elements, one and the same for all. There are four steps or stages: observation, analysis, classification, and inference. And at each of these stages error and mistake are possible. In the first stage we have observation—observation of (1) external objects by sense-perception, and (2) observation of internal phenomena, or the acts and states of the mind, by consciousness. And here, as we have seen and admitted, we are very liable to mistake—both in the mind and in nature—in consciousness and in the perception of the objects we think we see.

In the analysis and classification of our facts, the methods are somewhat different, and we are liable to errors of different kinds in the two branches of study, the study of mind and the study of matter.

In making our inferences the laws of logic are the same for both departments of knowledge. In the one direction we prove the reality of mind, the existence of God, and the doctrine of His Moral Government, by the same methods and with as much certainty in our conclusions, as in the other direction, we prove the existence of the objects in the world of matter, the fact of universal gravitation, or the theory of evolution.

The methods are in their essential features the same. The certainty is the same in the one case as in the other, so far as the mere grounds of logic and evidence are concerned; so far as our opinions and inferences are a mere matter of thought and intellect.

But in so far as the results in the two cases are a matter of the heart and of sentiment, they are not the same. We begin with the objective method. We observe external objects almost from the moment of our birth. We are always with them, and they with us. We test our opinions and theories by fact and experience daily. But in the other direction we begin to observe and study the facts of our mental activity only at a later date. We all find, at first at least, a great difficulty in grasping hold of them and keeping them steadily under our gaze, long enough to study them. We can make no diagram or model of them; we can have no dried specimens, or preserved preparations to aid us in our effort to get a clear conception, and form a careful analysis of the phenomena which we have to study.

It is no wonder, therefore, that material objects should seem the most familiar and real to us. Many of us have never heard of the facts and truths of mind. And many more who, in this age of irreligion and unbelief, have never been accustomed to hear the truths, or to practice the duties of religion. Hence, while *there* all seems familiar, here all seems new and strange, and to some extent improbable, if not even impossible.

One contrast more. The facts and truths of science impose no restraint upon our thoughts and actions—none, that is, except such as we have already learned to accept without complaint or murmur. But the truths of religion open for us a new world, and put a view and an estimate upon our life, our duties and our relations here that are new and quite unfamiliar to our minds. This new view calls for exertion, for self-denial, for sacrifices *here* and *now*, as the means to a glory which eye hath not seen nor ear heard, nor heart of man conceived, which can be fully attained only through the mercy of God and the grace of our Lord Jesus Christ, His most Blessed Son and our only Saviour and Redeemer, in that world to which we are all hastening, and for which this was designed and created chiefly if not only as a means of preparation.

LECTURE IV.

LOGICAL OBJECTIONS; HAMLITON'S "NO PROOF OF THE INFINITE," KANT'S "ANTINOMIES."

MARK XI, 35. Take heed therefore that the light that is within be not darkness.

LOGICAL OBJECTIONS.

I closed the last Lecture without taking advantage of the opportunity which it afforded me of saying something of the benefits of early Christian education and its relation to the general subject before us.

The prophet Jeremiah[1] foretold a time when " God would " put his laws into the hearts of the people and write them in their minds, and St. Paul[2] refers to this prediction as about to be fulfilled in the Christian Dispensation.

I think this implies something more than the mere hearing and learning so as to remember the words of divine truth. It rather describes that process with what we are now familiar, and by which these truths come to be acquired instincts—a sort of second nature—as the result of heredity and long use.

It is now a fact well known to modern science that, while man has *natural* instincts like the brutes, a large share of those he now possesses are the result of education. Those which constitute the dif-

---

[1] Jeremiah, xxxi., 33, 34.   [2] Hebrews, x., 16.

ference between the savage man of the woods and forests and the civilized man of the farms and of the cities, are of this kind. Those which constitute the difference between the men and women of these modern Christian communities and the men and women of ancient heathen civilizations, are also of this kind, and have been acquired under the guiding and controlling influence of Christianity. They begin in voluntary acts, performed from choice and conviction, and most often, not without self-denial, sacrifice and danger. These acts are repeated by persevering effort until they become fixed habits, and they are transmitted by the law of heredity to the offspring. In this way the virtues of these early believers have become so much a matter of habit and of course with us, that we forget that men and women have not always been such as we now see them, or that we are indebted to what Christianity has done for us, for this most beneficent change. Virtues which were then scarcely so much as thought of, which people were neither expected to have nor respected for having, have now come into vogue and are regarded as indispensable to respectability in any social community. And vices, of which St. Paul said it was "a shame even to speak,"[1] and which he even *commanded* that they should "not be

---

[1] Ephesians, v., 13, v., and 3.

once named" among Christians, have now no existence and no name among us.[1] Nowhere is idolatry professed and practiced; and men, even if they are not pure and clean in their lives, find it necessary to pretend and to appear to be so, in order to keep their places in society. Truth and honor, as well as every social virtue, are at a higher standard than they were then. This change hath God wrought for us, and it is the result of religious training under the influence of Christianity and the Christian church.

I think I have a right to allude to the facts of human history as furnishing both a proof of the existence of God and an illustration of His attributes. I shall say something more on this subject in the last Lecture. But as germane to the subject just alluded to, called "heredity" by modern scientists, I will take occasion before going any further with my general subject to say a few words more.

This is not the only case in which the attainments of modern science—attainments which have been made for the most part since the days of Paley and

---

[1] This great change in the moral sense and instincts of mankind is what but few persons appreciate. Nor have I ever seen it presented as I think it ought to be, as an argument in favor of the divine origin and claims of Christianity. See, for an exhibition of heathen sentiment on this subject, MAHAFFEY, *Social Life in Greece from Homer to Menander*. It became much worse after Menander. See also BECKER'S *Charicles*.

Butler—have afforded new and unexpected proofs of the inspiration and divine guidance of the early writers of the Scriptures and of the founders of the Jewish and Christian Dispensations. I refer now to one only.

We all readily see and acknowledge the wisdom and necessity of the isolation of the seed of Abraham, if there were to be kept in the line of his posterity the knowledge and worship of the one true God. But little thought, however, has been given to the opportunity which this isolation and exclusiveness gave to the law of heredity, just spoken of, to do its appropriate work among them. It did its work and made "a peculiar people"—peculiar in more senses than one—and that peculiarity became, in the generations from Moses to Christ, so thoroughly inwrought into their very natures that it has not departed from them yet. Everywhere they are still a peculiar people, isolated and exclusive.[1]

---

[1] As showing the effect of the discipline of heredity, I cite the following facts, which are found in Jewish history: The tendency to polytheism and idolatry, hitherto prevalent among all nations, became extinct with the Babylonish captivity. They have, and have had for two thousands of years, no *drunkards* among their men and no *wantons* among their women. They have no scrofula or leprosy, though leprosy was once not uncommon among them. Cases of insanity and idiocy are exceedingly rare. In all cases of epidemics, as plague, cholera, scarlatina, diphtheria, etc., they are singularly exempt. RICHARDSON, in his *Diseases of Modern Life*, p. 19, and

The operation of the same law, or rather the influence of Christianity *under the same law*, in regenerating[1] the race and transforming them "into the image of Christ," was as necessary, and apparently as much a part of the divine plan, as the preparation for Christ's "coming" had been under the old Dispensation. But geographical or local isolation was here out of the question. The gospel must be preached to all nations, and all, or as many as would listen and should be converted must be gathered into the fold. Hence, in order that "heredity" might have a chance to do its appropriate work, a *Spiritual Discipline*, not only as a means of enforcing the new modes of life and habits of thought *within* the church, but also as a means of excom-

---

following, gives the following statistics by way of contrast: Deaths under 5 years, *Jews*, 10 per cent., *others*, 14. Average age, *Jews*, 48 years and 9 months, *others*, 36 and 11 months. One half the *Jews* reach 53 years and one month, of *others*, the half reach only 36 years. Of the *Jews*, one quarter live to be over 70 years, and of *others*, not over one quarter live to be 60 years old. Diseases of the lungs, as consumption, are exceedingly rare. These are certainly remarkable results. They show what religion and morality—morality upheld and sustained by religious faith and discipline, can do for man.

[1] The word "regeneration," and its equivalent in Greek, $\pi\alpha\lambda\iota\gamma\gamma\epsilon\nu\epsilon\sigma\iota\alpha$, occurs but twice in the New Testament, and in the first instance, St. Matthew, xix., 28, I think it refers manifestly to a change in humanity collectively and as a whole, rather than to the renewal of persons each in his individual capacity. The other place in which the word occurs is Titus, iii., 5.

munication and exclusion for those, who after due efforts to retain and guide them, and after all due forbearance and patience with their unavoidable infirmities and weaknesses, would not live a Christian life. *Within* the church they would be a means of defeating the operation of this law. *Out of it*, their influence for evil in this line would be at an end, or work at least among those who, and whose posterity, were to pass away; and church fellowship and association would be among those only in whom the influence of the Holy Ghost and the co-operation of their own wills would be at work in the same direction in this slow but sure and inevitable process of regenerating humanity and transforming the believers into the likenesses of Christ, their Divine Head.[1]

Christians, whose eyes and thoughts are turned in that direction, will see in this, perhaps, a reason for the stress that is laid upon church unity and harmony among its members, and, by way of contrast, the severity of disapprobation with which the "sins of heresy and schism" are spoken of, and the terri-

---

[1] GALTON, in his work on *Hereditary Genius*, p. 357, and following, contends that *from this point of view* the institutions of celibacy and monasticism during the Middle Ages was a great disadvantage to Modern Europe. They withdrew the most intellectual, the most gentle, and the most refined of both sexes, as clergy, monks and nuns, from the ordinary sphere of life and of *parentage*, so that the race was propagated by the coarsest, least intellectual, and most animal part of the population.

ble effects that are ascribed to excommunication and separation from the communion of the Church. These sins tend to defeat one great object of the Church, the regeneration of humanity as a whole, as effectually as the sins of uncleanness and blasphemy prevent the sanctification and salvation of the individual soul of the offender.

I. But let us proceed to our main subject, the Logical Objections to the validity of the Methods of Natural Theology, and the importance of the results which may be reached by pursuing them.

I have considered the physical objections, and those that have been urged on grounds of psychology and metaphysics. And it is worth noticing that the men who have urged them have evidently done it for a purpose, and that when that purpose is not in view, they speak and act in regard to these very doctrines as though they held the common views of mankind on the subjects; common sense triumphs over their philosophy.

1. The point which I propose next to consider is one that is purely logical in its character. I will state it in words which I will cite from Sir William Hamilton, although it is but due to him to say that there appears—after a most careful scrutiny—reason to doubt whether in using these words he is ex-

pressing his own views and is not rather giving an abstract of what he supposes to be the views of Kant. His words are as follows:[1] "Things in themselves,—Matter, Mind, God,—all, in short, that is not finite, relative, the phenomenal, . . . is beyond the verge of our knowledge. . . A knowledge of the unconditioned is declared impossible; either immediately, as a notion, or mediately as an inference. A demonstration of the absolute from the relative is logically absurd, as in such a syllogism, we must collect in the conclusion what is not distributed in the premises."

I have said that in using these words Hamilton *appears* to be giving expression to the views of Kant. And yet Hamilton seems to hold the same view himself, and to accept all of its consequences. Anyhow in this matter his professed disciple Mansel has accepted this view and carried it out to the utmost extreme of statement and illustration.[2]

Two things, however, must be observed.

(*a*) While Hamilton says he thinks the reasoning complicated and the reduction incomplete, he says,

---

[1] *Philosophy of Sir William Hamilton*, Appleton's Ed., p. 458. The article was first published in the *Edinburgh Review*, October, 1829, under the title of *Philosophy of the Conditioned*, and *Refutation of the Various Doctrines of the Unconditioned, especially of Cousin's Doctrines of the Infinito-Absolute.*

[2] MANSEL, *Limits of Religious Thought Examined*, Bampton Lectures, 1858, Lects. II. and III.

also, that "Kant has clearly shown that the idea of the unconditioned can have no objective reality—that it conveys no knowledge—and that it involves the most insoluble contradictions" (p. 459).

(*b*) In the second place, we must observe that Hamilton's whole line of argument, which is understood to be a demonstration of the impossibility of any knowledge of God by the methods of Natural Theology, is based upon, and is an illustration of the doctrine here enunciated with regard to "any syllogism" that may be claimed and used as proving His existence or attributes. Mansel so understood the doctrine of Hamilton, and urges it with great force in his well-known work, *The Limitations of Religious Thought.* And Herbert Spencer so understood and applied it in that criticism of his which I have quoted in a preceding Lecture.[1]

And yet Kant and Hamilton and Mansel were all of them earnest Christian men. One of them, Mansel, was a high dignitary in the English Church. And "the philosophy" of Hamilton has been extensively favored and accepted rather, as I think, however, because he was known to be an earnest Christian believer, than from any appreciation of its intrinsic merits. It is felt and accepted, without question, that the "philosophy of a good Christian

[1] *First Principles*, Pt. I., chap. iv.

man must be a good Christian philosophy." But I think that the world is beginning to realize the fact that in his concessions, chiefly, as I think, through the influence of Kant, Hamilton gave away the whole case, as Kant had done, in the hope and belief that he was placing Christianity on impregnable grounds.

It is well to note carefully the terms of the statement. It does not say in precise terms that any syllogism that should claim to prove "the existence of *God*" would involve the fallacy in form that is described; but only that every syllogism that would prove or demonstrate *the absolute*, would involve such a fallacy. This distinction is practically lost sight of by our modern agnostics, and quite possibly it is of no value in itself.

Kant and Hamilton are two great names in all matters of logic; possibly the greatest that the world has seen since the days of Aristotle. One therefore naturally hesitates long, and considers well his ground, before calling in question any dictum of theirs.

The words used describe what the logicians call an "illicit process." But as a matter of fact there can be no illicit process of the *minor* when the subject is an individual term, as any word used to denote the Supreme Being must always be. Nor can there be illicit of the *major* when the conclusion is affirmative—which must always be the case when we predicate any attribute of God.

It is perhaps, therefore, on the whole, most likely that these critics had no definite idea of the fallacy which they intended to ascribe to the reasoning by which we would prove the existence of God.

1st. Let us then observe, in the first place, that Spencer's argument, which I quoted at some length in the first Lecture, is not based on a syllogism, or any form of syllogistic reasoning. It is what is technically called an "immediate inference" from the co-ordination and contradiction of terms. His argument is, as the idea of silence implies that of sound, and the idea of light implies the idea of darkness and proves its reality as something that has been cognized and experienced in some way, and by some means, so the idea of "the finite," "the relative," "the conditioned," implies the idea of the Infinite, the Absolute, the Unconditioned; the very fact of their being finite *phenomena* which we can see and handle implies the reality of infinite and absolute *noumena*, which we can neither see nor handle, or in any way make subjects of immediate observation.

Observe, he does not say, or claim, that *we can prove*, by any form of syllogistic reasoning, their existence. Not at all. He assumes the ground of his argument as implied in the very laws and possibility of thought, as one of those axioms which we must assume in all processes of reasoning, and which, because they are primary and self-evident, there can be no method of proving that will make them more certain than they were before we began our pretended demonstration.

But in the next place I wish to emphasize the fact that in the *a posteriori*, the outward or objective line of argument, by which we prove the existence of God, and of which I spoke more especially in the first and second Lectures, we do not attempt or claim to prove His existence as "the absolute," the "infinite," or "the unconditioned," but only as God, the First Cause and Creator of all things.

Now it is certainly one thing to prove His existence as First Cause and Creator, and quite another thing to prove Him to be infinite or absolute or unconditioned. In the first case we are using terms that are technically positive; terms that indicate His existence, by the very attributes, by the exercise and manifestation of which, we prove that He exists at all.

Let us then distinctly notice at the outset, that the expressions "the Infinite," the Absolute," "the Unconditioned," and such like, are not terms that are at all adequate or practicable for the purposes of logic and of reasoning. What we may say of any object, if we speak truly and intelligently, depends upon what that object is, its *essentia*, the τὸ τί ἦν εἶναι of Aristotle, which is always indicated by the noun that we use as its name, and never by any adjective, which can at most denote an additional *differentia*.

It is indeed true that the differentia becomes part of the essentia of the more limited subject when the adjective is so joined to the noun that the thought or the description of the object is incomplete without it. Then, in accordance with Aristotle's dictum, *de omni et nullo*, whatever may be predicated if the noun *without* the adjective may be predicated of it also after it is limited by the adjective, and much more may be said after and in consequence of such limitation. Thus, whatever may be said of man may be said of *black* men as well, and much besides. But without the noun we have no subject definitely before the mind.

If, now, these philosophers, when they speak of "the Infinite," mean that incomprehensible Being whom heaven and earth obey, and Him only, and use this form of expression out of reverence for the sacred Name, we can appreciate their motive and respect them all the more highly for it. But we must understand what they mean.

As a matter of mere logic it is evident that any adjective may be used to qualify more than one noun, and that it may qualify so many nouns, and nouns denoting such different subjects, that no one thing may be predicated of them all except the adjective itself. Thus we may speak of things as infinite until all that can be said of them all is that they are infinite, not indeed in number, but that they agree and are alike only in possessing this one property of infinity. If, then, we will speak of "the infinite" as a subject, all that we are authorized to say of it, or them is that they are infinite. We must therefore understand their terms. To assent to their statements without doing so would be like giving an unlimited letter of credit to a spendthrift who neither knows the extent of your resources nor cares for your wants and necessities.

2d. The terms "infinite," "absolute," "unconditioned," are certainly negative in form.

Let us consider for a moment what these terms mean, and what is the process of thought by which we arrive at them.

What I see and handle is finite.. Each object has a limit at which it begins to be, and it extends from that limit to some other point or limit at which it ceases to be at all. Now this is true of all the objects we see. And we generalize our observation, and say that all *material* objects, all objects that are seen *in space* must be finite.

What, then, do we mean by saying that anything is infinite? How shall we find out what is the meaning of the word? I know of no way better than Plato's, his "accustomed method,"[1] as he called it. In this way we consider the several objects that are called by any one name and thus find, if we can, what they have in common; and that will be the true, though the most general meaning of the word.

Men speak of space as infinite, and so, likewise, of time and of number as infinite. But I think that the process by which they get at this adjective is essentially the same in all these cases. All *visible* objects are finite, and could not be seen unless they were so. But we imagine space, which is not visible nor yet tangible. Hence we cannot suppose it to end anywhere; for, fix any limit as you please, and where you please, and you cannot but suppose that space extends beyond. Hence we say it is infinite, or has no limits.

So with time. Name any date or event and we cannot think that time does not extend beyond it— did not begin before and will not last after it. Hence we say time is infinite.

With regard to number, the case is not quite so clear. Cousin has in fact argued that there is an essential difference between what he calls the numer-

---

[1] *Republic*, B. X., c. i., εἰωθυῖα μεθόδος.

ical and the ontological infinite.[1] The numerical infinite should rather, as he thinks, be called "the indefinite." We begin by supposing any sum or number, and then suppose it increased by addition or multiplication until it becomes what we call infinite. What it has become, in fact, is so large or so small that a little more or less will make no *practical* difference for the matter in hand; or possibly so large or so small that we cannot tell or imagine how large or how small it is.

But Cousin fails to tell us what the ontological infinite is, or what we mean by the word. And I doubt very much whether it has any meaning but the one above assigned to it. Now, all these meanings of the word are the same in their import, they relate to quantity; and when we call anything infinite we mean to say that it is so large that we do not know how large it is, and cannot imagine or suppose it to be larger.

The word "absolute" refers rather, as I think, to quality than to quantity. We may say of water that it is absolutely pure; we should hardly say it is infinitely pure. We say of space, as above noticed, that it is infinite, or infinitely large, but we should hardly call it absolutely large.

[1] *Course of the History of Philosophy.* Course for 1828-9, 2d series, Vol. II., Lect. XVIII., Chap. iii., in Dr. Henry's translation.

But neither of them are words that are obtained from any act of immediate cognition. What we cognize, immediately, must be finite, limited and conditioned. If it is infinite or absolute it must be proved to be so by reasoning from its nature, and not from any direct observation.

We predicate of objects: (1) that which we see them to be, and (2) that which we can prove them to be by reasoning from their nature. I see this paper, as opaque, and because it is opaque and reflects the light. I feel it because it is hard, and resists my hand when I press upon it. It *is* limited or finite, because both by sight and touch I perceive something besides it, around it and beneath it, which begins to be, where *it* ends or ceases to be. But I prove that it is divisible—divisible infinitely or without limit if you please—from its very nature as an object that is extended in space; and I predicate all these properties and say it is opaque, it is hard, it is extended and it is divisible, with equal confidence and certainty.

Now we have seen that we prove the existence of God, as a First Cause, and as such He must be spontaneously active. We see that He must be intelligent in order that all that he has done shall be in accordance with law and truth. We see that He must be powerful, in order to do all that we find it necessary to ascribe to Him in the construction and course of nature.

We have a good illustration of this method of argument in the discovery of the planet Neptune, spoken of in the last Lecture.

Now in precisely the same way we find God acting spontaneously, with intelligence and power—great power—and some one asks, Is He infinite? We say He is not finite, because we do not and cannot conceive Him to *begin* to be at any point of either space or time, or to *extend as material objects do*, and of necessity must from some one point of space to some other point. His omnipresence is not conceived or accounted for in that way. Now, if we choose to denote the *not being finite* in this sense by the word "infinite," then surely we may say that God is infinite. But the affirmation is based on an immediate inference from the meaning of the word finite, and not on any syllogism that can involve any illicit process, whether of the major or of the minor, or in fact any other fallacy in form.

So with the word "absolute." If we generalize our experience of all visible and tangible things, and say they are all effects, dependent on causes that preceded them for their existence, and upon other things still for the continuance of that existence, and then say that God cannot be dependent, like these objects, on anything else, either for an origin or for the continuance of His existence, and choose to express this thought by the word "absolute" and call Him absolute, there can be no logical impropriety in so doing; there is nothing absurd or fallacious in the process.

With regard to the word *unconditioned* we must say something a little different. In most respects it means, in this controversy, the same as the word "absolute." And in so far as that meaning is concerned, what I have already said of the word "absolute" is fully applicable to the use of this word also. God may be said to be "unconditioned" in the same sense as He may be said to be absolute. And in fact He may be said to be absolute in another and more popular sense of the word. He is absolute in that no one person or thing can resist His will, outwit Him, if we may so speak, or interpose any obstacle that will be felt to be an obstacle to the accomplishment of His purposes.

I have spoken of "absolute" as relating rather to the quality than to the quantity of an object. In the discussions to which I am referring, however, the word is used, as I understand, chiefly in reference to freedom from restraint and constraint, or necessary conditions and limitations to His wisdom and power. When we call Him absolute, we mean that

He can do as He pleases, is under no law or limitation, as I apprehend, rather than to speak of the quality of His attributes.

But in regard to His infinity, we mean to assert, as I conceive, that we know of no limit to the extent of His wisdom and power, or to the presence and reality of His being.

But the method of our proof should not be mistaken. We do not prove, or attempt to prove directly, from the phenomena of nature, His existence as "the Infinite" or "the Absolute." What we prove is His existence *as God*—a Being of wisdom, of power, and of spontaneous activity.

Do you ask, Is He infinite and absolute? I answer, This depends very much upon what you mean by the terms. He is both infinite and absolute in the sense in which these attributes can be inferred, from what we know otherwise concerning His nature. And that is all, I apprehend, that we can care to affirm of Him, and in that sense of the words our affirmation cannot be questioned or denied.

But "unconditioned" has another element in its meaning, or rather suggests another view of the attributes and relations of God. And in this sense it is used as the opposite of the word "relative," as well as the opposite of the word "conditioned." Hence to be "unconditioned" in this sense is to be out of relations to all other things.

We touch here a thought that has occasioned great trouble to the metaphysicians from Spinoza, at least, down to our own time. If God be in "conditions" and "relations" with other things, those other things must exist, and, as they argue, they must be, outside of Him, and limit His existence; and so He cannot be infinite. This is a central thought—the germ of Spinoza's pantheism.

Now this may involve a mystery which we can neither understand or explain. Certainly I shall attempt no explanation of it here, for it is not my claim that the method of Natural Theology can prove, or claims to prove, that God is infinite, absolute, or unconditioned in any sense of those words which can make their use liable to the objections that Hamilton, Mansel and Spencer have urged against them. I aim to show only that this method of argument proves His existence as First Cause and Creator, a Personal Agent, wise, powerful and good, beyond any limits that we can discover or conceive.

But in a certain sense of the word He is not unconditioned. No object of thought or of reality can be so. He is in the "condition" of being an object that is thought of, and of whom we think, whether we think of Him to affirm or to deny His existence. He exists "in relation" to all created things—the relation of creator to things created.

He exists in the "relation" to all *phenomena* which we have denoted by the word *noumenon* as that which they make manifest. And if either the doctrine of the Christian Revelation or those of Natural Theology are true, He exists "in relation to" us as our present Moral Governor and our Final Judge. And on the Christian basis, He exists in many most tender relations to us—in Christ as our Redeemer—in the Holy Ghost as our Sanctifier, to enlighten our minds and guide us in the paths of peace and the ways that lead to Heaven. He exists as all that can excite or inspire noble thoughts, holy aspirations, all that can give courage and hope; all that can afford strength and give victory at last.

And if He exists at all He must be "conditioned" and in some relations to other things. He must be in a "condition" to be thought of, to be loved and feared, to be the creator of whatever is created, and the coeval of whatever is eternal, if there is anything that is eternal but Himself. If there is more than one thing in the universe they must be in some relation to each other and limited in *logical*—though not necessarily in *ontological*—quantity, so that the one is not the other, and they may be two or more and not one only.[1]

[1] It is readily admitted that any two objects *that are extended and have the property of impenetrability* which is ascribed to all material

And yet Herbert Spencer, while protesting as we have seen most earnestly, and, as I think, most effectively, against the inference of Hamilton and Mansel, derived both from their psychology and their logic to the non-existence and unreality of what they call "the infinite," was led by his false psychology both unwisely and unnecessarily, as I think, into the worst feature of his agnosticism, the one feature, as I am inclined to regard it, which made of him an agnostic rather than a devout Christian believer. He spoke of God as included in the class of things which he called unknowable and unknown! But surely He of Whom it may be said that He is "omnipresent," "manifest in every phenomenon of nature," "working through its myriad agencies," and even in the mind of man himself, "producing in him" his highest and holiest "beliefs," ought not to be regarded or spoken of as altogether unknown to men. We have here, not as a confes-

substances, do limit each other, not only in logical but also in ontological quantity, so that neither one of them can be said to be infinite in any proper sense of the word. They are not only two objects, but both of them are finite objects. Philosophers, however, hold that space, which has not the material property of impenetrability, is infinite, notwithstanding the existence of material objects. They are thought to exist in space—without limiting it ontologically. Much more, therefore, may this be said of mind, and especially of the Divine Mind, to which even the material property of extension is not ascribed.

sion only, but as a contention rather, all that Natural Theology claims, or that its methods ask,— the existence of God, His agency in nature, His providence over all things, and His inspiration, if not even miracles, in the only sense in which the Bible claims them, or in which theologians have any occasion to claim or to assert their occurrence.

The case is the same in all its essential features, and in all of the principles of logic that are involved, as what occurs in our daily experience.

There is a man before me. I see his body, but of his consciousness, his thoughts, his mind, I know nothing except what is manifested to me by his words and his actions; these are the *phenomena* which manifest to me what is yet only the *noumenon*, his self. I readily interpret his words and actions to imply certain thoughts, feelings and purposes, and these are the states and acts of his mind or self. By them I understand that he is a person and not a mere thing; that he is wise and benevolent, has purposes and aims to accomplish, and some measure at least of power to accomplish them. Of course I may misunderstand him. And it is possible that he may intentionally deceive me. But no one doubts the general result, the inference that he is intelligent, is capable of purpose, and has purposes to accomplish, arrived at in this way, however I may misunderstand them, or he may have deceived me as to the particular thoughts and purposes he may have at the moment.

So with Natural Theology. The world and its facts and events are the phenomena that manifest unto us the attributes of God. Their existence proves His creative power. Their intelligibility proves His intelligence. Their harmony and the adaptation of one to another, and of part to part, proves His purpose in their creation, and their tendency to produce good results rather than evil and painful ones, proves Him to be good and gracious, as truly and by rules of observation and reasoning which are the same, as those that guide us in the study of the character and purposes of any of our fellow men.

But is He then "the infinite," "the absolute," the "unconditioned"? It depends entirely upon what you mean by these words when you ask the question or raise the objection. In any sense and in all the senses in which the words are positive and have any meaning, He is infinite and absolute. But in so far as they are negative or involve contradictions and absurdities, He is not the one nor the other. He is only good and wise and powerful, just and gracious, full of mercy and compassion, "not willing that any should perish,"[1] but rather that "all men should be

---
[1] 2d Peter, iii., 9.

saved and come to the knowledge of the truth."[1] And to this end He not only spoke in times past by the Prophets, but "hath in these latter days sent us His Son Jesus Christ, full of grace and truth, whom He hath appointed heir of all things."[2]

The question, then, is not whether we can prove the existence of "the Infinite" or "the Absolute" or "the Unconditioned." But it is rather whether we can prove the existence of God—not so much whether He is "infinite," "absolute," and "unconditioned," as whether He is at all or not. And when we cognize or prove His existence, by the very act by which we prove that He is we prove *something* of *what* He is. If I know anything directly by sight I know it to be opaque, extended, of a certain color. If I prove that God exists by any process or mode of reasoning, I know Him to be that by which in the process I prove Him to be at all, *possibly* infinite and absolute, but *certainly* First Cause, Creator and Personal Agent.

II. I pass now to the last part of this branch of my subject: Kant's Antinomies.

It is now a little more than a hundred years since Kant published his great work, the *Kritik der reinen Vernunft*. In this work he first published to the

---

[1] 1st Timothy, ii., 4.   [2] Hebrews i., 2.

world his now world-famous *antinomies*. These are contradictions, on which, as he claims, all knowledge and all opinions, of whatever kind, must rest as their basis. In a subsequent work, his *Prolegomena*, he repeated his *antinomies*, with some slight modifications of statement, but with the continued claim that they lie at the foundation of all that can be called, or claimed, as knowledge, scientific or otherwise.

1. Before he came to his *antinomies* Kant had worked out a theory of perception which left the reality of the objects that are perceived in the external world in doubt, and he had taught that, at best, we can have no knowledge of them as they are as things-in-themselves [*dinge an sich*]. He had also limited the application of the principle of Identity and Contradiction to mere definitions, "*analytic propositions, a priori,*" as he called them. And then, as if to complete the work of destruction, he declared the doctrine that all that we call or can claim as knowledge, whether in science or religion, rests at bottom and for its only foundation on one or another of these contradictions or "antinomies."

2. The second point in Kant's Philosophy that requires notice, is his rejection of the Principle of Identity and Contradiction for all synthetic judgments.

I have found no statement of his doctrine on this

subject, or of his reasons for it except the brief statement in his *Prolegomena*, § 2, and this seems very inadequate for so important a departure from the preceding doctrine on this subject, which seems to have been universally accepted.

Leibnitz had taught that all the propositions we can assert *as truth* or knowledge—as distinct from matters of faith or mere belief—rest on the two principles (1) *Sufficient Cause* and (2) *Identity and Contradiction*.

On the first depends all the truths of history and mere science. And we may have the principle under either of the two forms (*a*) *causa essendi* or the cause of its existence, and (*b*) *ratio cognoscendi*, the grounds on which we believe or acknowledge the proposition.

The Principle of Identity and Contradiction is the ground of all *absolute* truths. It is based on the nature of the subject with regard to which the proposition is affirmed and is obtained by the two processes, analysis and demonstration.

I make no mention here of the Principle of *Excluded Middle*, because I regard that as only a part of the means by which we apply the principle of Identity and Contradiction in what we call the indirect method of proof or refutation.

The Principle of Identity and Contradiction can

be easily illustrated sufficiently for our present purpose. Suppose we have the proposition $2 + 1 = 3$. The terms are not apparently identical. But we can write them thus, $1 + 1 + 1 = 1 + 1 + 1$, in which case the identity is apparent.[1]

Now this is true of every other proposition in mathematics, and in the science of logic. The only question or difficulty arises out of our dexterity or want of dexterity in the manipulation of the forms of expression. There is no difficulty in regard to the principle itself.

The same law holds also with regard to some of the fundamental ontological questions. I will instance two, both of which have already occurred to us in the course of these Lectures.

The first relates to the reality of the objects that constitute the external or material world. Take any one of and each of them separately and we may say of it, "*I perceive it.*" But what is *it?* a reality? If so, very well. If not, it is not-any-thing, not-a-

---

[1] Or if we put the statement into another form, we get a proposition to be tested by the principle of contradiction. Thus if we say $2 + 1 = 4$, we may write it $1 + 1 + 1 = 1 + 1 + 1 + 1$, in which it is obvious on inspection that the first term or member is not the same as the second; or, *if this is true*, three is not there, and it takes three and something else to make three, which is of course absurd and impossible if we use the word "three" in the same sense in both cases.

thing, no-thing, nothing. Thus we have, "I perceive nothing." But that is logically equivalent to "I do not perceive." Hence, if the act of perception takes place, and is not merely false perception, imagination, memory or dreaming, the object perceived is a reality.

Take, again, the principle of causation. "Every effect has or has had a cause." But the word effect implies that whatever is properly called an effect is a thing produced by some form or act of *efficiency*, which of course implies an *effector* (if we may coin a word), or an agent which caused its existence. Hence if there were no such agent, there could have been no such act; and what we have called an effect was not properly so called—it was not produced as the product of any previous agency, or any previously existing agent.

All of Kant's demonstrations rest upon and assume this principle; and it seems to be almost incredible and not at all well accounted for, that he could have denied and rejected this principle as he did in the passages of his *Prolegomena* just referred to.

3. The remaining subject is the Antinomies. These Antinomies consist of four pairs of propositions which are apparently contradictory each one to its fellow in the combination, and the relation of the one to the other—the "thesis" to the "antithe-

sis "—is such that while it is impossible for us to believe or even suppose that both of them are true, the one of them can be demonstrated to be absolutely true as well as the other, which is its contradictory opposite. In fact, it is Kant's claim that both of the propositions in each of the four pairs can be shown to be absolutely true, leading to the inevitable agnostic consequence that there is and can be no *absolute* truth anywhere.

Kant saw both the wide sweep and the profound depths to which his so-called *antinomies* extend. He says: "There are four of them and only four, and they are natural and unavoidable. There can be neither more nor less, because there are no more series of synthetic propositions which limit the empirical synthesis." "In them we have the whole dialectical play of the cosmological ideas which do not allow that any object that is not in accordance with them shall be given in any possible experience."[1] This language is a little peculiar, but as nearly as I can construe it to the common sense of mankind, he means to assert that there is no opinion, truth or statement, that can be made by man that does not in some way or another depend upon, and assume,

---

[1] I quote from statements given in connection with the statement of the Antinomies, and immediately before them as an introduction to them, Vol. II., p. 330, and following, Rosenkrantz's edition.

the truth of some one of these eight propositions, which he arranges in the form of four pairs of antinomies. After discussing them through some two hundred pages he concludes the discussion with these words:[1] "We can neither endure the thought nor yet protect ourselves against it, that a Being Whom we represent to ourselves as the Highest among all possible things should say to Himself, 'I am from eternity to eternity; besides Me there is nothing except what exists, is something [*etwas ist*], through My Will [*durch meinen Willen*].' *But where then am I?* Here everything sinks under us and the greatest Perfection as well as the smallest, floats before the Speculative Reason, without support, to which [reason] it costs nothing to allow them, the one as well as the other, to disappear, without the least effort on its part to prevent it."[2]

---

[1] *Kritik*, Works, Vol. II., p. 477.

[2] The quotations given above to show Kant's appreciation of the Antithesis, are taken from the larger work, "*Die Kritik.*" I give here, however, a few citations, in the translation from the latter work.

"No metaphysical act or subtlety of distinction hinder or avert [*verhüten*] their contradictory opposition, but they compel the philosopher to fall back upon the first principles of the pure Reason itself," p. 109.

"The Thesis, as well as the Antithesis, can be set forth by equally clear and irresistible proofs,—and I pledge myself for the correctness of these proofs—and the Reason sees itself divided against itself,—a state of things at which the skeptics rejoice—while the crit-

It is but fair towards Kant, however, to pause and say that he gives this only as the outcome of Reason —*Pure* Reason—the result of *speculative* Philosophy. But Kant himself wrote several other works in which he maintained, very strenuously, that man is *naturally* a religious being, and that, instinctively, he does believe in God and in the reality of the objects in the world around us, and he seems sometimes at least to regard this instinct as being as good a foundation for religion and morality as the Pure Reason or Philosophy itself could be. And yet the world knows but little of this part of Kant's philosophy, while everybody knows of his "Antinomies" and his Agnosticism.

Kant is a very difficult author to understand or to translate. We can never for many minutes translate so as to convey precisely the ambiguities that are in his German, nor always be quite sure that we have given in English that one of the meanings of which his phraseology is susceptible which is the best.

But such was to be the sweeping effect of his "Antinomies." And from that day to this no logician has ever been rash enough, so far as I have seen, to undertake to show precisely what and wherein

ical philosopher betakes himself to reflection with great uneasiness," p. 110.

consists the fallacy of his "demonstrations." Even Sir William Hamilton, who was perhaps the keenest man in this respect since Kant's time, admits them to be—in words that I have already quoted—"insoluble," "the most insoluble contradictions."[1]

These "antinomies" may be stated thus in the best translation that I can make of them:

FIRST PAIR.

Thesis: "The world had a beginning in time and is limited in space."

Antithesis: "The world, in regard to both time and space, is unlimited" (that is, had no beginning in time and is infinite in extent).

SECOND PAIR.

Thesis: "Everything in the world is simple."

Antithesis: "There is nothing in the world that is simple; but everything is composite" (made up of parts).

THIRD PAIR.

Thesis: "In the world there are free and spontaneously acting causes."

Antithesis: "In the world there is no liberty, but all is bound in the necessity of nature."

---

[1] Even Professor MORRIS, in his little work, *Kant's Critique of Pure Reason*, which is an admirable exposition of Kant's doctrines, evades the subject under cover of general statements, as it seems to me, rather gives a clear and precise exposition of the fallacy that lies in them, p. 236.

FOURTH PAIR.

Thesis: " In the series of causes in the world there is somewhere a necessary Being."

Antithesis: "There is nothing necessary in the world; but in that series of events that make up the world all is contingent" (accidental or casual).[1]

[1] I give these *Antinomies* in the original and in both forms, the earlier form of 1781 in the *Kritik*, Rosenkrantz's edition, vol. II, p. 338, etc., and in the form given in 1873 in the *Prolegomena*, vol. III, p. 109. The earlier forms are printed in the left hand column, and the latter opposite to them on the right hand.

FIRST PAIR.

Thesis, 1781.	*Thesis*, 1783.
Die Welt hat einen Anfang in der Zeit und ist dem Raum nach auch in Grenzen eingeschlossen.	Die Welt hat der Zeit und dem Raum nach einen Anfang (Grenze).
Antithesis.	*Antithesis.*
Die Welt hat keinen Anfang und keine Grenzen im Raume, sondern ist, sowohl in Ansehung der Zeit als des Raums, unendlich.	Die Welt ist der Zeit und dem Raum nach unendlich.

SECOND PAIR.

Thesis, 1781.	*Thesis*, 1783.
Eine jede zusammengesetzte Substanz in der Welt besteht aus einfachen Theilen, und es existirt überall nichts als das Einfache, oder das, was aus diesem zusammengesetzt ist.	Alles in der Welt besteht aus dem Einfachen.
Antithesis.	*Antithesis.*
Kein zusammengesetztes Ding in der Welt besteht aus einfachen Theilen, und es existirt überall nichts Einfaches in derselben.	Es ist nichts Einfaches, sondern Alles ist zusammengesetzt.

Now I think I can show, without going into any great depth of metaphysical profundity, or taxing you with any great effort to follow me and comprehend what I say, that there are really no "antinomies" here; no "contradictions," "insoluble" or otherwise; and that all the appearance of contradic-

THIRD PAIR.

Thesis, 1781.
Die Causalität nach Gesetzen der Natur ist nicht die einzige, aus welcher die Erscheinungen der Welt insgesammt abgeleitet werden können. Es ist noch eine Causalität durch Freiheit zu Erklärung derselben anzunehmen nothwendig.

Antithesis.
Es ist keine Freiheit, sondern Alles in der Welt geschieht lediglich nach Gesezen der Natur.

Thesis, 1783.
Es giebt in der Welt Ursachen durch Freiheit.

Antithesis.
Es ist keine Freiheit, sondern Alles ist Natur.

FOURTH PAIR.

Thesis, 1781.
Zu der Welt gehört etwas, das, entweder als ihr Theil, oder ihre Ursache, ein schlechthin nothwendiges Wesen ist.

Antithesis.
Es existirt überall kein schlechthin nothwendiges Wesen, weder in der Welt, noch ausser der Welt, als ihre Ursache.

Thesis, 1783.
In der Reihe der Weltursachen ist irgend ein nothwendiges Wesen.

Antithesis.
Es ist in ihr nichts nothwendig, sondern in dieser Reihe ist Alles zufällig.

It will be observed that the Antitheses, as stated in the later work, the *Prolegomena*, 1783, are much more brief and condensed, but substantially the same in their meaning and import.

tion and antinomy there is, depends upon and arises out of a fallacy in diction. Or to be more precise, the whole difficulty arises out of what is called technically an *Ambiguous Middle*, using the term in its broader signification.

I do not offer this solution as a mere conjecture, or as merely something that *may* be said by way of answer or demurrer to his conclusion. But I examine his illustration and argument, his *Beweis* and his *Anmerkungen*, and find that there are the two senses which he attached to the terms, one of them in one proposition and the other sense in the other proposition.

Allow me to explain in a few words precisely what I mean by an Ambiguous Middle.

We say, "Feathers are light; light comes from the sun," and the ambiguity of the word "light" is obvious. We say, "Money will buy whatever is for sale; a two shilling piece is money." Here the ambiguity is slightly different in form, but it is equally obvious on a moment's thought of what the premises must mean in order that assent may be given to them at all.

Take one more example. We eat what we buy in the market, but we buy raw meat in the market, therefore we eat *raw* meat, or eat our meat raw. Here, again, the ambiguity is apparent on a little consideration.

But in the case of Kant's "antinomies" these ambiguities do not lie on the surface so as to be obvious on a mere inspection. It is quite true, indeed, that we might conjecture or suspect them, from a mere inspection of the language Kant has used. That, however, could hardly be regarded as any satisfactory exposition. We must inspect the *proof* which he gives in order to see whether our suspected ambiguity is really involved in and lies at the foundation of his reasoning. And this is what I propose now to do.

To take his "antinomies" in order, and consider them one by one in detail. I begin with the thesis of the first pair. It reads, "The world had a beginning or has a beginning in time and is limited in space" that is, it is not infinite in either respect, but has its limits and bounds.

By the words "the world" in this case he means the objects and events that we see, the world-series, *weltreihe*, as he calls it. He argues, as I have done, that these *events*, occurring one after another, constitute a series, in which there must have been from the very nature of every *actual* series, a first term—a term before which there was no other.

In regard to the *objects* in the world he holds that as each one of them is limited no one of them can be infinite, nor yet can any addition or multiplication of them make infinity. Hence the world, *in this sense of the word*, is limited; the *weltreihe* is finite both in time and space.

But in the "antithesis" "the world is said to be, in regard to both time and space, infinite." Kant here uses the words "the world" to denote the world-idea, the *weltinbegriff*, as he calls it. And his argument is that the world as a series of events implies Something Whose existence is not an *event* in the world (the *weltreihe*) and Whose presence is not by *extension* from one limit or point to another, some Being Who is eternal without succession of time—*no older than He was*—and whose presence is an omnipresence without relations to space or place such as finite or material things have.

Now in all this Kant is but presenting the same line of argument as I have been stating and illustrating in these Lectures. The world considered as what it *is* is finite, but when considered as including all that it *implies*—that is, as the universe—it includes something that is infinite, not limited by time and space.

In the second pair the "Thesis" is in these words: "In the world everything is simple," but for "antithesis" he has, "In the world there is nothing simple, but everything is composite."

In discussing this pair I propose to take up and consider the antithesis first.

His line of argument and illustration is the one that is usually pursued to prove the "infinite divisibility of matter" and of space. Whatever is extended may be divided into two parts; these parts again into other and smaller parts and so on *ad infinitum*. Kant is here obviously speaking of *mechanical* or *mathematical* division. And, *in this view*, nothing is so small that it may not be considered as made up of parts into which it may be divided, and so it may be said to be theoretically divisible.

The word that is common to both propositions, and on which the supposed antinomy depends, is "simple," *einfach*, in German.

We have seen what he meant by it in the "Antithesis." But when we come to consider his argument and illustration for the "Thesis," we find he means by the term something very different. He is now referring to logical division.

The example which Kant cites and dwells upon mostly is the self or the person. "I," he says, "am *einfach* or simple. I cannot be divided into two persons, nor yet into any two parts of one person." He also cites space as an example. "We cannot," he says, "divide space into parts. We should only make two spaces, which are integral objects and not parts of space [Nun besteht der Raum nicht aus einfachen Theilen, sondern, aus Räumen].

What he says of self is easily understood and appreciated. Space, however, is a less tangible object to deal with.

His line of remark and argument in regard to self may be extended to all things considered as individuals in a class. We divide genera into species, and species into individuals. But we can go no farther with our division in this direction, not, however, because the objects have become so small, but because they are individuals; because each of them is one and not two. I can divide this pen *mechanically* into parts. But I cannot divide it *logically* into two or more pens—two or more individual objects of the same species; not because it is so small, but because it is *one*, and not more, and division would not give us pens, but only parts of a pen. It is regarded, therefore, simple (*einfach*) in one sense of the word and not in the other.

In considering the third pair, I take up the "antithesis" first, also. It is, "In the world there is no liberty, but all is nature."

Here the line of argument is such as is usually employed to prove the regularity and uniformity of the phenomena of nature. Whatever comes into being had a cause; a cause or a combination of them, that were adequate to the effect. These causes act uniformly, as inert matter of necessity must act. No piece or mass is able to *originate* any action except as it is acted upon; no one can, of itself, vary the intensity with which it acts. By "the world," therefore, Kant means in this case the world of inorganic matter exclusive of human beings.

But in the Thesis, which is, "In the world there are causes that act through liberty," Kant evidently means the world *including* human beings. For in the soul of man, as he argues, there is freedom and spontaneity of action. He appeals to his own consciousness and says he finds there "a dynamical first beginning of actions, which has no dependence at all upon the causality of any preceding one; that is, it does not in any way follow from [as having been caused by] it." And this freedom or spontaneity is opposed to the law of cause and effect which, as he says, "prevails everywhere in nature," meaning by that term the material world.

But surely here is no contradiction. There is, however, a manifest ambiguity in the use of the words "the world." In the one case he means the world *including* man, and in the other the world *exclusive* of man.

In the fourth pair I shall continue my usual method and take up the antithesis first, "There is nothing necessary in the world; but in the series of events that make up the world all is contingent." In the earlier work, the *Kritik*, this was stated somewhat differently. "There exists nowhere, either in the world or out of it, as its cause, anything whose existence is necessary." I think the change in the phraseology is important, as indicating some change in Kant's views. But in any case, his argument must be taken to indicate what he meant by the terms he used in the proposition he was trying to prove.

The important word here is that which I have translated "contingent." In the German it is *zufällig*. It may mean either that which is regarded as having come into existence by chance *without* any antecedent cause producing it, or that whose existence is of no great importance; or in the still more strict sense of the word, that the existence of which is not the result of any design and purpose, and so purely accidental.

But when reasoning to prove this proposition, Kant takes "in the world" to mean the *material* world, the world of visible and tangible objects, and he reasons, as any advocate of modern science might do, that every thing had a cause and occurs uniformly in accordance with law, and every thing has a place and use, and that there is nothing that is not thus produced; nothing by chance, nothing without a possibility of its explanation by reference to ascertained or ascertainable causes and laws.

And in *this sense of the words* "the world" there is no occasion that I know of to dissent from his views.

In the thesis, however, which is, "In the series of causes in the world there is somewhere a necessary Being," that is, a Being whose existence is neither caused nor yet contingent, Kant takes the words "the world" as he did in the antithesis of his first pair to denote the whole world or universe. And he argues, as I have done, that the very succession of cause and effect and the law of causation imply a First Cause, which is an uncaused cause, whose existence is "necessary" in that It or He cannot be supposed to be non-existent. Whatever is contingent and dependent, implies something that is absolute and necessary on which it can depend and from which it derived its being. Without something absolute and necessary there can be nothing that is contingent and dependent. The very idea is absurd and impossible.

Thus taking the second pair, which I will now consider the first in the logical order, we have the commonly accepted doctrine with regard to the objects in nature, namely, that they are individuals, and divisible into parts mechanically and perhaps chemically, and yet they are grouped everywhere into genera and species, each and every one of them being logically and individually simple or *einfach*.

If we take the other three pairs, the thesis of the first and the third, and the antithesis of the fourth, together, they affirm that the world of visible objects and phenomena is limited in time and space, moves on in accordance with uniform laws, and no one event comes by chance or without its adequate cause and meaning. Taking the other parts we have all the foundation for a Natural Theology that we can reasonably ask, the freedom of the human soul and the existence and attributes of God.

There is another solution of Kant's "Antinomies" which I feel obliged to suggest, which, although however commendable on the score of ingenuity and charity, will not, I fear, stand criticism.

Kant wrote after Locke's famous doctrine that all ideas are derived from sensation had begun to produce its legitimate effects. He was alarmed, and sought, as Reid had done in Scotland, to arrest the evil consequences that were becoming everywhere apparent. Now we may *suppose*—and to *suppose* it is all we can do—that what Kant really meant to say was that if, looking at things from Locke's standpoint and the basis of sensationalism, we take the thesis of the first, and the antithesis of the second, third, and fourth pairs, they are undoubtedly and demonstrably true. But if, on the other hand, we look at their opposites, the antithesis of the first pair and the thesis of the second, third, and fourth pairs from the standpoint of innate or *a priori* ideas, or as I should say, from the standpoint of an *insight into* the *nature* of *things*, they also are seen to be absolutely true. Hence as a refutation of Locke and Condillac, they are unanswerable.

But Kant apparently never saw, what I have endeavored to show, that the controlling words in the *Antinomies* have different meanings in the respective pairs, arising, no doubt, from the different points of view from which the two philosophers regard them.[1]

---

[1] I have intimated in the text that it is possible that Kant *may* have intended these "Antinomies" as a refutation of Locke's theory of the origin and nature of knowledge. He certainly has not made it clear, nor has he hardly left it possible for us to maintain that he so regarded them or that such was in any way a part of his intention in giving them forth to the world. Had that been his object, or had he clearly seen what I have attempted to show, it is impossible that he could have given utterance to the thought in the texts of the Lecture, or to that which I have just cited from the *Prolegomena*.

But in the *Prolegomena* there appear passages that look as though Kant himself had some glimpse of the solution that may be offered to his difficulties; thus he says:

"If we suppose the necessity, which we everywhere find in nature, relates only to the things as they appear, or their appearance to us, and that freedom belongs to the things themselves [dinge an sich selbst], there arises no contradiction," p. 114.

"The necessity which we see in nature must be the condition after which the efficient causes are known to be causes. But liberty, on the other hand, if it is the cause of certain phenomena, must be in respect to them a power which can begin to act of itself, or spon-

I can well imagine that you will be surprised at this result, and ask, "Is this all? can it be possible that Kant deceived himself and has for these decades of years misled the world in this way, by these, so obvious sophisms?" And I answer, it is all. It is now more than forty years since I first made my acquaintance with Kant's great work. I have had occasion to recur to it often since, and just now, with reference to this very solution of what Hamilton has pronounced "insoluble contradictions," I have re-read the whole discussion over carefully again, and I have, therefore, no hesitation in saying that this is all. And I think that we have here a true and satisfactory solution of what has been quite generally accepted as giving away, in advance, the whole foundation of knowledge, Natural Theology included.

On the other hand, if we eliminate the ambiguities and regard the eight propositions, not as constituting four pairs of antinomies, but rather as eight distinct propositions, asserting, as they certainly do, the most

taneously (*sponte*)," p. 115. "In the former case the conception of causality is a conception of natural necessity; in the latter, a conception of freedom," p. 116, note.

"It can be said without contradiction, that all the acts of rational beings, in so far as they are phenomena or matters of experience, are subject to the same necessity as the phenomena of nature; but the same acts, when considered in relation to the rational being and his acts, are free," p. 117.

fundamental principles of all knowledge, we have a broad foundation well laid and established, as it seems to me, beyond further doubt or controversy.

I think, therefore, in conclusion, that we may claim that there is no valid objection against the method of Natural Theology, and that the nightmare of agnosticism under which philosophic minds have groaned for these many years, has had nothing for its foundation or cause but a few obvious mistakes in psychology or palpable sophistries in logic.

We have seen that evolution does not fully explain any of the observed phenomena of nature. It is but a process and not a cause. It needs something to work upon and something besides itself to carry it on. The word may be a good name to denote the Divine Method in so far as it denotes a method at all, that is, in so far as objects in nature have successive stages and are evolved out of those that precede them. But there are gaps and chasms in the order of nature which no theory of mere evolution, without the agency of God, has yet been able to fill or to explain. And thus the phenomena of nature show that this Supreme Being, this First Cause and Creator, must be a Lawgiver. The laws of nature are His modes of operation, and the same phenomena suggest, too, in more ways than one, miracles, so as to make the belief in them easy and probable on the presentation of a fit occasion and sufficient evidence.

And I think we may safely say that we have found nothing in our review of the other class of objections, whether psychological, logical or metaphysical, to interfere with or cause distrust of the inference drawn from the observed constitution and course of nature.

And thus whatever we see or our hands can touch in nature, is a manifestation of God, of His nature and attributes, His will and purposes concerning us. And all things which we can see or know we may regard as the work of His hands, or the gifts of His grace; to be received with gratitude if they are favorable and conducive to our enjoyment, and to be submitted to with resignation and patience if they are sent for our chastisement, or to turn our feet into the ways of righteousness and peace.

My convictions in regard to the fundamental principles of Modern Agnosticism took a very earnest form at an early day of my life, and that earnestness has been growing in intensity with at least forty years of study. And if I were called upon to point out the three greatest epochs of evil in human history, the three greatest strategetic devices of the Adversary of all good, and the Enemy of the souls of men, I should name as the *first* that scene in Eden when he persuaded our first parents that there was no harm in doing wrong; and as the *second*, that early scene in the history of our race when he persuaded men from their simple monotheism into polytheism, with its many gods, and the doctrine that necessarily results from it, that one religion, or form of religion, is as good as another, and that none is as good as the best, if only the devotees like it as well.

But the *third* great movement in the same direction—and it seems to me that it must be the last—was the diffusion among speculative minds of those doctrines in psychology and logic from which the present agnosticism and irreligion has come, as an inevitable result.

The first of these great delusions made Bethlehem and Calvary necessary; the second has cost the race many thousand years of degradation, misery and struggle for recovery, and the third may possibly yet come to be regarded as that fuller manifestation of Antichrist,[1] which began, indeed, in the Apostles' days, but which is to attain its fullest manifestation and power only in much later times. Time and the future alone can tell what will come of it in the end. But this we know and may feel well assured of, that He Who "bringeth to naught the counsel of princes"

---

[1] 2 Thessalonians, ii., 8.

and "maketh the divines mad," will triumph in His own good time.

Well may we say in the words of Him Whose right it is to rule and to guide all men: "If the light that is within you be darkness, how great is that darkness? Take heed, therefore, that the light that is within be not darkness."

LECTURE V.

*THE MISUSE OF ABSTRACTIONS; THE ATTRI-
BUTES OF GOD; HIS PERSONALITY.*

Cor. II, 8. Beware lest any man spoil you through philosophy and vain deceit, after the traditions of men.

THE PERSONALITY OF GOD.

There is a deeper ground for the modern agnosticism and the objections to the Methods of Natural Theology than any I have yet reached, a sort of sub-soil, down into which it sends its tap-roots, and from which it may draw nourishment and support when all other means of supply shall have been cut off, or have failed altogether. To this I wish to devote a few words before proceeding with the main topic of this Lecture, which is the Attributes and Personality of God.

St. Paul, when writing to his son Timothy, and through him to all subsequent ages, thought he had occasion to speak of the danger that comes from "science falsely so called." He adds, however, the qualification, as it seems to me, as if he was sure that there could be no danger then, now or ever from anything that is science *truly* so-called. But when he speaks of the danger of being spoiled "through philosophy," he adds no such limitation or qualification to his warning. But he adds the words "vain deceit," as if he had but little hope of any philosophy that would not partake largely of that character. However, be this as it may, I think that any one, in view of the past, will be disposed to say that the warning was not without sufficient occasion.

To prepare the way for what I wish to say on this subject, the final topic of this Lecture, I will turn aside here for a moment and call to mind a few of the results that have been attained by the study of the history and the philosophy of language.

It has been found that language is both a product and a producer of thought. It is probably the case that most of the opinions that men hold have been produced in their minds by the language and the form of expressions by which the thoughts of other people have been conveyed to them, not merely by language in general, but by the peculiar forms of expression that were used.

We say, for example, "the sun rises"; and it is quite easy for us who have the use of our eyes to see how that form of expression came into use. But the blind, who have never seen the phenomenon that is indicated by these words, ascribe the motion to the sun none the less on account of the fact that they have never seen the occurrence they speak of. We say the sun gives light to the earth, and immediately, though unconsciously, we imagine light as a substance that can be given or sent forth from one body to another. We say the fire sends forth heat, and straightway we think of heat as some imponderable, invisible substance that passes through the air and enters whatever becomes warmed by the burning mass which we call the fire. And in this way most of our early opinions are formed.

In all the languages of modern times the words and phrases which we use were introduced before we were born. They convey to us, or rather reproduce in us, not only the facts, but the theories and explanations of the facts which were adopted by the men who first observed the facts or formed the theories. These facts and theories remain *as our opinions* until we begin to observe and think for ourselves. For the most part, and on most subjects, they remain with most men as their opinions through their lives.

Let us, therefore, look at the history and development of language for a moment.

The first human vocabulary consisted of very few words, each of which was probably used indifferently as either noun, adjective or verb. In course of time some of these primitive roots become particles, like our conjunctions, prepositions, etc. I have to do now with those only that remained and continued to be used as verbs or nouns.

And first I will speak of the nouns or the words that denote the things that we speak of.

All nouns seem to have been at first individual, personal, or proper names. Soon, however, they became general or common, and denoted no longer an individual object, but a class—technically a genus—as man, dog, beast, etc. This was the result of the mental process of generalization.

But another process began very soon in the course of the reflective mental activity of man. This was the process of abstraction, and it produced from verbs and adjectives, abstract nouns that denote mere modes and properties. Soon these abstractions were objectified and made the objects of thought, as from to live, life; from white, whiteness, etc. But in the earliest stages of all languages, as Coxe has well remarked, "men had no abstract terms." "They had formed no notions of *prudence*, of *thought* and *intellect*, of *slavery* and *freedom*. They spoke only of the man who was strong; who could point out the way to others or choose one thing out of many; of the man who was bound to another, or who was able to do as he pleased."[1]

The development and formation of abstract terms, however, began very early, and came into extensive use in all the dialects of civilized man.

---

[1] *Tales of Greece*, Introduction, p. 13.

Abstract terms, in the strict and proper sense of the word, denote only the properties and modes of things which have been made objects of thought, and not things themselves. But in many cases these abstractions are "objectified" and treated as concrete realities; they thus become fictions, and in this way they have played a most important part in the origin and progress of speculation. I suppose that no one will seriously contend at this day that the "ideas" of Plato[1] were anything but fictions. The same must be said of what is so much talked of in modern times as the "mental faculties." No one supposes or will admit, when we ask him the question directly, that they sustain any such relation to

[1] REID says, *Intellectual Powers*, Prelim. Essay, Chap. I, "When in common language we speak of *having an idea* of anything, we mean no more by that expression than *thinking* of it." "But philosophers conceive of an idea that is *in the mind;* . . . this is the philosophical meaning of the word *idea*. . . I believe ideas taken in this sense to be a mere fiction of philosophers," Hamilton's Ed., vol. I, pp. 225, 226.

In the early part of this century Cousin has expressed (*Cours de l'Histoire de la Philosophie*. Cours de 1829. Leçon 22, vol. II, p. 385. Wright's translation, vol. II, p. 339. Dr. Henry's "*Cousin's Psychology*," pp. 280, 282, 285) the doctrine of modern philosophy very emphatically. He says, "If by ideas be understood something real, which are intermediate between things and the mind, I say there are absolutely no ideas; there is nothing *real* but things and the mind with its operations." Again, "There are in nature neither propositions nor ideas." And once more, "There are then indeed no innate ideas really existing, because there are no ideas" in the Platonic sense of the word.

the mind as the bodily organs, the heart, lungs, etc., do to the body. And yet all our use of language implies such a relation.[1]

But in the physical sciences these fictions come to deserve more consideration in view of our present object. From "hot" as an adjective we get "heat" as an abstract term, and thus "heat" the fiction that

---

[1] Locke's foresight and warning on this subject are both interesting and instructive (*Essay*, B. II, c. xxi, § 6). He says, "The ordinary way of speaking is, that the understanding and the will are two faculties of the mind; a word proper enough if it is used as all words should be, so as not to breed any confusion in men's thoughts, by being supposed (as I suppose it has been) to stand for some real beings in the soul that performs those actions of understanding and volition." Again (§ 17) he says, "However the name faculty which men have given to this power called the will . . . yet the will, in truth, signifies nothing but a power or ability to prefer or choose. If it be reasonable to suppose and talk of faculties as distinct things, that can act (as we do when we say the will orders and the will is free), it is fit that we should make a speaking faculty and a walking faculty and a dancing faculty, by which those actions are produced, which are but several modes of motion; as well as make the will and understanding to be faculties . . . and we may also as well say that it is the singing faculty that sings and the dancing faculty that dances, as that the will chooses or that the understanding conceives. This way of talking, nevertheless, has prevailed, and, as I guess, produced great confusion." The fault has been, as he says, that "the faculties have been spoken of and represented as so many distinct agents." He illustrates the matter still further by supposing one to ask what it is that digests our food, and some one answers, "the digestive faculty," instead of saying the stomach. Or if one asks by what means we move, some one should say by "the motive faculty, which is to say that the ability to digest is the organ of digestion, and the ability to move is the means and instincts of motion."

is spoken of as one of the seven, eight, or ten "forces" with which evolutionists think they can explain all the phenomena of the material universe without "the hypothesis" of a God who shall be regarded as Creator and Superintending Providence, a Worker of miracles, an Inspirer of thought or the Author of a Revelation that can be binding upon the conscience and wills of men.

The earliest form of the verb was the active voice. But very soon there came into use reflexive forms as in the Hebrew Hithpael and the Greek Middle Voice, which from its very form indicated and declared not only that the act had been performed, but also that it terminated in the agent, as "I strike myself."

The next form that was developed was the *passive* voice, as it is called. Men learned at an early day in their progress, that many events occur and become apparent, the cause of which is not known to the observer. Hence a feeling of the necessity for some form of expression that would assert the observed fact without saying anything about the cause. The vexed and vexatious question, "Who struck Billy Patterson?" occurred early in the experience of mankind, and developed the feeling of a necessity for some form of the verb that would assert the fact without incurring the risk or the responsibility of saying who performed the deed. Hence the passive voice, "he was struck." And this became ever after the form of caution and non-committal, and the middle voice gradually went out of use as a distinct form of the verb among all the European nations; and whenever we have occasion for it, we avail ourselves of a reflexive pronoun, as *self* in English, *se* in French, and *sich* in German.

These reflex forms are in common use in French and German, and indicate a frame of mind or form of mental activity quite unlike that to which we are accustomed who speak the English language, and many of them seem very odd, and even absurd, to us.

Thus in a recent work on physiology, written in the French language, the following examples, beside many others that might be cited, occur within a very few pages: " Ligneous tissues *form themselves*," "water *forms itself* in the tissues," "carbonic acid gas *forms itself* in the lungs during respiration," " heat *transforms itself* into muscular movement;" the "ligneous tissues," "water," and "carbonic acid" are indeed real causes, and are denoted by concrete terms. But assuredly they do not "form" or "make themselves."

A German writer settles the much disputed question of the origin of the soul by saying, "Souls form themselves (*sich ausbilden*) from the constituents of the body." This may do for a myth, but it is not science or philosophy. Nor does it seem to me to be very good poetry.

I cite but one example more. Montesquieu, in speaking of certain social conditions, says that when these occur among young people "*a marriage will make itself*" [*il se fait un mariage*]. Now this may be true in France and of the French. But among English-speaking people marriages are made by the parties to the contract, and there is usually too much that is interesting, if not vexatious and discouraging, to allow them to forget that they were the principal agents in bringing about the happy result.

But such forms of expression are of so frequent occurrence in French and German books that they appear to excite no surprise, and they seldom attract attention.[1]

---

[1] I cite one more, the distinction of nouns in reference to gender. In the old European languages—the Latin and the Greek—besides some regard to the sex of the objects, the distinction was based chiefly on the form and termination of the words. But in the modern French there is no *neuter* gender, and all nouns are either masculine or feminine. In German, beyond objects in the animal world, where gender is a reality, the words are also distributed between the three genders, chiefly in reference to their form. In English, however, no word is of any one gender on account of its form. The names of inanimate objects are always neuter and others often and to a considerable extent change form to suit the gender, as

But I think there can be no doubt that such forms of expression are injurious to the mental culture. They imply, and as I think they tend to *promote*, a want or clearness of insight into the true causes and the laws of the phenomena they describe.

When an object is before us, it exists already independently of any volition or mental action of our own. We *see* it, if it is visible, and *feel* it if it is within the reach of our hands. It existed before these acts of ours, and is the cause of those sensations by means of which the acts of perception are performed. Other persons cognize the object as well as ourselves, and it is the same thing to us and to them and for all observers; and hence the ideas or notions formed of it will be the same, or very nearly the same, for all. But if not, the object is appealed to to verify and to correct those ideas.

If we generalize the ideas thus formed, it is done by the omission or elimination of properties that are peculiar to individual objects and retaining those that are common to all the objects we include in one class and denote by a common name. But the process is one of exclusion or elimination of properties, and not one of addition or increase. We include in

---

actor, actress, master, mistress, etc. This peculiarity of modern European languages, as well as the orthography of the English, will have to be changed before the millenium is fully realized.

the general term or idea no property that was not obvious in the objects that we thus class together.

And all the terms thus obtained are concrete terms, the general no less than the individual or proper nouns.

But if we fix our attention upon some one of the properties, modes or actions of the objects thus perceived, we *objectify* it and make it an object of thought. And thus the idea we form of it is denoted by an abstract term, as whiteness, hardness, etc. In this case the mental activity *precedes* the object of thought, and in fact creates it.

The ontological difference between the objects denoted by abstract and those denoted by concrete terms, is easily pointed out, and when once seen, it is seen to be of the most fundamental importance.

Thus take "whiteness." We cannot imagine or suppose it to exist without or apart from some *thing* that is white. But take any white thing and we can imagine or suppose it to be of some other color, and so on with all the objects in the world until we come to think of a world in which there is nothing that is white and no whiteness. So of life; we cannot imagine or suppose it to be a reality distinct and apart from some thing that is living or alive. But we can imagine a world or a universe such as this is supposed to have been in its nebulous state, with no living thing in it.

Hence we call those objects of thought, properties or modes, which we cannot suppose to exist or think as existing, except as properties or modes of something which we regard as substantial. And we regard those as substances which we can think of as existing, not indeed without properties, modes or relations of some kind, but with properties and relations different from those they now have.

Thus if we take all the objects of thought that are denoted by abstract terms, we can apply the test above indicated to them all, one at a time and separately, and imagine a world in which that one is not present; but we cannot imagine a world in which it could be present without something else, some substantial thing of which it is a mode or property.

It will thus be seen that the difference between the two classes of objects of thought is, for all ontological purposes, quite fundamental; substantial realities are the things that God has made, while the world of abstractions is purely the creation of man himself.

So far as the primary and simple properties of objects are concerned there is comparatively little danger of error; but in regard to the more complicated relations of objects the danger becomes very great. It is hardly possible that any two persons will understand such terms alike, and very likely no one will understand them right.

If now we will analyze the sentences where the departures from the literal use of languages which represents objects as they are and events as they occur, or at least appear to be and to occur, we shall find that we have (1) the suggestion of some events that never occurred, and (2) the ascription of others to causes that have no effective existence anywhere.

In a very interesting and instructive scientific work which I have just read, the author says of the sun, that "it throws up immense quantities of matter in a gaseous form, which passes millions of miles into the open space and then, cooling by *the radiation* of its heat, it becomes vapor or dust, and falls back in an intensely luminous condition, constituting, perhaps the photosphere, which is all that we see of the sun." But I ask what becomes of the heat? He answers, "It *is radiated into space.*" But the question arises, is heat a *thing* that can be radiated? Is there any act of radiation? You accept, I suppose, the modern doctrine that heat is only "a mode of motion." How can a "mode of motion" be radiated? What actually occurs is, the matter becomes cooled. In what way, perhaps you may not be prepared to tell us. But the explanation you give assumes what is confessedly false. You have embarrassed science by the recognition of an event that never occurred and a substance that exists nowhere.

But I have been feeling for some time that you will ask, what has this to do with your subject? I answer, much every way. I have been trying to prepare the way for a satisfactory presentation and a fair appreciation of the criticism I have to make. And with this I will now proceed.

1. In the first place, this use of language, or rather the philosophy out of which it grew and *which it tends to perpetuate*, takes from our argument all foundation, and leaves us nothing to stand upon.

I have alluded to this fact before in a preceding Lecture. Suppose we agree with the Evolutionist in accepting his postulate of matter in existence in a gaseous or nebulous state, as he supposes it to have been, and we ask him who or what shall start into condensation this inert mass and begin the process of evolution. He thinks the answer easy enough. It may have been, he says, gravity, or it may have been chemical affinity. Either would bring the other, and with them, revolution on an axis, and with the condensation which the affinity would produce, there would come heat and light and electricity, and we have at once, or at least very soon, all the "forces," so-called, that Spencer asks for as a means of explaining all that has occurred since.

But "gravity" and "affinity," what are they for real causes? The terms are clearly abstract in form and appearance. Are they real causes or only modes in which something or Somebody else acts? If not real entities we have, by referring to them, no explanation of the phenomena, no account of what actually occurred; or rather we have words and a form of expression which suggest what did not occur, and call into existence and activity agents that have no independent effective existence and cannot act at all or anywhere.[1]

So when the first living thing appeared on the

---

[1] Force, as the word is here used, is, in fact, as purely a fiction as any one of the gods of heathen mythology. We use the word as a concrete term when we speak of wind and water as forces used to propel machinery. But in this connection the word is abstract. We speak of "the force with which the earth attracts the moon," but the force is not a thing, a reality distinct from the two—earth and moon. It is not even a property of either of the objects, but only a quality, or quantity rather, of their action, the one upon the other. We might with as much propriety, in a purely philosophical point of view, speak of any other abstraction in the same way. Whiteness, for example. It can neither be increased nor diminished, only when the snow melts the 'whiteness becomes invisible. Or of light. When night comes on there is just as much light as before only it cannot be seen; it has in fact become darkness. So force that is "latent" or only "potential" is a force that *may be*, but is not now; for all *practical purposes* it is non-existent—purely nothing.

In this view, the doctrine of "the indestructibility of force" is about the same as if one should maintain, as a part of his philosophy, the uniformity of the width of that "imaginary line" which we call the Equator; and insist that it neither is, nor can be wider in one place than in another; that it never can have been either broader or narrower than it is now in any period of past geological time. If any one should undertake to maintain such a doctrine I do not think that we should care to dispute him.

earth—(the current philosophy would say when "*life first appeared*" or "made its appearance")—we have, indeed, an unusual, and, at that time, an unprecedented combination of the four elements, oxygen and hydrogen, carbon and nitrogen. But how did the new compound become a living being?

If we may speak of "life" as something that was before "latent in matter" or as existing somewhere else, and as then coming into the new chemical compound as a fifth element, we do indeed say something that is "verbally intelligible." But is life something that exists independently of any living thing, and can act and *vivify* what was before and otherwise inert and lifeless?

Or, finally, when man made his appearance, whence and how came the soul or mind? Does that consist of mere abstractions? Is it only intelligence and memory and will? or is it a substantial something that understands, and remembers and wills, and which, when it comes into the human body, makes an intelligent human being? We believe it to be a substantial thing that *comes* into the body or *is created* in it and makes of the body a living man. Otherwise it must consist of mere abstractions.

And this is what our modern men of science propose to make it. In fact, there has been a growing tendency in this direction since Locke's time. Hume declared it to be " but a bundle or collection of perception or impressions."[1] Lewis calls it an "abstraction,"[2] Dr. Hammond[3] calls it "a force developed by nervous action," like "heat or electricity." John Stuart Mill says, "Mind is nothing but the series of our sensations,"[4] and he adds on a subsequent page that "this series of feelings " *is aware of itself*." But yet he adds (p. 256) that "our notion of mind is a notion of a *permanent something*, contrasted with the perpetual flux of the sensations," "a something which we figure as remaining the same, while the particular feelings through which it reveals its existence change."

Precisely so. And this "something" it was which Professor Garver's experiments disclosed, and which we always find as that which not only "underlies" sensations, but perform the acts of thinking.[5]

---

[1] HUME'S *Essay on Human Nature*, vol. I, p. 233.
[2] LEWES, *Problems of Life*, vol. I, p. 281.
[3] *The Brain not the only organ of the Mind*.
[4] *Examination of Sir William Hamilton's Philosophy*, vol. I, pp. 253, 258.
[5] A third view makes mind mere "force." Thus Dr. Hammond in *The Brain not the Sole Organ of the Mind*," says, p. 5, "By the term mind, I understand a force developed by nervous action. It bears the same relation to the gray nerve tissue that heat, or electricity, or light does to chemical or mechanical action." "Why mind should result from the functionation of the gray nerve tissue," etc., etc.

This, as I have said, may be conceived and understood—though it can be regarded as true only in a modified sense—of thought.

For all these acts of perceiving, thinking of, which these philosophers admit that we are conscious, and which they claim to regard as the immediate objects of consciousness are—like evolution itself, of which we have had so much to say—only *processes*, only and merely processes. They are not causes, forces, or agents; they are not substances that can exist by themselves. There can no more be thinking without a something that thinks, than there can be evo-

But it cannot be understood of mind. The one is an agent, the other a product or mode. The one is denoted by an abstract term, the other by a concrete term. Replace the word "I," or ego, by what is here taken for its synonymn, and the absurdity becomes apparent at once. We have for "I think," "thought thinks," for "I choose," "choice chooses." Thought without a thinker is as impossible as creation without a creator, writing without a writer.

And I do not think that Dr. Hammond really believed his own definition. He certainly did not, if he understood its meaning. The title of his address is, *The Brain not the Sole Organ of the Mind*. Now if he had been treating of heat and of the sun, he certainly would not have said *the Sun not the Sole Organ of the Heat*. But rather, as I suppose, "the Sun not the only, or sole source of heat."

And yet Dr. Hammond professes to regard mind and heat as belonging to the same kind of entities—both to be denoted by abstract terms, although he uses the one, "mind," as concrete.

Nor is it true that thought and volition are produced by "nerve activity" alone, and without something besides, as the cases cited in the first part of the third Lecture prove. There is "a something else" that sometimes excites and controls nerve action, and is sometimes controlled by it. And the two, although for the most part in harmony, are sometimes antagonistic to each other.

lution without something that causes and produces the evolution as well as a subject matter that is evolved. These men use the word mind as though it were the logical equivalent of the word thought.

Nor do the substantial objects of the material world fare any better. "Matter," says Stuart Mill,[1] "may be defined a permanent possibility of sensation," and this definition he repeats in several places as though it were the result of much deliberate consideration.

But the "possibility of sensations" must be *in us*, where the sensations are produced, and where only they can be real. And if that is all that there is of "matter" and material objects in his philosophy, we cannot wonder that he finds nowhere any satisfactory proof of the existence and attributes of God.[2]

Herbert Spencer, to escape the argument from the nature of matter to the existence of God, says,[3] "Our conception of matter reduced to its simplest shape is that of co-existent positions that offer resistance." But positions! what are they for causes?

---

[1] *Examination of Sir William Hamilton's Philosophy*, vol. I, pp. 243, 264, and elsewhere.

[2] Mill, however, speaks of matter in one place (p. 271) as the "permanent *cause* of sensations." But he does this apparently without any consciousness of the incompatibility of the two statements.

[3] *First Principles*, Pt. I, § 63.

Does he mean *things* in position, or atoms in relation to and acting upon one another? If so his pretended definition is but a subterfuge, or way of an attempted escape from the deistic argument. If not, he means nothing, and his pretended philosophy evanishes into nothing and mere senselessness.

John Stuart Mill gives us another illustration. Besides the definition of matter already given he says,[1] "When a physical phenomenon is traced to its cause, that cause, when analyzed, is found to be a certain quantum of force combined with certain collocations." But Mill's "collocations" are no better than Spencer's "positions," and no worse. They are out of the possibility of argument. Does he then mean atoms that are collocated and acting on each other with force more or less? If so, we have all that we ask; if not, his words are senseless.

Herbert Spencer asks, as all that he needs to explain the universe, these five elements or postulates, Matter, Motion, Time, Space and Force. But motion is only a mode and no "substantial reality." Time and space, if anything more than mere "fictions," are only conditions. But force, what is that? the word is ambiguous, and in this ambiguity lies its power for use (shall I say mischief?) in this connection. We speak of wind and water and steam as

[1] *Theism*, p. 144.

forces that propel machinery, and we speak of them as the forces of nature, or natural forces. In this way we are accustomed to the word as a concrete term, and are not, therefore, shocked or surprised at its use. And if Spencer means to use the word *in this way*, what he means by force and what his philosophy demands is, and can be, nothing less than God Himself, the God in whom we as Christians believe.

But the word has another logical quality, and in this lurks the mischief. We say the earth attracts the moon, and attracts it with a certain force. We call that force gravity, and in fact Spencer has left us no escape from this meaning, for he says that this force exists and acts in seven different forms and under as many different names, Heat, Light, Electricity, Magnetism, Cohesion, Affinity, and Gravity. All of these are abstract terms, and they denote either "mental abstractions" or fictions, such fictions as are needful in science, although no "substantial realities" of which I will say a few words more soon.

Hence force, if it is not God, is either a fiction or an abstraction, a mere mode or degree of the motion, and the motion itself is only a mode of the matter, so that all that Spencer's postulates amount to, when reduced to their substantial value, is matter in motion or moving with a certain force. And of course if it moves or is in motion at all, it moves *with a force* greater or less according to the rate of motion. But Who or What put it in motion? Surely not the motion itself. Nor yet force in his sense of the word; for so understood it is but the mode or degree of the motion, the force of the motion, or better still, the force of the moving matter.

And thus we have for Spencer's system of the universe one reality, matter, and four abstractions or fictions to one reality. And perhaps this is about the portion of truth to fancy, of worth to worthlessness, that future generations will be willing to accord to his speculations.

Now it is obvious that this use of abstract terms leads us at once into a region of fancy and of mysticism, where anything can be affirmed and nothing can be successfully denied or contradicted; since the "philosopher can retire into a nebulosity of words and phrases, where no logic can follow him and no sagacity can detect him."

Every philosopher with whose works I am acquainted makes complaint and enters his protest in one form or another against the use or abuse of abstract terms. To cite only one, a notable case on more accounts than one, I will refer to John Stuart Mill. He says,[1] " All experience attests the strength

---

[1] *Examination*, etc., vol. I, p. 247.

of the tendency to mistake mental abstractions, even negative ones, for substantive realities." And yet this same philosopher resolves both matter and mind into mere abstractions, as we have just seen, defining the one "as nothing but the series of our sensations," and the other as "a series of feelings which is aware of itself." But surely "sensation" and "feeling" are abstract terms—"*mental* abstractions," therefore, I suppose, as I know of no other kind.

We sometimes meet with a man whose use of language very soon satisfies us that he is color blind. It is said—I do not know how true it is—but it is said that persons with a good ear for music often become unable to distinguish between harmony and melody on the one hand, and discord on the other, by having their organs of hearing habitually and for a long time accustomed to hear discordant sounds.

We know something like this to be the case with the moral sensibility. He that carefully studies the right and wrong of acts and sacredly and earnestly regards and obeys the dictates of conscience, becomes not only strong to do, but quick and clear-sighted to see, what is right and becoming for him to do. On the other hand, he that neither tries to see, nor makes any effort to do, what is right soon loses, to a great extent, if not wholly, the power to distinguish right from wrong, as well as the sensibility to feel and appreciate the difference between them and the importance of doing right when it has been pointed out to him.

These facts indicate and illustrate a law of human nature. And it is applicable in the case before us. The habitual use of language, such as I have described, tends to confuse that insight into the nature and relations of things upon which all science that is not "falsely so called," and all philosophy which is not mere "vain deceit," must depend. It fills the pathway of the earnest thinker with obstacles. It raises questions and problems where there need be none. *It makes atheism easy.* It enables men to hold and to defend themselves in holding any opinion that caprice, constitutional idiosyncracy, personal ambition or self-interest may incline them to adopt and proclaim as their own.

All the nouns that may be used to denote the things of which we speak may be referred to five classes: (1) those that denote *material* objects or matter; (2) those that denote souls or *personal* beings or mind; (3) those that denote *abstractions;* (4) those that denote recognized *fictions;* and (5) the One Name or the many names that denote the One Supreme Being.

Of the third class, *abstract* terms, I have said all that

is necessary to indicate their character. They denote no objects that we need to take into account in our investigation of the facts and phenomena of nature for the purpose of finding therein the indications of the existence and attributes of God. They have their use, and their use cannot be dispensed with in any cultivated language, nor in any discussion of scientific questions. But denoting only properties, modes or affections, the objects they denote can have no *substantial* existence, can be no *real causes*, and can neither afford nor help us to any adequate explanation of the existence of anything. Our only concern with them in this connection, therefore, is to see that they do not lead us into a "vain deceit" where most of all we need a sound philosophy and science that is *not* falsely so called.[1]

---

[1] It is always comparatively easy to replace abstract terms by their logical equivalents. To do this, convert the noun into its adjective form and place after it some noun that is most appropriate. The word "thing" will always answer, although a term of much narrower comprehension is often preferable. Thus take the proposition, "light comes from the sun." Replace "light" by "luminous" and put things or matter after it and we have "luminous things or matter comes from the sun." If the proposition asserts precisely the same in this form as it did before the word is not abstract. Otherwise it is to be so regarded. So with "sound travels," etc. For sound, put "sonorous bodies," and we see at once the difference.

This law turns to our account in another way. As I have said, many philosophers in these latter days profess to regard the word

Of the next class in order, the fourth, fictions, it is necessary to say a few words. They consist for the most part of "objectified abstractions" used as though they were realities. In some cases, however, they are purely factitious, as Descartes called them; and Kant, agreeing with Descartes in this, has called them by the same name, and the word has come into general use. But in any case they denote no substantial realities, no real causes.

As belonging to this class I would name, by way of illustration, the Equator, which is a mere "imaginary line" used for some very necessary purposes in geography and several other sciences. As belonging to the same class we have the parallels of latitude, the tropics, and the meridians of longitude. They are not realities on the globe like the rivers and mountains, and yet they are of inestimable value

mind as an abstract term. But test it by our rule, and say "the mind thinks"—put it "mental substance thinks"—and the meaning is seen at once to be precisely the same as when the statement was in the first form; whence we infer that mind is only a name for mental substance, and not a mere abstraction.

In many cases, however, we should fail to get all the meaning that is intended in a passage when this use of abstract terms or fictions prevails. Suppose we say "sound travels," etc. By the method already indicated we find that "sound" is but an abstraction or a fiction. But suppose we regard the language as a metaphor and complete the implied comparison, and we have "the result is the same as if sound were a reality and did travel at such and such a rate."

in discussing questions of geography and the situations of places and things on the surface of the earth.

Of the same kind of realities are also the point, the line, etc., as used in geometry. No realities *exactly* corresponding to their definitions exist or can exist among the realities of nature.

To the same class of objects, as I think, must be relegated those two much discussed subjects, *time* and *space*. No realities exist or can exist that agree entirely with our ideas of them. The one is *supposed* to extend, without any other property but its extension, indefinitely in all directions—never acting as cause—having no impenetrability, and offering no resistance either to our hands, by way of touch, or to masses that are supposed to be moving in it, and whose infinity is not supposed to be limited by objects that are regarded as existing in it. And much the same may be said of time—with proper limitations with regard to the nature of the way of its extent—which is sometimes called *protension*, or rather, *extension*.

And if we adopt what Tyndall has declared to be the "modern idea" of scientific men with regard to them, we must relegate to the same category those so-called forces of nature, light, heat, etc., on which Herbert Spencer depends for his explanation of the universe. The sun is luminous, and we speak of light. Bodies are hot, and we speak of heat; and find it exceedingly convenient to regard heat and light as imponderable substances that may be emitted, reflected, radiated, refracted, absorbed, etc. But in this modern view they are no "substantial realities"; no real causes or efficient agents of any of the events that occur as phenomena either in life or in nature.[1]

We have then, after eliminating abstractions and fictions, the former as denoting only properties and modes, with no substantial existence, and the latter as mere creations of fancy for the sake of convenience in discussing questions of science and of philosophy, which, however, are no "real causes," only the three classes of objects remaining to be considered, namely, (1) material objects, (2) mental objects, (3) the one Supreme Being.

[1] In most languages there is no distinction made in their syntax or other laws and usages between abstract and concrete nouns. In English, however, the difference is well marked. We use the article before concrete terms, as when we say, "the heart beats," "the lungs expand." But if we are using an abstract term, we do not use the article before it unless it is followed by the preposition "of" or some limiting clause as, "the whiteness *of snow*," "the heat *that comes from the sun*," etc. Before the mere fictions, however, we use the article, as when we speak of "the equator," "the point," "the line," etc. Of course there are some exceptions or doubtful cases, such as "time" and "space." They are hardly abstractions, and yet we do not use the article before them except when the word is followed by a limitation, as "the space of," etc.

In this I leave the case of plants and animals out of the enumeration designedly, because I do not wish to either assume or reject, in this connection, Huxley's doctrine that animals are mere "automata." If they are so they belong to the first class named above, although, as Huxley would doubtless contend, and all must admit, the phenomena of animal sensibility and reflex action present some cases that are not in exact accordance with the laws of action and reaction in inanimate nature. They present, however, no facts of spontaneity, such as we see in man and the mind everywhere.

If, on the other hand, one prefers to hold to the old view that animals have consciousness, intelligence and voluntary action, they must be included in the second class I have named above.

The three classes of objects are distinguished as follows:

1. Material objects may be seen by the eye, or, if they are not visible, they may always be felt, as is the case with some of the gases, by the touch of the hand, and their presence is indicated by pressure and an effort at condensation.

2d. Then in the second class we have minds or souls, as in man. These are not supposed to be susceptible to cognition by the senses, but are manifest to each one for himself in his consciousness; and as existing in other persons, they are manifest through their influence upon the body and their control of the bodily organs.

I have spoken of minds or souls as in man. There may be souls in brutes and there may be other orders of intelligent beings above or below man, as demons and angels. But these are questions that are of no importance to my present purpose, and so I leave them without discussion, and shall so shape what I have to say that it will make no difference which way one decides with regard to them.

3d. And finally we have the One Supreme Being Whom we call God. And in this class, if class it can be called, there is and can be, as we believe, but one Being.

Let us consider each of these classes of objects separately by way of resuming the object that is more immediately before us—the existence and attributes of God.

Objects in the first class named above have well defined limits to their actions and modes of causation. Without going at all into detail—and the details would make up the whole body of scientific facts, truths, and laws—we can easily indicate the outline that limits their agency. This limits, also, the use we may make of them in our attempts at explaining and accounting for the phenomena that fall under our observation in the study of nature. This is the law of inertia.

It may be well to state this law in outline. This can be done in three propositions.

1st. Whatever is at rest, if anything is ever really so, will remain at rest until moved or put in motion by some object acting as cause or force outside of itself.

2d. Two elements that are not in a state of chemical action on each other will not begin to act until they are acted upon by something else that changes their condition or relation to one another.

3d. Two substances acting upon each other, as the earth and the moon, by gravity, or oxygen and hydrogen in the molecules of water, will not and cannot vary the intensity or force with which they act, spontaneously and of themselves, without some change in their condition or in their position, in relation to one another.

Now this is the *nature* of matter, the limit to the activity or agency of all mere material objects, whether particle or planet, atom, molecule or mass. The law is inevitable and inexorable; without it not a general fact or law, or a truth of any one of the natural sciences could be affirmed—there could be no natural sciences.

But when we come to objects of the second class,

we find a different nature—we encounter *spontaneity* of action. It is not merely that man is always or for the most part active; for this is very likely the case with every atom and every mass of inorganic matter. But we find here action of another kind, and under an entirely different law. Explain it as you will, no one denies or doubts the fact. And with this spontaneity we find, also, intelligence, reason, memory, and choice, as the result of deliberation. Explain the phenomena as we will, and include in this class animals or exclude them from it, as the theory you adopt may incline you to do, admit or deny the existence of demons below man in the moral scale, or angels that are above him, as you may find reason for doing, there is in any case no denying or doubting that we find these peculiar phenomena in the life and activity of man. And they *are characteristic* of him, they constitute for him a distinguishing mark, and indicate for him a nature that is essentially *distinct from*, and, as we say, *above* that of any of the masses of mere inorganic matter.

But the moment we attempt to account for the observed phenomena of nature, we find occasion for something higher than mere matter; something higher, also, than mere primordial nebulous matter When the atoms of man.

first began to combine and move, there was a necessity, as we have seen, and as evolutionists admit, for something besides these atoms. The law and nature of inertia prevailed then as now, or they were not matter, but mind or spirit; this law of inertia ruled then as now, with inevitable force and inexorable uniformity. Man was not there, nor was he in existence then, to start them into motion and activity.

And besides this, the occasion called for something far beyond the intelligence and power of man. Even now he knows and can at most understand but very little of what was then done; and many of the things which were then done, and which he understands and explains, or thinks he does, he lacks the power to perform.

Now, as we have seen, spontaneity and inertia are respectively the differentia of mind and matter. So, undoubtedly, there is some one characteristic of God which constitutes for Him an essentia (and I use the word here in its technical sense), and essential distintion and difference between Him and either human beings, on the one hand, or mere inanimate objects on the other. And as man has many things in common with matter, so, doubtless, God has many things in common with man. He is intelligent, and spontaneous in His activity, as men are, so that men are said to have been created in His image or likeness.

But besides and beyond all the attributes which He may have in common with man constituting our likeness to Him, there is and must be something that constitutes essentially His divinity, His ουσία, for which we have at present, perhaps, no name. Of this we see *manifestations* in His omnipresence and foreknowledge, as we call it for want of a better name. Herbert Spencer says, as we have seen, that since " we are obliged to regard every phenomenon as a manifestation of His Power, we are obliged to regard this Power [or Being] as omnipresent." But omnipresence cannot be effected by extension from one place to another, for whatever is extended is of necessity limited, and has form and outline.

So, too, Whoever is omniscient cannot be wise and know things as we do. His thoughts cannot have had a beginning in time as all our thoughts must have. For thoughts and events cannot come and go as they do for us and with us. He to Whom events come and go in the order of succession and time, was *once* young and is now growing old. But God—with the utmost reverence be it said—is no older than He was.

All this may pass our powers of comprehension, and doubtless it does, but it is nevertheless proved to be true and constitutes, or rather grows out of, that which constitutes His distinctive characteristic, as inertia does that of material objects, and as spontaneity of action does that of human minds.

And yet while spontaneity is a differentia and characteristic of mind as contrasted with matter, it is not a ground of distinction between man and God. And in fact it is a fundamental law of logic that when we have three co-ordinates it is impossible to find a property which will be a differentia of any two when compared with each other that will not be common to both of the other two. Otherwise there could be no three distinct species in any proper classification of objects.

Getting rid of abstractions and of fictions, whenever the cause of scientific truth demands it, we get rid of what Tyndall calls "the slave labor" of the so-called imponderable agents. We clear the field of all purely mythological creations of fancy, and we have the world of matter with its masses and molecules acting directly and immediately on one another—the world of mind with each individual soul acting in a visible body, but acting under the law of freedom and spontaneity, and above all and over all, One God, a Supreme Being, a Creator and First Cause.

In this we begin with the seen, and pass to the unseen, the limited and the temporal, and then pass to the recognition of Something that is infinite and eternal.

Our chief dependence in this line of investigation and argument is upon the idea of causation and the relation of cause and effect.

It may be that some of us have never considered the wide-spread and fundamental character of this principle. All knowledge of objective or substantial reality depends upon it.

In mathematics, we *assume* the unit, the point, the line, etc., and deducing from them, by insight into their very nature, certain self-evident axioms, as we call them, we proceed to demonstrate the truths that are not at first self-evident. Thus if three straight lines meet in three points they make a triangle, and we can demonstrate from this conception of the nature of the triangle all the truths of trigonometry. But the triangle is an ideal figure, a fiction, and we cannot prove by any means or methods known to pure mathematics, that there is any object that is triangularly shaped in this world or anywhere else in the universe of real objects.

But for our knowledge of reality, everywhere, we depend on the principle or idea of causation. I know that this paper or this book exists only as it produces or *causes* within me the sensations of color, form, etc., by means of which I perceive the object. And the same is true of all the properties of which a knowledge is gained by the six senses.

And then we learn other properties of bodies as we see them acting on one another, and causing the changes, mechanical or chemical, which we see around us. And without such action and change we learn nothing of these relative properties of objects.

So, too, with mind. We know it only as it acts as agent or cause, producing those phenomena of thought and feeling and will, that we are conscious of within us. And only as it thus acts as cause or agent do we know nothing of it except, perhaps, what we may learn of it by the physiological method spoken of in the first part of the third Lecture.

The same is true with regard to the First Cause. We know Him to exist and we know of Him—His attributes and modes of action—just as we do of all other things, by what He does, and with as much certainty, so far as our knowledge extends. Whatever we cannot account for by ascribing it to mere matter because all matter is inert; and whatever we cannot account for by referring it to the agency of man, who, though not inert, is yet ignorant and weak and limited in time and space, we ascribe to God, Who is not inert, and Who is neither ignorant nor weak; or rather, we thus prove—starting from the same facts and pursuing the same method—that there is a Being who is neither inert nor ignorant nor weak, nor yet confined by limitations and conditions of time and place. And this result we attain as surely as we can prove and as certainly as we can know that there is the power of thought within us, stars over our heads, or the earth beneath our feet.

The method is one and the same in all the cases. The process may be longer and the steps more in number in one case than in the other two; just as in mathematics the steps are more numerous and the process of reasoning is often much longer in the more remote conclusions than in the earlier propositions in algebra and geometry. But the conclusion is no less certain for any one who fully understands the methods and the process. Hence, if there is a cause, an immediate cause anywhere, there must be a First Cause somewhere. And He must be eternal and everywhere present.

This I say as a matter of mere logic and reasoning. But the assent to this doctrine, and the realization of it in our hearts and lives is quite a different matter. It depends upon processes and means that are entirely different from logic and mere reasoning. He that will do His will shall know of the doctrine, and know it, *too*, by that knowledge which is of the heart and not of the head and the mind alone.

I have alluded in a former Lecture to the important psychological fact that we depend mostly for our knowledge of objects around us upon the two senses, sight and touch. By what we thus gain we are able to imagine objects as they are, and thus we get that sense of reality which accompanies our thoughts about them.

And I sometimes think that our relation to God, so far as the sense of the reality of His existence is concerned, considered in a purely intellectual point of view, is very much as would be that of a man in relation to external objects, who has not either of these two important senses, sight and touch. He could hear the sounds they make, as we do. He could smell the odors that they give off and that are wafted to him on every breeze that he inhales. But the objects themselves, he sees not and cannot see. Their form and solidity he knows not, for he cannot feel them; he cannot touch them with his hands, nor yet has he any of that "muscular sense," as it is sometimes called, by which he can feel their hardness, their solidity, and their ability to resist his pressure. He could have no idea of them. He could form no conception of their form or shape; he could not imagine how they would look or feel or in what manner they exist. And yet, he is always hearing their sound and their voice. He perceives their varying and ever-changeful odors, although themselves he sees not and cannot see; he feels not and cannot feel. And yet to him they are real. And I doubt not he could cultivate a sense of their reality that would in time come to be equal to that which we now have.

Considered as a mere speculative dogma, there are but very few, if any, persons that deny the existence of God or avow themselves atheists or mere blank materialists.[1] Their chief objection is to the acknowledgment of the personality of God and the exercise of a Moral Government over them. This is the obstacle that always and everywhere, and in every human heart, stands in the way of our appeals and of our logic, of our reasoning and of our entreaty. And it stands there until something which you may call, if you please, an interposition of divine grace, occurs to bend the will and bring it into subjection to Christ. And in my opinion, not even by Christian education, however early begun, and however systematically and unremittingly persisted in, not even, as I think, when preceded by and based upon the grace of Holy Baptism, do we altogether and wholly remove this obstacle out of the way before the child

---

[1] Thus TYNDALL, *Vitality* (Fragments Ed. 1878, p. 459), "In tracing these phenomena through all their modifications, the most advanced philosophers of the present day declare that they ultimately arrive at a *single Source of power*, from which all vital energy is derived."

comes to be old enough to renew and ratify the promises that were made in his name, or for him, when he was received by the minister of Christ as "a child of God and an inheritor of the Kingdom of Heaven." If the child lives to come to that age he must *voluntarily* submit and *consciously* choose to do the will of God rather than to follow the devices and desires of his own heart and pursue the dictates of his own will.

This, however, is a moral obstacle, or cause of disinclination to the recognition and acknowledgment of the Personality of God with which we are not here specially concerned.

There is, however, an influence of a mere intellectual character which comes more directly in the way of these Lectures, and to which, in closing this Lecture, I refer.

We all form an idea of the Supreme Being in our early years, whether from the pious teachings of parents and sponsors, or from the chance expressions we happen to hear in the market places and byways of life. The idea we thus form is very human. We imagine God as having a human form and a visible abode, and quite likely as possessed of human passions, caprices, and infirmities, such as we see men have. But as we grow up and reflect on the subject, we soon come to see that He can have no human "form, parts or passions." He cannot be said even to have a throne, or to sit upon one, except figuratively. To be omnipresent He must be invisible to the bodily eyes; to be omniscient He must have modes of thought entirely unlike our own and beyond our comprehension.

We thus find it necessary to get rid of the idea of a bodily, visible form, and of a local habitation for Him who is God over all.

But this is not all. We derive our idea of personality from the observation and study of man. And we are accustomed to reckon as among its elements man's infirmities and weaknesses, and quite possibly their caprices and their sins, and whatever we least respect and are most likely to hate. And in popular phraseology these peculiarities are often spoken of as constituting "the personality" of the individual.

And in this, I think, lies the greatest difficulty of the case.[1]

---

[1] TYNDALL, after having admitted that "the most advanced" philosophers in tracing the phenomena of nature find at last a "*single Source of power*," says, *Fragments* Ed. 1878, Introduction, p. 336, "When I attempt to give the Power which I see manifested in the universe an objective form, (?) personal or otherwise, it slips away from me, declining all intellectual manipulations. I dare not, save poetically, use the pronoun 'He' regarding it. I dare not call it Mind. I refuse to call it even Cause. Its mystery overshadows me; but it remains a mystery, while the objective (?) forms which

Let us then inquire what really constitutes personality? What is its essence, and what are only its accidents?

Persons and things; these are the two great and co-ordinate subdivisions of all objects that have substantial reality. Things are inert; persons are more or less spontaneous in their activity. Spontaneity of action implies intelligence, to understand and know what one is doing, and that consciousness which acts of intelligence always implies. It implies sensibility, also, or the susceptibility to feelings, or motives, as distinct in their nature and different in their mode of action from the "forces" that operate in nature and upon mere inorganic matter. It implies the power of purpose and final cause, that is, the working for ends and aims of which the agent is conscious, and for which he can direct his energies and powers, and for which, also, he can to some extent make use of and direct the objects and forces of nature.

Now when this intelligence is limited and imperfect, there will be changes of purpose according to, and as resulting from, increase of knowledge with

---

my neighbors try to make it fit, simply distort and desecrate it."

It is manifest, I think, that by "*objective form*" he means a visible, bodily form, and that when he speaks of "*personal*," he has in mind *human* personality, with a form that is somewhat like that of human beings.

regard to the object that is pursued, as well as in the choice of the objects of pursuit. And persons of very weak minds may be very changeful because they have no fixed purpose.

And so, too, persons of imperfect character and changeful feelings may change their course because of a change in their feelings. All improvement in character implies some change. Repentance is a change that comes from consciousness of guilt and wrong doing. When we come to hate the evil we have been accustomed to do, we change our course, become inconsistent with our past selves, and we may seem to others as giving evidence of great weakness.

All these elements, however, are but the *accidents* of personality; connected with it as we see it in our fellow-men more or less, and conspicuous in them. But neither weakness nor wickedness, neither caprice nor ignorance, are essential to personality. They rather mar than make it. They indicate that the being whom they characterize is yet far, very far, from the perfection which he can and ought to attain.

And yet it is these very accidents of personality, these faults and imperfections, these signs of either weakness or wickedness, that the objectors to the personality of God seize upon as the ground of their objections.

Herbert Spencer says,[1] speaking of our progress in philosophy and scientific knowledge, "As fast as experience proves that certain familiar changes always happen in the same sequence, there begins to fade from the mind the conception of a special personality, to whose variable will they were before ascribed. And when, step by step, accumulating observations do the like with less familiar changes, a similar modification of belief takes place with respect to them."

Here we have the whole thing told, and the reasons for it fairly given. A "variable will" is taken as the essential constituent and the only infallible proof of personality. And as we do not see this manifested in the phenomena of nature, these men conclude that the *Noumenon* that underlies and "works in all the *phenomena* of nature," cannot be a personal Being.

Now, undoubtedly these mere accidents of personality, as we see it in man, are among the most conspicuous and striking manifestations of that which constitutes the difference between human beings whom we call persons and those lifeless objects around us which we call things. And often it is that the more capricious and abnormal these quali-

---

[1] *First Principles*, Part I, § 29.

ties are, the more strikingly do they manifest their "personality."

But assuredly He that is Omniscient need not change or vary His plans to meet any unforeseen emergency. In the constitution and course of nature there can be nothing that was not foreseen and perfectly understood from the first by Omniscience. And He Who is perfectly good and unchanging in His nature can have no occasion to change His purposes there where there is no power of choice or spontaneity of action to call for a change of purpose or of measures.

Hence there is nothing in the regularity and uniformity of nature to militate against the doctrine of the Personality of God the First Cause; nothing to prevent the so-called forces, gravity with the rest, from being regarded as only the constant exertions of His will and purpose in the world He has created.

It is in the world of moral and accountable beings alone—in the world where there is power of choice and spontaneity of action, there only and alone—that we must look for change of purpose and of measures. When man repents, God relents and forgives. When man errs, God instructs, by conscience in the inward man and by His Prophets in the community at large. In the early ages He did as any wise parent does and must do; He adapted

His instructions and His institutions to the infancy and youth of humanity, their moral notions and their powers of spiritual apprehension.[1] And the full measure of His truth and grace came only in these latter ages, and were manifested in all their fullness when the fullness of time had fully come, in the Person of the Son of Mary, His Blessed Son, and our only Redeemer and Saviour.

The whole objection to the Personality of God, therefore, in so far as it has any intellectual basis, grows out of what we call technically the *fallacia accidentis*, the fallacy of accidents. It mistakes certain mere accidents of personality for what is essential to personality itself; and not finding manifestations of these accidents in the phenomena of nature or anywhere in the works which we ordinarily ascribe to Him as First Cause and Efficient Agent in nature, these persons deny His personality altogether.

But we might as well deny that man is man on account of the color of his hair or because he might happen to have no hair on his head at all.

And this is perhaps all that these men mean when, in denying the personality of God, they say it is only because they mean to ascribe to Him and they do

---

[1] See MOZLEY's *Ruling Ideas in Early Ages* for some admirable thoughts well expressed on this subject.

it as a means of ascribing to Him "some thing that is higher than personality."

Herbert Spencer says, indeed, a little farther on in the discussion, "Those who espouse this alternative position make the erroneous assumption that the choice is between personality and something lower than personality; whereas the choice is rather between personality and something higher."

But *person* and *thing* are co-ordinates, both logically and ontologically—a co-ordinate pair. Like odd and even in numbers, what is not the one must of necessity be the other. Person or thing, one or the other, therefore, whatever exists at all must be.

Or if any one should say that there are three classes, we might then have the three, animals, things and persons. But it will make no difference with our argument, since, at any rate, persons are higher than either of the other two classes. And if we omit from our idea of personality wickedness and weakness, ignorance and caprice, as mere accidents, we can form no conception of anything that is higher than a person. And if one says that we may have proof of the *existence* of that of which we can have no idea or conception he is using language, the force and meaning of which he does not understand. If we know a thing by sense-perception, we know it by its sensible properties. If we know anything by consciousness it is the mind within us, and we know it by its activities. If we know anything by the law or process of causation, we know it by its adequacy to the effects it has produced. Hence in any view we cannot know that anything exists without knowing something of what it is.

And even Spencer admits all that is here implied,[1] —even though he calls God the Unknowable, he confesses that we know that He is omnipresent—that He is active in all the phenomena of nature, is present in our minds as the inspirer of all our highest thoughts and noblest aspirations. And surely we have in this all the essential constituents of personality, even the highest personality, that than which there can be nothing higher.

With all this considered it can be only a question of words whether we call this Being "the Unknowable," or the God Whom Christians love and adore.

Hence I think we may safely conclude that all the arguments and all the methods of argumentation by which we claim to prove the existence of God, proves also His Personality.

If God acted before all other actions and events, before all things, He certainly must have acted from Himself, or spontaneously. The first action could have been no *reflex* action like what we see in the

---

[1] *First Principles*, Part I, §§ 27 and 34.

nerve-centres of man and animals, nor yet any mere *re*action such as we see in the phenomena of inorganic, lifeless matter. In the First Cause, action could be neither the one nor the other of these two kinds. Hence our argument proves as fully and as certainly that the First Cause must have been, and and must be still, a Personal Agent, as it proves that He exists at all.

Of course we cannot ask or expect to come to any adequate conception of the character and attributes of God. His mode of being, of thought and of action, are beyond our comprehension. This we must distinctly admit and realize.

Nor is such a comprehension necessary for either Natural Theology or practical religion. We do not get such a comprehension even of the fundamental facts and principles of the sciences, not even in those that we regard as the most certain and the most exact.

And yet there is a way of looking at the subject, which, for these many years past has been of great service to me.

I, a finite being, see the objects around me from one point of view alone. One is on the right hand, another on the left, one before me and another is behind me.

But now suppose I could see these objects all at

once, and *from all points of space* at the same time, as if I were omnipresent I certainly could do. It is easy to see that in that case there could be no here and there for these objects, no "on the right" or "on the left," no one before or behind me. In a word, there could be no space-relations in or between them and myself.

In the same way I consider myself finite in the matter of mental comprehension. I have a thought now. I had another a moment ago; but that is gone now. Another will come, perhaps, in a moment. But they all come and go, and hence the idea of time and of a past and a future and of a succession in time.

But suppose my mind were so comprehensive that I could have all my thoughts and all ideas *present at once*, and *at all times*, in consciousness, as must be the case with one who is omniscient and eternal. Is it not certain that there would be in that mind no time-relations, no "before" and no "after," just as in the former case there could be no space-relations, no idea of space? This is doubtless beyond imagination, and hardly conceivable. But it may help us to believe what St. Peter says, when he declares, in speaking of God, "that with Him one day is as a thousand years and a thousand years as one day."

The great, the eternal I AM, may always speak in

the present tense of whatever was, is, or is to come, considered in relation to man and to human affairs.

God, then, is a person incomprehensible in His nature and mode of existence; but so like us, or rather we are so made in His image, that we conceive of Him under forms and modes more or less anthropomorphic. In this we are all essentially alike. We differ in degree only. From the feeblest infancy of the lisping child up to the broadest powers of comprehension ever attained by man, we think of Him to some extent as acting under limitations which we can easily show do not belong to His nature; we speak of Him as passionate, as angry, as changeful in His purposes. Something of this kind is necessary to give a sense of reality to our idea of Him and to make His name a power in its influence upon our thoughts and our feelings. A God too far removed from us is practically no god at all. Abstractly and absolutely the Personality of God is one thing and incomprehensible, but it is a fact none the less. Practically it is a different thing for each individual; according to his powers of comprehension, and his spiritual culture or lack of culture. Let us begin by regarding Him as wise and good and holy, and as we grow in wisdom and holiness the idea will ever move on towards perfection, leading us on, and drawing us by the power of its might, towards that state of being which we can always approach but never fully attain unto.

God is an infinite person. And by the expression we mean only that He is one Whose presence is not limited by time or bounded by space, whose intelligence knows all things, whose power is adequate to all things so that He can give His attention to and take care of all things, from the greatest to the least, from the suns and constellations that roll in heavenly space, to the sparrow that flutters and falls to her inevitable death; from the proudest earthly potentate that sets Him at defiance, to the humblest soul that sins and repents, turning to Him with a cry for mercy. To all and for all He is not only God and Creator, but a Father and Friend as well; a Father and Friend Who never slumbers nor sleeps; Who faints not and is never weary, and Whose mercies never fail.

LECTURE VI.

MIRACLES AND INSPIRATION AS OCCURRING IN NATURE AND INDICATED IN EXPERIENCE.

Luke XII, 56, 57. Ye can discern the face of the sky and of the earth . . . . why then do ye not even of yourselves judge what is right?

MIRACLES AND INSPIRATION.

At the beginning of these Lectures I spoke of two methods in Natural Theology—the *one*, the outward method, beginning, as it is commonly stated, with the objects in the outward world, leads back to a First Cause and Creator; the other, beginning with the facts, laws and conditions of thought, leads to the idea of a Supreme Being, Who is necessarily existing, is spontaneously active, but Who nevertheless does not act under the conditions and limitations of time and space as human beings do.

I might have said then, and I take occasion to say now, that this latter method branches off at a very early stage, perhaps one might say at the very beginning, into two entirely different channels, the one of which may be called the purely intellectual or logical method, and the other the method of sentiment and instinct. I have thus far pursued the first of these two methods; the latter, however, has been in vogue of late years and seems, in fact, to be growing in favor. The argument is that man's wants and instincts demand a belief in some such Being and that these elements of our nature constitute a ground for belief and action which is as legitimate as any other.

President Porter, in his late work, "*Science and Sentiment*," has put this argument in the strongest light that I have seen. The late lamented Professor Dimon, in his "Lowell Lectures," "*The Theistic Argument*," has exhibited the argument at greater length. And in fact all the later "apologies for Christianity" that I have seen are in this line of thought. And I have no disposition to criticise or to disparage in the slightest degree that line of argument.

But I should only express my conviction if I were to say in the words of President Porter (p. 21), "The heart can neither love nor trust what the head demonstrates to be untrue." And this means, as I apply the words, that if we cannot vindicate our belief by the other method, and leave it to rest on sentiment and the felt-wants of humanity alone, it is not likely to be much respected. Men of the agnostic school are likely to say as Tyndall has said:[1] "If, abandoning your illegitimate claim to knowledge, you place with Job your forehead in the dust and acknowledge the authorship of this universe to

---

[1] Appleton's *Popular Science Monthly*, Jan., 1879, p. 288.

be past finding out—if having made this confession, and relinquished the views of the mechanical theologian, you desire for the satisfaction of feelings which I admit to be in great part those of humanity at large, to give ideal form to the Power that moves all things—it is not by me that you will find objections raised to this exercise of ideality, when consciously and worthily carried out."

So, then, these men will allow us to have our religion if we ask it only as an amusement, a favor or as a "comfort" in our weakness. But if we claim for it any foundation in truth, or any binding force upon conscience, they will interpose to prevent it.

Revelation without inspiration is impossible; and inspiration itself is of the nature of a miracle.

A revelation, in any proper sense, must be a communication from a personal being. It must be made to the minds of men. It must be, in its first stage, an act or influence that is exerted inwardly and upon the mind. It may then become, through the words of the inspired man, a revelation or disclosure to others.

Truths received by immediate inspiration may be communicated by words and outward signs to others, and thus become the means of stimulating, elevating and guiding the minds of men and of communities of men almost indefinitely.

Now, to begin in our accustomed method, we start with recalling to mind the facts already noticed, that there are among those that are daily and hourly falling under our observation, these two classes; the one the facts of nature produced by inert causes, atoms, molecules or masses acting on each other in accordance with physical laws; and the other class, constituting what we call *voluntary* acts, acts that cannot be accounted for, and which nobody attempts to account for, without recognizing the agency of man as something different from mere physical or inert matter.

The acts of the first great class are all reducible to law. They can be stated, if I mistake not, in mathematical formulæ. But in any case, all these acts come under the domain of what we call natural or physical law, and the law is such that we can, alike, reproduce the past and predict the future, with little or no possibility of a mistake or of any exception from the rule.

But in human action it is otherwise. Here man chooses how he will act, and acts to some extent as he chooses or pleases to act. Hence no science—neither psychology nor mathematics—can tell how a man will act until the act itself has become a fact accomplished and so a part of the history of the past.

Hence the two domains, *Moral* Philosophy and *Natural* Philosophy, in the broadest acceptation of their meaning, are marked off and outlined from each other, by an insuperable barrier. They are different in their first principles and starting-point, and ever diverging more and more widely from each other because of the ever increasing influence of spontaneity in the one, of which there is nothing, not even the beginning, in the other.

Miracles are from their very nature voluntary acts, performed by a personal agent or being. And hence, too, as I think, every voluntary act, every act that arises from spontaneity is of the nature of a a miracle; something unforeseen by science, something that cannot be accounted for on scientific principles, if we insist upon using the words "science" and "scientific" with exclusive reference to *natural* science. Something is done for a purpose and with a view to an end such as could not or would not be accomplished in the ordinary course of nature without the intervention of mind, whether by evolution or otherwise. Miracles are the acts of Personal Agents and not the products of physical forces.

Miracles are in their very nature relative. When there was no living thing, growth and locomotion would have been regarded as both incomprehensible and miraculous, if there had been a crystal capable of intelligence to see and think about such phenomena.

So, too, in a world of intelligent beings where all are deaf the man that could hear would be all the time performing what would be regarded as miraculous.

And even any of the phenomena of inanimate matter, if it should occur only once, and we should be unable to assign to it any adequate cause or give it any satisfactory explanation, would be, in the estimation of all men, a miracle.

Thus if we look from mere matter up to animal life, or from the level of mere animal life up to the intelligent voluntary activity of man, we see in either case a region of miracles.

Now, omitting for the present the element of rarity and novelty in the occurrence, what we find common to all the events, that are or would be called miraculous, is the intervention of a force or being that is higher than that which is found to be active in the region below.

What I want to have specially noted is that in all this, so far as we have thus gone, there is no contravention, suspension or violation of the laws of nature, in the phenomena which, as we have seen, would be regarded as miraculous in these various cases.

In the phenomena of animal organization and life there is no violation or departure from the laws of chemistry and mechanics, but there is a new force at work combining the elements and using the laws in ways that had not been before observed.

So in human life and voluntary action, the laws of nature prevail. There is, however, a new force—the human mind—guiding them. And although it cannot suspend or counteract those laws, it can give new directions and new combinations to their modes of activity, so that results that could not occur in nature without such an agent, are all the while occurring with his presence and constitute what we regard as the sphere of human action.

We have already gotten, as I trust, something of an idea of the sphere and characteristics of human action. We have seen that its phenomena imply, besides physical strength, something of intelligence, purpose, and spontaneity of action. But the mind, which is the substance of these attributes, is only a force in, and acting upon and among, the inert masses of matter, and always in subordination to their nature and the laws of inert matter. This nature and these laws man does not and cannot change. He may *violate* the laws, but if he does so he suffers the penalty. *He* cannot, however, suspend the law; and *they* will not show mercy or favor, forbearance or forgiveness, to any one who transgresses them.

But this does not explain away all miracles; it only proves the necessity, in order to a true miracle, that there should be an adequate agent, a *nodus deo dignus*. If God be present, all things are possible. In this view the Incarnation, the miraculous Conception and the Resurrection of the body itself, although miracles of the most marvelous kind, are seen to be possible to a Divine Agency.

One method of procedure would be to assume some one act that is acknowledged to have been miraculous if it occurred; and prove its occurrence historically. And this method must be pursued, I apprehend, by those who undertake to discuss and present the Evidences of Christianity. But my object is of a different nature. It is to prove that even the phenomena of nature present us proof of miracles; so that from a right view and a thorough comprehension of the facts of nature, we should be led to *expect* miracles rather than look upon them as impossible, as our modern agnostics do, or as too improbable to admit of any satisfactory historic proof, as Hume and the infidels of his day professed to do.

And it is quite possible that my statements with regard to the nature of miracles and of the principles that are necessary to prove and account for their occurrence, will not be all that is necessary for one who is writing concerning the miracles that have actually occurred as recorded in the Old and the New Testament.

As I have said, miracles are relative, and as much that is considered as miraculous, when regarded from our point of view, ceases to be so when looked at from a higher level, so much that is and will be regarded as miraculous in one age will cease to be so regarded in another.

There is reason for Comte's division[1] of the history of the human progress into three stages. They occur in the life of every man as well as in the progress of the history of the race. They may co-exist to some extent, and they are in any case, as I think, to be regarded rather as having a logical than a chronological basis; they certainly overlap and reach into each other chronologically, so as to co-exist the one with another; and to some extent all three of them exist together, both in the life of the individual and in the history of the race.

The first stage Comte calls the "theistic" or "the theological"; the second the "metaphysical" or the philosophical, and the third the "positive" or scientific.

---

[1] *Introduction*, Vol. I, pp. 2-7, Martineau's Edition.

In the earlier or theological stage, men knew but very little of science, and were intensely religious. Hence they ascribed nearly all the phenomena of nature to an immediate Divine Agency, and this made nearly every occurrence a miracle in their estimation.

We now know a thousandfold more of this age than we did when Comte wrote. We know that men were then "unconscious monotheists"—saw God everywhere and in everything. We know now, too, how their "unconscious monotheism" developed into a pantheism, with its peculiar cult and forms of nature worship; or into polytheism, with its myths, its temples, and its idol images, and finally its fetichism.

With the progress of time, however, man, having noticed the uniformity and the regularity with which many events recur, ceased to wonder at them. The idea of a uniformity in nature with which man could not, and God or the gods would not interfere, began to prevail. In this way a large share of the phenomena of nature passed over from that class that were regarded as of divine origin, or as implying direct *personal* agency, into the class that excited no wonder and called for no gratitude in thus accounting for these phenomena.

And these early philosophers, like the impetuous

youth of our day who aim to be wise before their time, instead of the slow and cautious process of observation and induction, hastened to conclusions and resorted to creations of fancy. They found invention easier and far more expeditious than discovery.

But in the third stage, as Comte describes it, philosophers begin to be more skeptical. They begin to see that the creations of fancy are rather fictions than facts, and lead to a mythology rather than to a scientific knowledge of anything. Then comes the age of "positive philosophy," when men, rejecting all idea of divine interference and all the abstractions and fictions of the metaphysicians, give themselves up to the study of facts in the more cautious method of scientific induction, in which they will accept nothing as matter of science nor believe anything as matter of faith that they cannot test by experiment and observation.

Now this historic review has a relation to the subject before us that is very pertinent. In the first stage all, or nearly all, was miracle. In the second nothing was miraculous, because all things were explained either by mythology or referred to abstractions. And in either case and alike they were under the control of him who undertook to explain them. Nothing was easier than to invent myths, unless it were to create a new abstraction that will do the work for us. And thus no fact or phenomena could be seized upon or used as a means to prove the existence of God.

But with the "new age," the "positive" age, the age of exact science, we are in a different position. We *know* now what matter, whether it acts as atoms, molecules or masses, can do; or rather we know the limits that mark off certain things that it cannot do. Within the range of what it can do, there may remain, and there doubtless does remain, a well nigh infinite amount of truth and fact yet to be discovered. But we know the limits to that domain, the boundaries of activity which it can never pass.

I have pointed out in a preceding Lecture and somewhat insisted upon *one* such act or event in the past history of the earth. We may as well call it creation, for if the Self-Existent First Cause did not then call matter into being from nothing, He certainly did act to set its inert, and at that time, inactive atoms into motion and activity. From a state of "universal death" and "perfect equilibrium or rest," He caused the atoms to begin to act directly upon each other; and the result was molecules and masses, with heat and light, affinity and cohesion, and gravity of masses, as "*modes of motion,*" mere phenomena of their activity.

And this was a MIRACLE in the very highest sense that we can attach to the word.

I consider this proposition proved beyond any further need of argument. Of course the proof may need explanation, reiteration, and illustration, until it shall have become familiar to the mind and its force is fully realized. We have then the existence of God as a Creator and a Miracle Worker, proved by an argument which I think is as rigorous in its logic and as inevitable in its conclusions as any one of the Propositions of Euclid.

With this I think we leave, at least I am willing to admit that we leave, the ground of absolute certainty and enter upon that of probability—a probability approaching more or less nearly to absolute certainty as the case may be.

And here two fields open before us. The one is the field of nature as it appears to us in its present phenomena and in its past history as disclosed to us by the geologist and palæontologist; and the other is the field of human history. Of the first I will speak in this Lecture and reserve what I have to say, or rather what I shall have time to say of the other, to the next Lecture.

And for the purposes of this Lecture, as well as for those of the next Lecture, I want to have it understood that I think I have a right to claim, and that I do claim, that there is a presumption in favor of the doctrine I am about to attempt to prove, arising from what we have already proved concerning the existence and attributes of God. Plato argued, as I have before said (Lect. I), that it was absurd to suppose God, such as we know Him to be, both in intelligence and in activity and power, to be either indifferent to, or inactive in, the affairs of this world, and more especially the affairs of men.[1] Aristotle,[2] also, as we said, Lect. II, held that God is essentially active, and is virtually the active cause and force in all of nature's phenomena, that it is contrary to His nature to suppose that He could be otherwise.

And it seems to me but fair to assume from what we have seen that He is essentially active in His nature, and that having begun a work with evident purpose, He will continue to carry it on to its final and foreordained result, and to go on with our discussions, with a strong presumption in our favor derived from this source.

1. The first case I will cite as coming under this head, is the appearance of the first living thing on this earth. I have already spoken of this occurrence in a preceding Lecture, and do not intend to repeat what was then said.

The combination of the four elements, oxygen,

---

[1] *De Legibus*, B. X, c. xi.   [2] *Metaphysics*, B. XI, c. vi.

nitrogen, carbon and hydrogen, called protoplasm, is known to be an exceedingly unstable compound. It cannot exist at a temperature much above the boiling point of water. And if I mistake not, no chemist has yet been able to produce it by any process that is merely chemical or mechanical or both combined. Nor, as I understand the matter, can it be kept together long, except on the condition that the compound is either a living being or so intimately connected with some living organism as to be preserved by that connection from the inevitable dissolution that would follow its separation and elimination from the system, or its death.[1]

I am well aware that claims have been set up and are, or were a few years ago, being pushed with a good deal of persistence, of the reality of what is called "spontaneous generation."

This is the name given to a process by which it is claimed that living beings of the lowest order can be produced without any living parentage, the process consisting in taking some animal or vegetable tissue, reduce it to a jelly or a pulp and putting it into a jar which is afterwards hermetically sealed, with no atmospheric air in it except such as has been heated to at least the boiling point. It is claimed

[1] Perhaps I ought to make an exception of those cases in which living tissues are preserved by the arts and agency of man, as desiccation, etc.

that in this case there could be no germ of a living thing in either the air or the pulp, so that if animalculæ make their appearance it must be a case of spontaneous generation—animals without parentage.

That animalculæ have appeared under such circumstances after a few days admits of no denial. And the dissent from the conclusion comes from a doubt whether *all* germs had been destroyed, and the weight of authority, even including those who will not admit of any *miraculous* creation, is against the claim of spontaneous generation.

But to my mind a more important fact is, that these men, so far as I know, claim to use and need to use matter that *had once been organized into living tissues.*

This fact is material; for if we concede the fact of spontaneous generation *out of such material,* or if the efforts to produce it from such material should ever hereafter prove successful, it will not help the case of the unbeliever; since we are referring to a time when, confessedly, there had been no previous organic tissue out of whose decayed, or decaying, protoplasm the new being could be produced.

I have said that no chemist has yet been able to produce protoplasm, or at least any living thing, whether cell or tissue. Nor can he tell how, or by what process, chemical or mechanical, or both combined, such a result can be produced. And what is more, he cannot tell why he cannot produce it.

This does not indeed prove that its production was a miracle, or the result of an act of immediate Divine agency. But it does prove that scientific men have no right or ground on which to deny that it was a miracle. The argument is all against them, and will remain so until they can explain how the first protoplasm was produced, and how, having been produced as a chemical compound, it became a living being.

Now it is readily admitted that this case does not afford, like the one last considered, an *absolute demonstration* of miracles or divine interposition. It is readily admitted that in the progress of scientific discovery we are daily advancing *towards* a solution of this difficulty in one way or the other. Here, then, there is a mere possibility, in the technical sense of the word, that we may come to know how to make living protoplasm, if not certainly to make living beings.

But even if, in the progress of science, such a result should be attained, it will not impair the force of my argument so far as I can see. Man will only come to know how to do, and to do, what God did millions of years ago, when there were no human beings to do it.

And this is in accordance with the general course of events. Long before man was brought into existence some intelligent being, with spontaneous activity, must have done a good many things, the likes of which do not now occur at all, and many others which man can *now* do, in a small way. And in this likeness to God man is progressing all the while, by his discoveries in science and in the useful arts of life, no less than by his growth in grace, in his moral nature.

But on the other hand it must be considered also that as we approach this point there appears also, strong indications that we never can reach it. And these indications become more clear and decisive as we approach what seems to be the result. Like certain principles and formulæ in mathematics, we have experience on one side indicating and promising certain results, with the absolute certainty on the other that those results can never be realized.

It may be well to give an example or two by way of illustration.

Take for one the well-known series $1 + \frac{1}{2} + \frac{1}{4} + \frac{1}{8}$ and so on. It is obvious from inspection that as we go on with the series we approach nearer and nearer at every successive step, to a term which will be zero, and a time when the sum of the terms will be 2. But we know absolutely *from the nature of the series*, that no such result can ever be reached in fact, notwithstanding the confidence and expectations that may have been caused by experience to the contrary.

So with the hyperbola. We know that with every step in the increase of the abscissa, we are actually approaching the junction of the curve and its asymptote. Nothing can be clearer as a mere matter of experiment, or *a posteriori* knowledge. No expectation founded on experience alone could be more reasonable or worthy of confidence. And yet we know, from the nature of the case, that no contact is ever possible between the two lines.

Now there are those who would affirm that this is precisely the case with regard to the production of protoplasm and living beings without either pre-existing organic matter or divine intervention, and so by a miracle. But I think that is stating the matter rather stronger than the character of the argument, or our insight into the nature of the case, will fairly justify. It makes undoubtedly a strong, and an ever-increasing case of probability. But I think this is all we can fairly claim at present, and all perhaps that we shall ever be able to claim on purely scientific grounds.[1]

---

[1] I see no occasion to speak of this part of the argument in stronger terms than JOHN STUART MILL has done in his posthu-

The force of the argument is undoubtedly greatly increased by considering it in connection with the preceding demonstration derived from the origin of motion and change in the inorganic matter of which the universe consists. We have thus proved that there is a Being Who can thus interpose and create a "new thing," do something unlike what had ever been done before. We see also that such an act is entirely consistent with His character and attributes—it is like Him—to do just this thing, to produce living beings, and beings of a higher order one after another on the earth, in its progress of becoming fit for the abode of man. I think that the consideration creates a strong, a controlling probability that He would do so.

Tyndall, with the "rapt vision" of a prophet, may have thought he saw in the nebulous mass of prezoic matter, and claim, as he does in his famous Belfast Address, that he did "discern in that matter . . . the promise and potency of every form and quality of terrestrial life."[1] But he saw nothing of the kind,

---

mous work, *Theism*, p. 170. He says: "As mere analogy, it [the argument for the existence of God from nature] has its weight; but it is more than analogy. It surpasses analogy exactly as induction surpasses it. It is an inductive argument." "It is, for reasons known to inductive agencies, the weakest of the four [kinds of inductive arguments], but the particular argument is a strong one of its kind."

[1] *Fragments of Science*, Ed. 1878, p. 524, and again in modified phraseology, p. 546.

except in fancy and by way of a dream. Eliminating the poetry and taking the residuum of fact, what he saw, or might have seen, in that incandescent mass, was the chemical elements of which organic beings are made, and the fact that they might unite, or rather *be united*, into protoplasm and living cells. And this he might well say; for nobody doubts that the material elements were there; and the fact that they were, some of them, united into protoplasm, and afterwards became living animals, has become a matter of geologic history.

But he has not told us how they became united into living cells and organized into sensitive, moving beings, with life and death, reproduction and persistence of specific forms. And this is the question which just now mainly interests us.

I have spoken of this subject before, but there seems to be occasion to recur to it again. Three, and only three, hypotheses are supposable.

1st. The atoms "acting directly on each other," as he says they do, united to form molecules; the molecules acting in the same way and "without the intervention of slave labor" or any foreign force or agency, *united themselves* to form cells and tissues which, somehow or other, became living beings, and thus the beings created themselves.

2d. The next hypothesis is that life, as a foreign

substance or element came, somehow, into this inorganic, or rather unorganized mass, united the elements in most mysterious ways and *formed for itself* a habitation and a dwelling place, which it might continue to occupy until by some process, unknown to us, it might choose to leave the body it had formed to the decay which results as soon as life is gone, from the natural repugnance of those elements to remain united.

3d. The only other supposition is that God united the elements and made of them when He had so united them, living creatures, with life as "a mode of motion," a *mode* of being and existence only; just as is the case with color and temperature, density and form.

The second of these hypotheses which, in the words already quoted more than once, are "verbally intelligible," is ruled out by the advance of mankind to what we have called the "positive" stage, the age of exact science. We are left, therefore, to our choice between the two, the 1st and the 3d, with the probabilities, considered from a purely scientific point of view, preponderating immensely to the latter; preponderating, in fact, so far as to amount to what we call a moral certainty.

And that, if it so occurred, was certainly a miracle. At any rate it was an event which, like the

Incarnation and Atonement, occurred then once for all. It had not occurred before; it has not occurred, so far as we know or have reason to believe, since. There was good reason why it did not occur before; there is no reason, so far as we know or can imagine, why, if there is any *natural* tendency in the elements so to unite, there have not been constantly occurring such unions from that time to this. The conditions, the physical conditions, all the conditions except that of time, or mere chronology in the progress of the ages, must have occurred many millions of times since the first living cell appeared on the face of the earth, and yet no such event is on record or known to have occurred.

It is, I think, a well established principle of science, that whatever nature has done man can do in his turn when he comes to know the laws and conditions on which the event occurred in the course of the world's history. This is what we are doing all the time by our "experiments." We know of no condition in nature, whether of heat or cold, of drouth or moisture, that has occurred in the past, on any scale however large or small, that man cannot reproduce on a small scale in his laboratories now. He has solidified hydrogen by his cold. He can produce heat sufficient to resolve the most stable compounds into their component elements. But he has found as yet no way to produce living protoplasm. This, so far as we yet know, God only can do.[1]

2. I turn now to another branch of the subject, different in some respects, though kindred in others.

Until quite recently it was the belief of nearly all men that all the animals that make up a *species* were descended from one pair; and that the descendants of any one primitive pair, constituted one of the classes of animals recognized in Natural History as a species.

This view was thought to imply, in the case of the primitive pairs of each species, a special creative act, which was, of course, of the nature of a miracle.

But in these latter days it is claimed that Evolution accounts for the origin of species, and that there has been no creative act, no interposition to produce the protoplasts of a new species, since, at latest, the origin of protoplasm.

But to this claim I interpose the following objections:

---

[1] The old heathen poet, LUCRETIUS, though a thorough-going Evolutionist, felt none of the modern difficulties on the subject. He said that in the earliest times *crescebant uteri, terræ radicibus, apti*, and that when the children had been born in these flowers of the plants, the earth poured forth from its open veins or pores a liquid like milk just as women do now from their breasts, and thus "the

1st. There is no proof and no *claim*, so far as I have seen, that any new "species" has actually been produced under human observation or within the sphere of human knowledge. Evolution, therefore, when considered in this point of view, can be considered as nothing more than a mere hypothesis, a mere conjecture awaiting proof. For it is readily admitted that evolution and development may take place in the successive stages of the same individual, with no change of the individuality, however, and without creating so much as a presumption, or a probability, or even a plausible conjecture that by the same process one individual could be changed into another, or transformed from one species into another with difference of kind.

I am well aware that questions may be raised here as to the meaning of the word species.[1] I ask no

---

earth afforded nourishment for the infants," Book V, line 808 and following.

[1] There is much ambiguity in this controversy in the use of the word "*species.*" In *Logic* the word may be used to denote any class, and any class will be either genus or species, just according to the point of view from which we regard it. But in *Natural History* is is quite otherwise. A certain class is called a species, and any one who should call it anything else, as genus or variety, would exhibit thereby either an ignorance or a disregard of the established usage.

There are, however, two other terms that are of importance in this connection, "varieties" and "hybrids." A variety is a sub-species, and may possibly be as well marked and as permanent in odds on this score. I use the word in the same sense as these scientific men do themselves whenever they are talking or writing Natural History, Botany or Zoology, and are forgetful, for the moment at least, of the exigencies of their controversey with "the theologians." And I say that no one of them has claimed, so far as I have seen or heard, the origination of what he calls, or claims to have called, a new species, within the historic period and under human observation.

We know very well that great diversities and constantly increasing diversifications are all the while occurring under the influences which Darwin has so well described among men and animals under domestication.

It may be well to dwell on this point for a moment.

And as the first example, I will cite that of the Machin family, known as the "*porcupine man.*" [1]

---

its characteristics as a species. Varieties can undoubtedly be produced and have been produced under our observation by (1) perpetuating some congenital peculiarity, as in the case of the Ancon sheep, or (2) by a much slower process like what Darwin describes.

Hybrids are the result of crossing and intermixture of different species. It is doubtful if they ever occur in the natural condition, and their permanence or perpetuity anywhere is much doubted, and even strenuously denied. See QUATREFAGES, *Human Species*, B. I, chaps. vii and viii.

[1] PRITCHARD, *Natural History of Man*, Noyes' Edition, Vol. I, p. 86, etc.

He was covered with a coat of quills like a porcupine. More than half his children and a part of his grandchildren also inherited this peculiarity from him. Had this trait been "cultivated" by the well known process of "inter-breeding," it would have become the characteristic of a variety, if not of a distinct species of the human race, as well fixed and permanent as the color of the negro's skin or the shape of the Mongol's head and eyes.

As another case, we have what is known as the "Ancon" sheep. The first animal of this variety was born in Massachusetts, 1791.[1]

He was characterized by very short legs. By inter-breeding, a variety was produced which came to have a permanent type and would have lasted to this day, doubtless, if it had not been superseded by a more valuable variety of sheep.

Again, in the Falkland Islands and other places, the horses soon become very much undersized, mere ponies, and remain so as long as they continue on the islands.

Now if one chooses to call all the diversifications and varieties which thus arise from congenital peculiarities, "environment," climatic and other physical influences of the kind, cases of evolution, to dispute him would be only a dispute about words.

---

[1] DARWIN, *Variation of Animals and Plants Under Domestication*, Vol. I, p. 104.

Nevertheless, these congenital peculiarities or marks are to a large extent unexplained and inexplicable on any purely scientific grounds. They *may be*, for aught we know, or are ever likely to know, the means which God uses to diversify the animal and vegetable kingdom.

But this does not explain the origin of those more fundamental and permanent traits that divide off the groups that Naturalists call Species and Genera.

Evolution, as established by experience and observed fact, does not cover the whole ground. And to ask that it shall be considered or accepted as doing so in this state of the discussion is to beg the whole question, and that, too, while facts and considerations of the most stubborn and unyielding character stand against it.

3. My third point is based on the discrepancy between the Zoological and the Geological Series.

The advocate of Evolution, from a purely Zoological point of view, will refer you to the order of development, and arrange the several species in that order. Beginning with the lowest, the one that is nearest to mere protoplasm, which may possibly be the *amœbæ*, he will place next to it in the ascending order some animal so nearly like it that you can hardly see the difference, even with eyes trained to discern such things. And so on up to the highest

—man. Even if there are some intermediate species or "links" missing, he will expect you to admit, in view of the possibility that they may yet be discovered, that the series is complete. He will then call your attention to the very slight differences that are observable between any two of the species that he has thus placed together in the order of their ascent from *amœbæ* up to man. And perhaps you will find no difficulty in admitting that these differences are no greater than you have often seen and supposed to have been produced by "environment" and other elements of physical causation, which call for no special wonder and no thought of miraculous interposition.

If now, however, we turn our attention to the Geological or Chronological Order, we find quite a discrepancy. Let the Zoologist range his group in the order of the numbers from one up to as many thousands as he may happen to have, and it is seen at once from the Geologist's order of succession that these species did not make their appearance in the same order as the Zoologist's classification demands. Instead of their making their appearance in what is the Zoologist's order, 1, 2, 3, etc., they come in a very different order. It may be that he has made, and must make in fidelity to his science, a succession in which what the Zoologist calls the first did not appear on earth until after what the Geologist has called the fifth, and the sixth of the Zoologist's order was not the next to make its appearance in the order of time, but was perhaps the fifteenth or twentieth rather. Hence we have to account for the changes, not from the first in the Zoological Series to the next one above it, but to one that is many degrees removed from it.

In confirmation and illustration of this point I cannot cite many examples. I give a few, however, in a note,[1] and would cite a work by E. Ray Lankester, in which he shows that *degeneration* from higher to lower species is as indispensable to the theory of evolution as the advance from the lower

---

[1] I give the following, taken from an unknown author, which I believe to be correct:

"In the vegetable world mosses are inferior to the lycopodiæ and ferns, but they come in later. Ganoids are among the earliest of the fishes, and yet they are of the highest orders. Trilobites are crustaceans of a high order, and yet they are among the very earliest. Monkeys, although much higher in the Geological scale, appear before the ox family."

The *Machairodus* is an obstacle to any theory of mere evolution. It appeared in several species in widely separated districts, as Nebraska, (N. A.), Brazil, (S. A.), in France, in Greece, and as far east as India. It was of the cat family *Felidæ*, as large as any known lions or tigers, more "specialized" and perfect in form than most of the later species. It appeared early in the Tertiary at or near the close of the Eocene period, and with nothing before it in that great family from which it could have been derived by any process of mere evolution or development.

to the higher stages. And especially would I refer to Dawson's "*Chain of Life in Geological Time.*" He states among his conclusions this as 6, p. 260: "Groups of species as genera and orders do not usually begin with their highest or lowest forms, but with intermediate and generalized types, and they show a capacity for both elevation and degradation in their subsequent history." And he gives examples of this throughout the whole book.

We have thus seen that the new traits and peculiarities that have actually occurred under human observation are not such as Naturalists regard as characteristics of species, or as constituting what they are disposed to call a new species in their ordinary mode of classification.

We have also seen that what we have to admit as accounted for by evolution, is not the slight differences that distinguish one species from another allied species in the *Zoological* classification, but the far broader and larger differences that distinguish remote groups one from another, since this latter and not the former was order of sequence in geological times in which they made their appearance.

4. But I have another point still. Dawson says, the 10th of his conclusions, "Palæontology furnishes no direct evidence, perhaps it never can furnish any, as to the actual transformation of one species into another."

But I wish to add a more serious objection still. Even in those cases where we have a series or succession of species, of the same genus in the same place, we have no proof of lineage or genealogical descent.

It is claimed that in the case of the *Equidæ*, or horse family, we have a good illustration and proof of Evolution. It was to this series that Huxley had reference when he made the declaration cited in the early part of the first Lecture. We have in the Lower Eocene the *Eohippus*, a small animal about the size of a fox, with canine teeth, and three toes on the hind feet, and four, with the rudiment of a fifth, on the fore feet. After this, in turn, some eighteen or twenty different species, until we come to the *Equus* proper in the Post-Pliocene and Modern period.

But there is not the slightest evidence or proof that the later species were descended lineally and genealogically from the earlier. This is all presumption and assumption.[1] To one prepossessed with the

---

[1] The fallacy of all these advocates of Evolution consists in the *assumption* of the Major Premise and an immense elaboration of the Minor Premise. They *assume* that whenever there has been a succession of species in geological time in the same place, there has been evolution or derivation of the latter from the former species. The proof of the Minor Premise—that is, cases of succession with a progress towards a higher, or possibly a lower type—is abundant and beyond doubt or question. In fact it never needed much proof. But the question is, after all, as to the *Evolution* in the case. Did

theory of Evolution, it may indeed seem the most likely or the most natural way in which the change could have occurred, or the latter and more perfect species could have come into existence.

But the presumption is not *all* on their side.

If we look to the Ohio valley we see a race of white men there now. A few hundred years ago there were only the redskin Indians, and a few centuries before that the Mound Builders inhabited the same region. Did the redskins descend from the Mound Builders? That is not generally supposed to have been the case. And we *know* that the present white race are not genealogical descendants from the redskins, by evolution or otherwise. And yet we have just as much, and, as I think, rather more reason for thinking and asserting that the whites descended from the Mound Builders, though the redskins than that the Protohippus and the Equus of the Nebraska strata descended from the Eohippus or the Orohippus of the Lower Eocene.

Nor is this all. Scores of cases may be cited in which one species of undomesticated animals have appeared and driven away a kindred species and then occupied their *habitat*. I remember two that have occurred within my own observation. The

---

the latter species *descend genealogically* from the earlier? This is what yet lacks proof. And yet it is a point which most evolutionists fail to see; or seeing it, fail to appreciate.

"barn swallow" of my boyhood days has been driven away by a bird of the same family, with very different habits, but so like to my old favorite that the one cannot be distinguished from the other without rather close observation. So, too, I can remember the time when the rats that were the pests of my father's granary, were the English black rats. Now not one of this species is to be found in the neighborhood; they have been replaced by the Norway rat or wharf rats, as we called them when they first made their appearance.

Now, in view of such facts, there naturally arises a doubt whether Professor Marsh's series of the *Equidæ* do present a case, whether as proof or as illustration, of the evolution of a higher species from one that is much lower in the scale, and further down towards the primitive protoplasm and *amœbæ*. Nay, as I claim, the presumption is wholly against the theory. *We have no case*, as Dawson says, *of the evolution or derivation of one species from another*, that has actually *been made* KNOWN *to us, either by personal observation of the change or by palæontological proof that it actually occurred.* But we have as matter of observation and of history, many instances of species succeeding species or varieties, one after another in the same locality, by displacement and superposition, and not one by evolution

It seems to me, therefore, that we must hold to our old doctrine of special interpositions—of miracles—with the origination of each species of animals from the earliest dawn of animal life until the most recent times.

Many lines of investigation tend to show that there is a limit to the possibilities of variation among the progeny of any one pair. There are limits in affairs which nature does not, and apparently will not, and which at any rate man cannot, pass over. Subject individuals to *gentle* influences as they grow up, and they yield and are moulded by them to some extent. Let the influences become more violent and the subjects of them die.

But even if long continued they soon reach their limit. As Bouverie Pusey has well shown,[1] if influences of this kind could cause the beak of the rock-pigeon to grow from a quarter of an inch long to the length of five-eighths of an inch, in the last 200 years, there is yet a limit to the length which the beak can be made to attain. Under no possible circumstances, by no combination of influences, and in no length of time, can it be made to reach the length of four or five inches, to say nothing of several feet. *Est modus in rebus.* There is a limit in the very nature of the case, in all human affairs, and in all the affairs of nature as well.

[1] *Permanence and Evolution*, p. 15 and following.

In mere inorganic matter and the changes that have taken place in it, the case is otherwise. If the bed of the sea is found to have been elevated a foot in a century, we have a basis on which we may compute the elevation in a million or any other number of years. Or if we know, by any means, how fast a deposit is increasing in depth, we have an element for calculating vast periods of past time.

But it is not so with living organic beings. The child grows at a certain rate in infancy, but he soon reaches his utmost limit of size. And so it is with the development of any part or organ of a living body. Great length of time does not seem to be much more effective than a shorter period.

There seems to be a limit or a boundary surrounding and hedging in the posterity of every pair, over which no influence of nature, and no violence or caprice of man, can ever carry them. As they approach these outer limits, individuals become infertile; and when they reach them they become absolutely sterile.

No origination of what is recognized as a new species is *known* to have occurred in the human period or in any past period of the world's history.

There are groups—call them species or what you will—between which no interproduction has occurred so far as we know, and between which none is believed to be possible.

And interproduction between even the most similar species is infrequent, abnormal, and not likely to produce a permanent stock. The *general* infertility of hybrids is acknowledged by all.

And now just in proportion as the knowledge or influence of these facts increases, and they are gaining very fast just now, so fast does the " probability " of divine interpositions—miracles—all along the geological history of the earth from the azoic age to the close of the tertiary, at least, increase and grow towards an absolute certainty.

It would thus seem that while there have been great departures from the type of the original stock in many, perhaps in most, species, there are limits and bounds which this process of variation cannot pass.

Take the domestic dog for an example.[1] So far as we know he appeared with several other of man's best friends and companions about the point in geological time that man did. For six thousand years he has been the companion and trusted friend of man; more completely domesticated and more thoroughly subject to man's influence probably than any other animal. We have seen him under all possible variations of physical " circumstances," " influences "

---

[1] See WALLACE, *Contributions to the Theory of Natural Selection*, p. 293.

and "environments," in climates as cold as the ice-age, and in those that are as hot as the carboniferous or the early Tertiary; in regions as dry as Sahara, or as moist as Mesopotamia and the banks of the Amazon; as high as St. Bernard, and as low as Holland. We have seen man petting, coaxing, "interbreeding" and doing everything that ingenuity could suggest or violence enforce. And we have dogs indeed; dogs in great variety, from the smallest terriers and spaniels up to the Newfoundland, the Chinese pug, the Italian greyhound, the bulldog, and the Dalmatian coach followers, the ferocious bloodhound and the gentle, affectionate setter. But they are all dogs, nevertheless. With all that man can do; with all the aid of most bountiful nature, and these thousands upon thousands of generations of dog-life and periods of reproduction, we have had as yet nothing but dogs—varieties of the dog species. These influences, no one of them nor yet all of them combined, have as yet produced or "evoluted," from dog parentage, a cat or a rabbit, a guinea pig or a squirrel—not even so much as a rat or a mouse—*ridiculus mus.*

I think the case must, therefore, be considered as hopeless, and the argument in our favor about as strong as demonstration can make it; as strong, at least, as reasonable men expect or ask in the practical affairs of daily life.

Having said so much in this one direction, it is but fair that I should say that I have no intention to deny Darwin's great law known as "the struggle for life with the survival of the fittest." In fact, I do not see how any one with his eyes open and his thoughts about him can deny it. There are born into the world a given number, we will suppose, of rabbits in one spring. To live they must (1) escape enemies and (2) get food. Now doubtless whatever makes one of these puny animals the best able to do these two things makes him "the fittest" to live—that is, the best fitted—and so the most likely, to live and be a progenitor next season. And thus by the law of heredity *his* posterity would be better "fitted" to survive and perpetuate the species than the offspring of those who had been his inferiors in this respect. And thus we have an improvement in the species with varying adaptation to circumstances and environment.[1]

---

[1] It is claimed, however, that there is a serious offset to this line of argument; that while the peculiarities of each species of animals are for the most part favorable to the animals in "the struggle for life," there are others that are of a different character. The horny scales on the tail of a rattlesnake have been cited as an example. Whenever the animal becomes excited and about to make any effort, these rattles make a noise, and the noise is alike a warning to the prey that he is about to seize to satisfy his hunger, and an invitation to any enemy that may be in the neighborhood seeking to take his life. How, therefore, these rattles could have come by *Evolution*

But what I represent as unproved, or having as yet the immense probability, a probability amounting almost to an absolute certainty, against it, is the claim that there has been produced *in this way* and *without Divine intervention*, those more permanent features and characteristics which Naturalists are agreed in regarding as constituting *species* as distinct from the less important features which serve to mark off and distinguish mere varieties from one another.

But as to man! what of him and his origin? I introduce what I have to say on this subject with the following words from Huxley,[1] which, coming as they do rather in the nature of an admission than of a contention, are entitled to great weight: " Man, intelligent man, existed at times when the whole physical conformation of the country [England] was totally different from that which characterizes it now... But when it comes to a question as to tracing back man further than [the drift], and recollect drift is only the scum of the earth's surface, I must confess that to my mind the evidence is of a very dubious character... I don't know that there is any reason for doubting that the men who existed at that

---

it is difficult to see. But regarded as the result of a creative Power, we can believe that they were added to the animal rather for the benefit of others than for any advantage or help to himself.

[1] *Dublin Address* in *Appleton's Popular Science Monthly*, Oct., 1878, p. 676.

day were *in all essential respects* [the italics are mine] similar to the men who exist now."

Here are two points for consideration; each of them of the greatest importance to our present purpose: the one relates to the time of man's appearance on the earth—his antiquity, and the other to his condition at that time, as bearing on the question of his creation or evolution.

For many reasons it will be best to take up the question of the date of his origin first.

In the quotation from Huxley we have it brought down to some period since the close of the Glacial Period. Dawson also says,[1] "The only necessity for supposing an earlier appearance arises from the requirements of the hypothesis of evolution."

Nicholson also makes a similar statement in regard to the antiquity of man, referring his origin to Post Glacial times,[2] with no evidence of an earlier date.

It becomes a very important matter, therefore, to determine, if we can, how long ago, in astronomical time, that Age came to its close.

Fortunately for us we are in a better condition to answer this question now than we were only a few years ago.

---

[1] *Chain of Life in Geological Time*, p. 239.
[2] *Ancient Life History of the Earth*, p. 365.

The doctrine that the Ice Age depended upon certain astronomical combinations, so ingeniously urged by Dr. James Croll, has been completely disposed of by Wallace in his recent work, *Island Life*. He has shown (1) that the difference in the amount of heat between these extreme periods is very small, not more than about three degrees Fahrenheit in the annual average of temperature for this latitude in our coldest month,[1] and (2) that there could have been no ice accumulation or general glaciation at any time in the past without (*a*) greater elevation than we have now in Great Britain and northeastern North America, nor without in addition to this (*b*) a greatly different location and flow of the ocean currents.

And Tyndall had shown as long ago as 1865[2] that

---

[1] This is given by WALLACE as the result of his computations, *Island Life*, p. 123.

[2] *Heat considered as a Mode of Motion* p. 206.

It has been estimated (WALLACE, *Geographical Distribution of Animals*) that in order to provide vapor enough to produce the ice that covered the polar regions, the entire ocean must have been reduced by evaporation 2,000 feet in depth.

This computation, however, was made when it was supposed that the Glacial Period was due chiefly to astronomical causes, and prevailed at the same time in both hemispheres alike. The later view is that it prevailed in the Northern hemisphere only at that time, and did not extend more than half round the globe; as there was none in Asia east of the Ural Mountains, or in N. America west of the Upper Missouri. This would reduce the two thousand feet probably to something less than five hundred. But that is enough to show that there must have been great heat in the tropics, as well as great cold nearer the poles, as Tyndall maintains.

cold alone is not all that is necessary to produce glaciation. We must have heat as well to cause the evaporation that is necessary to supply the water that is to form the ice.

We turn then to compute from the best data we have, the length of time that has elapsed since the close of the Ice Period and the beginning of the Present Age. The best computation that we can make at present gives from seven to nine thousand years.

And it seems to me to be especially worth remark that the Bible chronology, as given in the Septuagint version, is about the same, 7,290 years.[1]

---

[1] Dr. SOUTHALL has considered this subject very carefully in his two works, "*The Recent Origin of Man*," and in the more recent work, "*The Epoch of the Mammoth and the Appearance of Man.*" Both of these works have been ridiculed and scoffed at; but I have seen no serious attempt of refuting their conclusions.

Dr. Southall disposes in the first place of all the facts that have been claimed as proving the great antiquity of man, and then proceeds to consider the question in view of the real facts in the case. In what follows I have made free use of his materials and am greatly indebted to him.

The data consist of measurements that have been made of changes that have taken place since the close of the Ice Period. They are, of course, to some extent, based on estimates of rates of erosion and accumulation. I have before me the results of such computations in eight different places—three in this country and five in Europe. I give them below, with the names of the authority, and the two estimates, the highest and the lowest, where I have more than one, and an average of them all at the bottom.

It must be remembered, however, that there was no Ice Age in the north of Asia, nor much if any in

In America.	Authority.	Least.	Highest.
St. Anthony's Falls,	Winchell,	6,276	12,103
Lakes Michigan and Huron,	Andrews,	5,300	7,500
Falls of Niagara,	H. S. Williams,	11,886	
In Europe.			
"The Wash" (East of England),	Skertchley,	7,000	
Danish Peat Bogs,	Morlot & Lubbock,	6,400	10,000
Saône Valley,	Ferry & Arcelin,	7,000	10,000
St. Nazaire (on the Loire),	Kerviler,	6,000	
Solutré (East of France),	Ducrost,	7,000	8,000
Average of all the estimates,		8,028.	

Considering the fact that these changes must have been more rapid in the earlier stages than they have been since, it seems likely that the smaller number is more nearly correct than the larger. And the smaller is in fact a little less than the Bible chronology as given in the Septuagint version, which is about 7,300 years.

Dr. SOUTHALL, in his work, *The Epoch of the Mammoth and the Appearance of Man*, in view of these facts and others like them, comes to the conclusion, p. 382, that these facts indicate only about 6,600 years.

Of course it is not intended to deny that these astronomical changes alluded to do exert an influence on the temperature, but only that of themselves and alone they can neither produce nor prevent glaciation or Ice Age. Of these causes or cycles there are two: (1) the varying eccentricity of the earth's orbit, and (2) the precession of the equinoxes. The first is very unequal in its periods of recurrence and *may be* connected with those alternations that are known to have occurred in the temperature of the earth in past geological time. Thus it has been claimed that the ages cold and warm have succeeded each other as,—printing the names of the warm in italics—Cambrian, *Silurian*, Devonian, *Carboniferous*, Permian, *Jurassic*, Cretaceous, *Tertiary*, Glacial, the *Present.*

But in the other cycle, that occasioned by the precession of the equinoxes, the last period of great cold occurred about 10,000 years

North America west of the Missouri river. Hence, as man doubtless originated in Southwestern Asia northeast of the head waters of the Euphrates and Tigris, he may have existed, and probably did exist, there for some time before he made his appearance in Europe. Of this, however, I need not say anything in this place.

Our second point was the condition of man at this early period, in its bearing on the question of his evolution by mere natural means out of some of the orders or species of the animal world below man.

ago. And although there was no glacial period in the north of Asia, it was doubtless somewhat colder there then than it is now.

We have in connection with this a similar tradition among the early Aryan population, which is probably not less than four or five thousand years old. It is to the effect that their ancestors, who lived then in the high lands of Hindu Cush, were subjected for several hundred years to great severity of climate, ten months of winter in the year. Was this a tradition of this cold period? If so, it would carry back the date of their existence to something like ten or twelve thousand years. And this is the earliest point to which any known date would seem to carry it. See, in reference to this tradition, RAWLINSON's *Ancient Monarchies*, Vol. II, p. 432.

Since the foregoing note was written I have received, what I believe to be, the latest work by Principal DAWSON, who is certainly the *best* authority on this subject in America, and as good as any in the world. The title of the book is *Fossil Men and their Modern Representatives*. He reiterates his statements of the high character of the earliest men that we know anything about as having lived on the earth. And in regard to the antiquity of their origin he says, p. 246, "What evidence the future may bring forth I do not know, but that available at present points to the appearance of man, with all his powers and properties, in the Post-glacial age of Geology, and not more than from 6,000 to 8,000 years ago."

Early man was, as Huxley says, "in all essential respects" like the men of our age, equal to the average of civilized men in all that indicates elevation in the scale of being and mental capacity; they were far above the lowest of the savages that we now meet with in some parts of the world.

We have thus Huxley's admission rather reluctantly made. Dawson[1] says, "With such views the skeletons of the most ancient known men fully accord. They indicate a people of great stature, of powerful muscular development, especially in the lower limbs; of large brain, *indicating great capacity and resources.*" (The italics are mine).

Nicholson says,[2] "As to the physical peculiarities of the ancient races ... little is known... Such information as we have, however, ... would lead to the conclusion that Post-Pliocene man *was in no respect* [the italics are mine] inferior in his organization to or less highly developed than many existing races. All the known skulls of this period, with the single exception of the Neanderthal cranium [which is now acknowledged to have been abnormal and idiotic] *are in all respects* average and normal in their characters."

---

[1] *Chain of Life*, p. 241. See also MITCHELL's *Past in the Present*, everywhere. And still better, DAWSON's *Fossil Men*, which has been received since the above was written.
[2] *Ancient Life-History of the Earth*, p. 364.

I cite but one more authority on this point, and that is one which will command very considerate attention, Herbert Spencer, and I quote at some length. He says[1] that "Evolution is commonly considered to imply that in every thing there is an intrinsic tendency to become something higher, but this is an erroneous conception of it. . . If environing circumstances change, the species changes [in general traits] until it re-equilibrates itself with them. . . Only now and then does the environing change initiate in the organism a new complication and so produce a somewhat higher type [species]. . . When the habitat entails modes of life that are inferior some degeneration results. . . Direct evidence forces this conclusion upon us. Lapse from higher civilization to lower civilization made familiar during school-boy days is further exemplified as our knowledge increases; . . . many large and highly evolved societies have either disappeared or have dwindled to barbarous hordes or have been long passing through slow decay; . . . thus then the tribes now known as lowest [note the word, as "lowest"], must exhibit some social phenomena which are due . . . to causes that operated during past social states higher than the present."

In connection with this, I note the fact that so far

[1] *Principles of Sociology*, Part II, Chap. viii, § 50.

as we know, so far as any discoveries or researches have brought any facts in the case to light, there were none of the quadrumanous animals in existence at the time when man appeared, from which man could have been derived, that were of a higher grade or order than those that are in existence now.

To suppose, therefore, that the first human beings —our ancestors—were born of quadrumanous parentage, is to suppose what is as improbable, what is in fact as absurd, and from a scientific point of view, as impossible as that a human child had been produced and nursed up to maturity by parents belonging to any order of the present quadrumana, the gorillas, chimpanzes, or orang outangs, of to-day, or by any of the monkeys, apes, or baboons of the Asiatic or African forests, the swamps of South America, or the islands of the Pacific Ocean.

Nor does there seem to be the slightest prospect or promise that further discoveries will bring to light anything to diminish the chasm that now exists between man and any of the species or orders of the animal world below man; the tendency and the prospects are all in the other direction. Hence as the matter stands now the descent of man by way of evolution from any of the species of animals that now exist, or that are known to have existed in the past, would be no less a miracle than his immediate creation out of the dust of the earth, as most Christians believe that he was created.

We have seen that Dawson says, and no well informed man will contradict him, I think, that there is no necessity or reason for supposing man to have been on the earth more than the eight or ten thousand years that have elapsed since the close of the Glacial Period, except what arises out of the necessity for supporting "the hypothesis of evolution." And I think we may now add that there is neither necessity nor reason for believing him to have come into existence by any natural descent from any parents of a lower species of animals except what arises from a disposition to maintain that "hypothesis." And I think we may add that there is no disposition to maintain that hypothesis in its extreme or atheistic form, except what comes from an unwillingness, whether conscious or unconscious I cannot say, but an unwillingness to acknowledge the personality of God and the reality of His moral government of the universe.

I have no theory to offer on the subject. My present purpose does not require that I should explain the mode of man's origin. My object has been rather to show that no explanation has been offered which proposes to dispense with creation and miraculous interposition that is at all satisfactory and consistent with the facts that are known in the case.

And if one should claim that the peculiar characteristics of humanity came into existence as a congenital abnormity or monstrosity, like the quills of the porcupine man or the limbs of the Ancon sheep, the phenomena would not be explained thereby. We know no better how such traits are produced than we do how the first protoplasm became a living animal, or how to make a man out of the dust that is beneath our feet.

II. I come now to another branch of the subject of this Lecture—Inspiration. I shall treat it very briefly and say the less of it because the topic belongs more properly to a Treatise on Revealed Religion.

I have said that Inspiration, in the sense in which I am now using the word, must be of the nature of a miracle as I have defined the term miracle.

I think that a strong presumption arises in favor of a belief in inspiration, both general and special, from what we have proved with regard to the nature and attributes of God. We have seen that the material universe can be but a realization of His thoughts and purposes. He has acted on matter, even if He did not create it, moved and moulded it to His will. Inert as it is it does not appear to have any power either of resistance or impenetrability as against

Him. It is as plastic and as yielding as if it were only His thoughts or volitions, as some philosophers have claimed, and He works *in* it and upon it. He has shown His presence and power, His agency and intervention in physical nature, whenever it was necessary to produce some new thing, the protoplasm of which all animal tissue is made, or the first pairs of all permanent species. And He *made man;* "In His own image created He him." Shall we hold that He works in nature and in accordance with the physical laws, or rather *in* those laws in the inorganic world and not in the mind of man? He manifests His purposes, and works to do His will, in the instincts of animals; does He not work also in the reason and conscience of man, the only *rational* being that He has created that is within the sphere of our observation?

In human history, also, God has manifestly a plan and a purpose, and for the execution of this purpose His influence on the hearts and wills of men is as necessary as it was to start the primordial chaos of nebulous matter into the manifold operations, chemical, mechanical and biological, which were necessary that, in the process of evolution and development, we might have the state of things in the midst of which we live.

I like to quote Herbert Spencer when he says

anything that is to my purpose, as he often does. He says,[1] "He [the philosopher], like every other man, may properly consider himself as one of the myriad agencies through whom works the Unknown Cause; and when the Unknown Cause produces in him a certain belief, he is thereby authorized to act out that belief... Not as adventitious, therefore, will the wise man regard the faith which is in him. The highest truth he sees he will fearlessly utter, knowing that, let what may come of it, he is thus playing his right part in the world, knowing that if he can effect the change he aims at—well; if not—well also; though not so well."

Could the fact of inspiration and an overruling Providence be more fully declared? "The thought and belief that is in him" is the product of the Unknown Cause—of God—and let him act accordingly, and let what may come of it, the outcome is the result of an overruling Power "that is not ourselves working for righteousness." He will overrule and graciously forgive our mistakes also, if only we will be faithful to our convictions. Really, I can hardly see how a Christian man could have said this better. Here is Inspiration and an overruling Providence fully confessed.

I believe there is no man who has lived, or tried

[1] *First Principles*, Part I, § 34.

to live, a religious life, who has not had a faith in such divine guidance and overruling Providence, a faith which, whatever it may have rested upon at first, became so confirmed by experience that no argument, or line of argument, could shake it. It had become part of his experience, part of his innermost consciousness, a part of his identity, as completely in, and as inseparable from it, as any fact or recollection of his past history.

I remember an instance that stands out among the most distinct recollections of my early life, which is quite in point. It was a bitter cold afternoon of a December day. The steamer *Lexington* was lying at the wharf ready to start for New York. One of the greatest men that our country has produced had occasion to be in Washington early the following week. He was on his way to the landing with his satchel in hand, ready to take the boat. But on a sudden the thought came upon him, "I won't go to-night, after all." He turned on the sidewalk, though in sight of the boat, and went back to his home. He could give no reason for his thought, or for the consequent change of purpose that ensued. He went home and slept soundly for the night. But in the night, at sea, when off the coast of Rhode Island, the *Lexington* took fire, burned to the water's edge, and finally went down in fifty fathoms of water.

All on board, save two or three, perished in the flames or were whelmed in the freezing waters, and our friend could not have been one of the few that escaped had he been on board.

Now I suppose that in the present state of our means of psychological analysis, nobody can *prove* to the satisfaction of one that is skeptically inclined that here was a special interposition of God. And perhaps it is best that we cannot. There must be left a place and a work for faith, if man is to attain the highest of which his nature is capable.

What is the relation of the Divine Efficiency to the present and ordinary phenomena of nature must ever remain, as I think, a matter of speculation and mere opinion. Two theories only, as I think, are possible: the one holds, with Tyndall, that the atoms and masses of matter "act directly on one another," and the other holds that God is the One force and Agent; so that in the strictest expression of the truth, we should say that He acts in all action, and the several forces, heat, light, and such like, are but names for different modes or forms of His activity. Substituting for the word God, the term "the Unknowable," which seems to be a favorite expression with this class of philosophers, this last view would seem to be the one that is preferred by them and for which many very explicit passages could be cited.

But when we come to consider the relation of God to the minds of men, the matter becomes still more difficult.

There are two fundamental differences, each presenting a class of difficulties of its own, which I see no way at present of overcoming.

1st. The first is, we have no certainty that the atoms or particles of matter have any *independent* existence so as to be able to "*act on each other*" in any proper sense of the words instead of being mere modes of God's action. But with the minds of men the case is otherwise. Although created and dependent for the origin of their being, they have *now* a certain independence of existence, and act, to some extent, as "first causes."

This we know of them by the very means by which we know that they exist at all, just as I know that this paper is white by the means by which I know it exists as anything external. Hence, in knowing that minds exist I know that they exist with the power of independent spontaneous activity.

2d. In the second place, mind and matter are different in kind and are distinguished and co-ordinated by the two properties, spontaneity and inertia. We can therefore reason easily from matter *as inert* to many things that mere matter, whether as atoms, molecules, or masses, cannot do; and hence we have in certain cases, by one of the surest and best known canons of induction, very certain proof of the intervention of an agent that is different in kind from matter.

But as between the mind of man and God, the difference, *so far as our present inquiry is concerned*, is only one of degree. Both are intelligent, and both act with spontaneity. It is true that one is finite and the other infinite. But "finite" and "infinite" do not co-ordinate them as objects in ontological reality. Terms to be co-ordinate must be of the same logical quality; if one is concrete the others must be concrete also; if one is positive the other cannot be negative. But the terms "finite" and "infinite" do sustain precisely this latter relation to each other; the one is positive and the other is negative, in form at least. And in so far as we can attach any clear and comprehensible meaning to the two terms, they denote difference in degree only, and not difference in kind as co-ordinates, whether logical or ontological, must always do.

Hence to find cases of inspiration, and proof that they are really cases of inspiration, we are not to seek for or find something different in kind from what the mind of man *ordinarily* does. On the contrary, acts of divine influence must be the *same in kind*, and differ only in degree from what ordinarily occurs in human consciousness. If man knows without inspiration, inspiration can only increase his knowledge. If without the direct agency of God, man knows and can know something of the nature and attributes of God, even "His unseen, or eternal power and godhead," by way of Natural Theology, then by the aid of inspiration he can see and know more of the attributes and purposes of God, even to the tri-unity of His nature, including the personality of the Son and of the Holy Spirit. If man has something of foresight, inspiration can make him a prophet, and enable him to foretell the doom of Babylon and Tyre or to predict the birth of the Son of Mary in Bethlehem of Judea.[1]

The question then arises, precisely what can the unaided mind of man do in these directions, and what is the limit, if indeed there is any, beyond which it cannot go? Fix this limit, settle upon it

[1] It is very possible that this and other statements in this connection may be thought to imply a theory of Inspiration which I do not intend either to teach or to deny in this connection. I am not writing as from the facts and phenomena presented in the Holy Scriptures, or to explain them. I am writing rather from the Natural Theology point of view. If, therefore, the Scriptures present instances of inspiration in which the prophet had visions and uttered words which he himself did not understand, there is nothing in my statements, nor do I intend to say anything, that is inconsistent with such facts. And I think that what I have occasion to say will serve as a basis on which to erect any higher view of inspiration that may be found necessary.

so that all men will be agreed in accepting your determination, or so that you can defend it against all adversaries, and we can prove miracles of inspiration, acts of direct and immediate divine influence upon the mind of man or within his mind, as clearly and as unanswerably as we prove acts of supernatural intervention in the realm of nature, and upon mere inert, inanimate matter. But this will be difficult, perhaps impossible. At any rate I shall not attempt it; arguing, as I now do, from a purely Natural Theology point of view. With a revelation as a proved or as an accepted fact, the case would be quite different.

All that we can say now is, therefore, that inspiration as a special divine influence, acting upon the mind of man, frequently or otherwise, as the case may be, is shown to be a possibility, nay a probability rather, and a thing to be expected, looked for and welcomed, whenever a special emergency or occasion for it shall occur. But the fact of inspiration in any particular case must be left, I fear, as a matter of faith and opinion, of probability and moral suasion, rather than demonstrated as a matter of scientific or absolute certainty.

And to me, the fact so well known, thanks to some of the more recent investigations in this line, that all men and all nations of men, if we except perhaps a few of the least unsophisticated philosophers of the more civilized races, have always believed in such communications and influences, is a strong proof—strong enough to overcome, and more than overcome—all the doubt and distrust on this point, that has been raised, cultivated and inculcated by modern skepticism. All nations and all people have had their prophets. All believe in prophecy, all believe in God, and none of them believe that He has left Himself without witness. All gladly acknowledge that their highest wisdom, their best thoughts, and their holiest aspirations are from Him who is the Father of Spirits and the Source of life and of light to all His creatures.

But precisely where is the distinction and what marks off as a boundary line the thoughts and feelings that are of God from the freaks and fancies of our own minds, no one perhaps can certainly tell in all cases, so long as they are mere matters of his own consciousness.

But undoubtedly experience and the developments of history will, in time, discriminate between the two—false-perception, hallucination and the creations of fancy on the one hand—all of which represent error and delusion—from the results of true and genuine cognition and insight on the other. *True* predictions will come true, and be verified by subsequent events. *True* insight, and its discoveries and revelations, will exert an elevating influence on mankind, and form an epoch in the history of men, from which all events, that are legitimately influenced by them, will move on a higher plane. And that Something has been at work in this way in human history from its very beginning is so plain that I cannot see how any one can read that history attentively without admitting the fact. With these facts in view we may say with a thoughtful sage of old, "Surely there is a spirit in man and the inspiration of the Almighty giveth him understanding."

LECTURE VII.

PROVIDENCE AND MORAL GOVERNMENT; INCOMPLETE WITHOUT CHRIST AND CHRISTIANITY.

PSALMS LXXIII, 15, 16. Then thought I to understand this, but it was too hard for me until I went into the sanctuary of God.

PROVIDENCE AND MORAL GOVERNMENT.

I think it a fair inference from what we may consider as capable of proof by the Methods of Natural Theology, as exhibited in these Lectures, that there must be, in this world at least, a Providence and a Moral Government. And to these topics I invite your attention in this, which is the last Lecture in my course.

And here, as elsewhere in these Lectures, I have aimed not so much to set forth and prove the doctrines of Natural Theology as to vindicate its Foundation and Methods. I have assumed that you know already pretty much what has been said and taught by the great divines, the noble line of witnesses all along in the Christian Church; and I have aimed at limiting myself, pretty closely, to the task I had undertaken, namely, the vindication of the *Methods* of Natural Theology rather than its truths.

During these Lectures I have said but little of the proof and illustrations of what are sometimes called the Moral Attributes of God, or His goodness and benevolence. I have directed attention chiefly to the two of His attributes which are of a different order, namely, His Wisdom and His Power, and to the spontancity of His action; these are manifested in those phenomena of nature which inert matter cannot produce, such as the beginning of the present evolution, the origin of living protoplasm, the beginning of new species in the vegetable and animal world and such like, which man, the only spiritual or spontaneously acting being whose acts fall under our observation, was not then in existence to produce.

But the goodness of God must be chiefly if not exclusively manifested in the life and history of man. Here, however, we encounter the difficulty spoken of in the last Lecture. We deal here with acts which are certainly similar if not the same in kind as man can perform and is to some extent constantly performing, as the result of human choice and spontaneity of action.

Human history is indeed a part of the general process which we call Evolution. But it can hardly be regarded as presenting us with a proof of a Creator like what we derive from a consideration of the material universe. But with this exception, I think that human history and human life and experience is the field to which we must look for our fullest and best proofs and illustrations of the Moral Attributes of God.

Ascribe what you will to the influence of "environment" and physical conditions, etc.,—and their influence has certainly been very great—and ascribe all that you can or may to the voluntary selection, and choice and conscious purpose of the people, individually and personally, or to their rulers and guides, and yet there remains a large residuum of influence that can be ascribed to God only, and accounted for only on the supposition that there is an overruling Providence that "shapes our ends, rough hew them how we will."

Thus in regard to the influence of physical environment, I think it perfectly certain that no such environment or influence could, by any possibility, have produced either (1) the religious instinct in man or (2) given him his first idea of God. But nothing is more manifest in history than the fact that such influences have been very powerful in giving form to man's theism and his mode of worship. It led from unconscious monotheism to *pan*theism and to *poly*theism in theology, and to idolatry and fetichism in worship. It gives to one's religion a gloomy and sombre tone in some countries and climates, and a cheerful, hilarious tone in others. But such influences cannot have given origin to the instinct and the idea on which all religion and theology are based or out of which they have grown.

History is to be studied as a whole, a grand drama, whose parts are consecutive and well planned. Or, to change the figure, as in the study of some great cathedral or other structure of man's skill and device we find much indeed that is determined and controlled by the climate and by the condition and laws of nature, in regard to the materials to be used, the size and proportions, etc., of the building, beyond any power of choice or selection by the architect or the workmen. Set aside what we will and ascribe it to these causes. Then again, each workman has some power of choice and comprehension of the work he is doing; and this adds something to the appearance and detail of the finished work. But in all, above all and over all, there is the thought and the will of the architect, which may be seen more conspicuously, perhaps, than anything else by any one who looks at the structure with anything of the eye of an architect.

And so in history. In the history of any nation that has risen to civilization and influence, and still more so in any comprehensive view of the history of man taken as a whole, the most important influences that have been at work, the most efficient causes, or cause, in producing the great and final results, cannot be found in "environment" and "physical conditions," nor yet in the foresight and choice of man. Everywhere there are signs and proofs of an intelligence far above that of man; of a will and purpose more persistent and unchanging than his, and of a force to overcome obstacles and to shape the course of events that shows a determined earnestness in carrying out a preconceived plan and reaching results that were ordained before the foundation of the world.

I have no time to illustrate this principle fully by examples. I cannot, however, resist the temptation to refer to two or three facts or laws, as suggesting most important influences.

1st. At our earliest glimpse of history outside of the Bible, man was already very far gone from a righteousness which, if it was not "original," was at least ideal—a righteousness of which we all have some conception. We find many—not all—tribes without the arts of civilized life, even the art of agriculture, living in geographical centres where the supply of food such as was available for them had become insufficient. A crisis came; a turning-point had been reached. All had sagacity enough to see the importance of labor, of industry, of frugality and economy. Would the stronger exercise the self-denial and make the exertions which labor and foresight demanded? or would they indulge their own appetites, eat their fill, and leave the weaker, their wives and children, their parents and disabled brothers and sisters to suffer privation and starve? If the latter, savagery, with all its beastliness and cruelties, would ensue and remain their condition. But if love for kindred and compassion for the needy was strong enough to induce them to impose upon themselves the toil of labor, the self-restraints of abstinence, the thoughtfulness of frugality, foresight and economy, for the love of wives and children, the weak and the infirm, there was a step in advance, a beginning of civilization, and a higher life.

But it was the necessity for labor that brought it about. It did not come from choice or as a pursuit of pleasure, nor yet from any choice voluntarily made in view of the great benefits to mankind that might ensue from labor and frugality. And yet the necessity for labor, as it was at the beginning, has done more than any one thing else to promote that civilization and moral elevation among men which we enjoy to-day. It has wrought under the law of heredity a change in man's nature, so that he is now constitutionally and instinctively an industrious and working being. That is, he will work—all that are good for anything, the "fittest,"—will work *voluntarily* in view of the enjoyment which the products of his labor will bring to him and his.

2d. Another point of suggestive inquiry and consideration is found in the origin and nature of government.

As man is not naturally, especially in his savage state, inclined to toil and industry, so he is not inclined to submit to the will of another, for the good of the whole, or even for his own good. The wisdom and necessity of submission to authority, is a lesson which he has learned by long experience. We cannot doubt but that at first ambition, the lust of power, the disposition to tyrannize over others, was more prominent in the hearts of those who assumed control, than any more impersonal or unselfish consideration for the good of others. But the mass submitted of necessity and because they could not help themselves. And in this way they learned submission through the ages past. They have come to see that loyalty, which was at first indeed *ad regem*, and has only in these last years become *ad legem*, is one of the first of virtues, one of the most indispensable of mental habits. They who appreciate it and will reverence and obey law *for the sake of the law*, may be for a time under a government where all are politically equal before the law, and the greatest amount of civil liberty may be enjoyed. But for all others some form of despotism and tyrannical control is still a necessity.

But men in the beginning did not choose the submission to which they were subjected. Some of them may have seen its necessity, but most of them did not, nor could any form of government or administration which they would have chosen from any appreciation they may have had of its effects on them and their posterity, ever have accomplished the result that has now been obtained.

3d. I refer for the last instance to what is more germane to my general subject in these Lectures.

Man is essentially and everywhere a religious being. The religious instincts are the strongest and most ineradicable of any in his nature.[1] In quiet times men may be governed and guided by self-interest alone. But for men, as for nations and countries, and for nations and countries as for men, there come times of passion and excitement, when the plainest and most obvious dictates of self-interest and common sense are disregarded—passion rules for the hour. But above all other passions, and as able to subdue and control them all, arises the religious instinct whenever it has been roused to a pitch of intensity which we call enthusiasm, or

---

[1] Even Tyndall says in words that are more energetic than graceful, "The world will have a religion of some kind, even though it should fly to the intellectual whoredom of spiritualism." *Fragments*, Ed. 1878, p. 355.

rather, fanaticism. Then is not only self-interest forgotten, but all the angry passions are put into abeyance; ambition, pride, and even resentment or revenge are laid aside, and men sacrifice all but themselves, and even themselves, so far as this world is concerned, to the one absorbing object of their fanatic zeal.

Now this peculiarity of man's nature has been used with tremendous power in the past ages of the history of our race. Men have claimed to come from God, or to rule and guide with a divine mission or sanction. And not one of the governments of the past has arisen or stood and endured without allying itself with the religious sentiment of the people.

This sentiment has doubtless given power and influence for evil to despots and impostors. But it has been one of the most efficient and most indispensable means of maintaining even the best governments and of bringing about that change in the constitution of man and the instincts of humanity which distinguish the civilized from the savage man. It has enabled the great rulers and leaders to bring to bear upon the minds and hearts of men a power that is vastly superior to any of the threats and torments they could inflict.

And this, too, has been a means of elevating

man. It taught him to look to something higher than this world affords, did much to prepare for that "fullness of time" when his thoughts and faith, his fears and his aspirations should be directed to Him who is a Spirit and who would be worshiped in spirit and in truth, when bloody sacrifices should no more be needed, and the priesthood should be chiefly instructors and guides in matters of conscience, and every one a "priest and a king" for himself to God in a certain sense, and that, too, the most important sense of the words.

And here again, that which has been the most influential, and the most influential because "the most needful for the time," when it was in vogue, was never an invention of the men of the age. It was never wholly or to any great extent a matter of choice with the masses except as that choice was the result of a conviction or of a fanaticism that had been enkindled for a purpose, and that, too, often by a designing impostor. No system that ever accomplished much good for man was chosen, kept up and continued by a popular choice, the majority determining whether they would have this man or this religion "to rule over them" or not.

Now in all these cases it is obvious that that which has been the most needed and has proved the most useful and efficient in bringing man from the degradation of his early, not to say his first, for I do not believe it was his first, condition, has been something that has kept him in subjection, compelled him to do and to submit to that which he would not have done or submitted to from mere foresight and choice without such necessity or compulsion. The involuntary and unwilling submission, however, produced its effect in the altered habits of the individuals who were then forced to practice these virtues; and they have been transmitted by the law of heredity, spoken of in an earlier Lecture, to us and the men of these latter days.

And thus we see that our modern civilization depends not only on the *intellectual* advance of the race in what is apparent in our arts and sciences, but there has been going on, underneath all the more obvious facts and events of history, a gradual change in the nature of man himself. This change has been indeed twofold or in two opposite directions, one downwards towards savagery and beastliness, and the other in all the civilized races, upwards towards civilization and a higher plane of life.

These changes, those of them that are for the better at least, have been going on very much in accordance with the laws which the evolutionists advocate. There has been a Power or an Influence at work in them, that has gradually wrought a change in human nature so as to render much possible now, in science and religion, in politics and in morals, that could not have been introduced with any prospect of success, at any earlier stage of human history. Has there not been a providence in all this?

But it is time to go on with our main subject, Providence and Moral Government and the objections to them.

The main points of the objections that are chiefly urged are two, namely: (1) to a Personal Providence, and (2) to the fact of a Moral Government that is exercised on the principles of righteousness and justice and in the spirit of good will or benevolence.

Such objections discourage prayer and worship, instill into the minds of all a distrust of moral principles and of any rewards, either here or hereafter, for righteous deeds, except such as are seen to be manifest in prospect and which, as is often supposed, can, for the most part, be secured better by prudent foresight and expediency, with possible trickery, deception, pusillanimous submission to those in power and such like means, than by the nobler means of a higher morality.

Of these Pessimists, the two names that are just

now the most conspicuous, perhaps, are Schopenhauer and John Stuart Mill.

The pessimism of Schopenhauer evidently began in personal feeling, and led to a theory, such as only a German could form, from which his system results as an inference. He was unhappy, unsuccessful. Things did not go at all to suit him; and so he invented a theory of his own. Starting from Hegel's point of view that all reality is included in the *about-to-be* (*das Werdend*), Schopenhauer thought to improve upon it by adopting the notion that Will is all. "Matter is nothing but Force; Force is nothing but Will"—Will become apparent as presentation or *Vorstellung*, or phenomena in the mind of the thinker. For the *das Werdend* of Hegel he would substitute *das Wollend*, mere will-power, or activity. Thus far his philosophy is not so bad as many other systems that we could name.

But when he comes to practical views, he overlooks the fact that the one creative Will is guided by wisdom or acts from a sense of justice and love. In his view, whatever is, is a manifestation of will or willfulness, and of course anything and everything that has a will of its own is to be regarded only as seeking its own—its own ends and pleasures. Hence for the weaker there can be nothing but misery and defeat.

Schopenhauer is, however, but little known among English-speaking people. The best known representative of pessimism among the English is John Stuart Mill. I shall therefore refer to him chiefly, not only because he is the best representative, but also because he presents in his writings *all* the objections of this kind that have been presented at all and in fact all, so far as I can see, that the case admits of.

The objection is easily stated: there is pain and suffering in this world. If God could prevent it and would not, there is an end to all idea of goodness and justice. If He would prevent it and make all creatures perfectly happy and cannot, there is an end to all idea of His infinite power or omnipotence.

"If," says he,[1] "the Maker of the world can do all that He wills, he wills misery, and there is no escape from the conclusion. If He willed that all men should be virtuous, His designs have been completely baffled." Again, p. 38, "Not even on the most distorted and contracted theory of good which man ever framed by religious or philosophical fanaticism, can the government of nature be made to resemble the work of a being at once good and omnipotent."

[1] *Nature* in posthumous works, p. 37.

Again, in a later part of the volume, p. 112, he says, "It is impossible that any one who habitually thinks, and who is unable to blunt his inquiring intellect by sophistry, should be able, without misgiving, to go on ascribing absolute perfection to the author and ruler of so clumsily made and capriciously governed a creation as this planet and the life of its inhabitants." "The Author of the Sermon on the Mount is assuredly a far more benignant Being than the Author of Nature."[1]

I presume it will hardly be considered as coming within the fair range of argument to allude to the

[1] Mill, in his less "*atra bilious*" moments, thinks that among the attributes of God, as manifest in nature and human experience, goodness or benevolence is on the whole predominant over other motives of a different kind. The pleasures and the pains have a conservative tendency, the pleasures being so disposed as to attach to the things which maintain individual and collective existence, the pains so as to deter from such as would destroy it," Theism, p. 190.

"Yet endeavoring to look at the question without partiality or prejudice and without allowing wishes to have any influence over judgment, *it does appear* [the italics are mine] that granting the existence of design, there is a preponderance of evidence that the Creator desired the pleasure of His creatures... Even in cases where the pain results, like pleasure, from the machinery itself, the appearances do not indicate that contrivance was brought into play purposely to produce pain ; .. there is, therefore, much appearance that pleasure is agreeable to the Creator, while there is very little if any appearance that pain is so, and there is a certain amount of justification for inferring, on the ground of Natural Theology alone, that benevolence is one of the attributes of the Creator," p. 192.

personal character and habits of these pessimists. But yet I think that some notice should be taken of it, for wherever there is complaint there is surely something wrong; so that if the thing complained of is not at fault the complainant himself is certainly so, so far at least as the act of making of the complaint is concerned. Now I do not know that any one of these complainants has ever been distinguished for the highest moral or spiritual excellence, or has even secured any considerable number of followers who would willingly trust the affairs of the universe in his hands, with any expectation that they would be on the whole any better managed than they are now.

Pessimism has existed as a sentiment in sporadic cases, in all ages of the world. Always there have been men and women who have felt and thought that their trials and sufferings were more than they could bear.

With us, and in all the higher races, this view of life reaches, in isolated cases, its proper issue in suicide, when the victims of misfortune come to the conclusion that not to be at all is better than to be as they are, or in any condition they can hope to realize. And we regard all such cases as bordering upon, if not already entered into, that state of mental disease which we call and treat as insanity.

Often does it happen that their sufferings and misfortunes have come from no fault of their own, no events or acts over which they had or could have had any power of control. Such cases appeal to our tenderest sympathy and make us hesitate in our speculations and theories.

And to my mind, one of the saddest things in all human history is the fact that the hundreds of millions in Asia who are called Buddhists could have ever taken such pessimistic views of this life and the best that it can offer, as to accept their mysterious Nirvana[1] as a boon. Whether we regard it as total annihilation or the extinction of all conscious individuality or not, the result is the same; the case is one of unspeakable sadness.

[1] It has been suggested and, as I think, satisfactorily *proved* that Nirvana did not mean originally, and was never intended to mean, entire annihilation. The founder of the religion had in view a twofold nature of man like what the Christians have in mind when they speak of "the spirit" and "the flesh" and the contrariety between them, and by Nirvana the Buddha meant only the extinction or annihilation of "the lusts of the flesh," the carnal nature of man. Hence it is only by a later perversion that the word has come to mean entire annihilation of the conscious being. At first it meant resignation. "When a man can bear everything without a word of complaint," says Buddha, "he has attained Nirvana . . . thus is Nirvana the greatest happiness." See MAX MÜLLER, *Science of Religion*, p. 142. And yet I suppose there can be no doubt that the great mass of the Buddhists, the ignorant, degraded and miserable portion of them do regard Nirvana as an utter extinction of their conscious being.

Now I have no skill at making evil appear to be good, and no ambition for distinction in that direction. Nevertheless, something may be said in favor of pain. It has its place and function in the world.

I think it may be safely said that pain is always a sign of something wrong, besides itself. It shows that something has been done that calls for amendment and remedy, or that something is being done, or is about to be done, that calls for foresight, circumspection and efforts at avoidance.

In the lower and purely physical sphere, pain is proof of something wrong, some disease or injury to the tissues that calls for attention. And even when remedies are painful it is only because they are in themselves considered a violation of the laws and conditions of well-being, the use and application of which can be justified only on the ground that they are *remedies* and means for curing or removing an evil that is greater than that which already exists. Hence the surgeon's knife is as painful when it removes a diseased limb or opens an abscess as if it were used needlessly and for the mere purpose of torture. The law is general, and were this not so there could be no general law.

But it is asked why should there be pain in the animal world? If there were no pains of hunger and of dying there would be no effort to secure food and to avoid danger; and the species would speedily come to an end. If, on the other hand, food were so abundant that life could be prolonged without effort, or if the animal were to be spared the pains of death and allowed to live forever, the world would soon become so full of the one species that there would be no room for another and for a succession of the higher orders, as we see that they came into existence in the course of geological time: there could have been no evolution.

If now we raise our view to the next higher plane, the moral and intellectual, we find that the painful, or malevolent passions have their place. When one is angry, for example, there is *something* wrong. Either an injury has been done, which, in the interest of righteousness and general well-being, call for indignation and resentment, or we ourselves are in the wrong, angry without sufficient cause. And in this latter case there is something wrong in ourselves, our own conduct, something that calls for a remedy as much as in the former case, although the remedy will be of a totally different kind and in a very different scene of action.

Something the same may be said of all the varied forms of the evil or malevolent passions—of envy, of hate, of revenge, of jealousy, and of even spite itself. They come of wrong, indicate and prove the existence of wrong, and call for a remedy even if they do not always clearly point out the proper remedy. We may "be angry and sin not," although we may be angry and commit a great sin. But the anger is always proof of something wrong, and, by consequence of, something requiring to be changed for the better.

But does one ask why there should be wrong doing or the possibility of it? I answer as the question has been answered so many times already, that without the *possibility of wrong doing* there could be no *liberty for right doing*, no moral freedom, none in fact of that *acquired* character and those higher, nobler virtues which we all recognize and admit to be the chief glory and distinction of the higher order of beings. Nobody doubts that purity and temperance and generosity and fidelity and courage and magnanimity, are better and higher and more desirable than their opposites. Or if there is anybody that doubts it, he is hardly a person to be reasoned with on such a subject as this. In the exercise of common reason and right judgment we all see that these virtues are the conditions of happiness in social life, as truly as the laws of gravity, of chemical and mechanical action are the necessary conditions of the orderly system and harmonious ongoings of the material world. Without them there would be no proof of the existence and agency of a wise, benevolent and all-powerful Being, whom we may worship and adore as God over all blessed forever.[1]

And not only pain, but even wicked men, have a work to do in a world where wickedness and wrong exist, which no other class of persons can so *fitly* do. Although not intending it and not conscious of the fact, they are doing God's will and are in some cases the very "fittest" instruments for doing it under the circumstances.[2]

---

[1] There is another thought connected with this subject that I think I ought to present for the consideration of the reader, and this I do without attempting to determine how far it is true, although beyond doubt there is some truth in it.

Happiness implies the possibility of its opposite, unhappiness or misery, and the converse, misery or suffering, implies the possibility of happiness; that is, they both imply a sensitive nature. We do not speak of inanimate objects as happy, nor yet are they miserable, they are simply insensible.

Nor, as I think, do we speak of one as happy who is not conscious of his happiness. We may regard him as *fortunate* and even speak of such an one as happy, but when we come to look into the matter carefully I think we shall admit that no one is happy who is not conscious of being so.

Now much that I have said in the first Lecture of co-ordination in cognition applies here. We can have no consciousness or thought of happiness except as it is co-ordinated with its opposite, pain or misery.

[2] The old Prophet ISAIAH had a very clear conception of this law of Providence, chap. x, 5-8: "O Assyrian, the rod of mine anger and the staff in their hand is mine indignation. I will send him against an hypocritical nation, and against the people of my wrath

It would seem, therefore, that what men so often and so loudly complain of is but a necessary part of a system, with which, perhaps, they are not altogether in harmony, and which, at any rate, they do not fully understand and appreciate.

Any attempt to judge of this world, in reference to the matter before us, must assume that it is a means to some end, and judge of it with reference to that end. If God had intended it as a place for mere animal enjoyment, or for the success of schemes of worldly ambition, I have no doubt He could have made it better than it now is; most any of us could have done so. At least such is the prevalent opinion. Men who take this view of life can see no reason why pain and ill health should have been made to follow upon excessive indulgence, or why all the hopes, " reasonable hopes " they will call them, of ambitious and aspiring men should not be realized.

We can clearly see, however, that if man is destined to another and a higher state of existence, and that if the moral and spiritual life is higher than the mere animal and worldly life, a world in which men that are, and intend to be, devoted to animal enjoy-

will I give him a charge, to take the spoil and to take the prey and to tread them down like the mire of the streets. Howbeit *he meaneth not so neither doeth his heart think so; but it is in his heart to destroy and cut off nations not a few.*"

ments and the pursuits of mere worldly ambition, would find themselves best provided for and things most to their liking would not be very well adapted to those who might have the higher aims of life chiefly in view. A world that would make the drunkard and debauchee happy and entirely satisfied in their line of enjoyment could hardly be adapted to the promotion of virtue and the higher objects and aims in life.

Now I am willing to admit that I do not see how from the mere facts of nature, without taking into account human experience, the incarnation, Christ and Christianity and all that precede it to prepare the way for it, with all that has followed it and is yet to come as its work, its work here and the results of that work hereafter, we can prove that God is infinitely good or altogether benevolent. We need some way to turn seeming evil into real good, and a world best adapted for spiritual purposes could not be satisfactory to those who are otherwise disposed.

I cannot, therefore, dismiss this part of my argument without intimating very strongly that our estimate of this world depends much, very much, upon the use we propose to make of it and the kind of life we intend to live in it while we remain a portion of its inhabitants.

The heathen religions of the world may teach us an important lesson on this subject. The heathen nations all believed in a god, and for the most part in "gods many." They never ascribed to them a very high degree of moral excellence. They never thought them altogether benevolent in their feelings and designs towards man. And not only their opinions and religious rites were influenced by this view of the character of their so-called gods, but their whole life was tinged by it. For the most part their religion afforded no encouragement to a high standard of morals, and little or no hope for a future life that could be in any important particular better than this.[1]

---

[1] One of Mill's arguments against the goodness of God, as a proof of a want of either goodness or power to do what, in Mr. Mill's estimation, would have been a far better thing to do than has been done, is derived from the low state of civilization, the savagery and ignorance that prevailed so long in the early ages of mankind and still prevails among such savage tribes as the Bushmen and the Andaman Islanders. Mill sees no reason why they might not have been made at once equal in civilization and all the attainments of modern science, political economy included, to modern Englishmen, or possibly a little better than some of them.

But there *is a point of view* from which even the Bushman and the Andaman Islander, if they live up to such light as God has been pleased to give them, are to be preferred, in their lowly and miserable condition, if happiness alone is to be regarded as "our being's end and aim," to the most advanced Englishman, with his agnosticism and blasphemy. They are happier now and here, and have a much better chance, as I think, for the "hereafter."

The Jews are said to have been the only people that had any idea of sin and ill desert so that, in the light of this consciousness, they could see and acknowledge that God is just and righteous in all His ways, and good in all His dealings with men.[1] But even they did not, and could not, see and realize this truth as we can, who live in later times and who now see in His Son Jesus Christ the fuller manifestation of His goodness and love. In this complement of the revelations and manifestations of His plans and purposes we see the full exhibition of His attributes, so that there is no longer any occasion, or any disposition, to doubt among those who have experienced the grace which He brought to light in the Gospel.

The Christian view of life, when once thoroughly adopted, changes the whole aspect of the case. *It cures all pessimism* and takes away all disposition to complain.

Amidst the sadness and the sorrow, the disappointments and the discouragements that come to

---

[1] The Patriarch JOB speaks of the pessimists of his day as condemning God that they may "appear to be righteous themselves," Job, xl, 8.

Nor did the Psalmist become a pessimist on account of his misfortunes and sufferings. He could rather say, "O my God I cry in the day-time, but Thou hearest not and in the night season I take no rest. And Thou continuest holy O Thou Worship of Israel."

all thoughtful people, there is nothing like the contemplation of the life and death of Christ, the Divine Son of Man, what He did and suffered for us. The one thought takes all bitterness out of the heart. No event on earth has exhibited such a depth of tragic pathos, none has had such power to touch the heart with infinite tenderness. And all subsequent history, the experience of believers, the conversion of the heathen, the success of missions, now, to-day and everywhere, justify the divine foresight of Him Who said, signifying what death He should die, "And I if I be lifted from the earth will draw all men unto Me."

The laws under which we live may be referred to several groups, systems or codes, each of them having some peculiarity of its own.

1st. All the laws of number and quantity are absolute: two and two will make four, and will not, and cannot, make five, however much we may wish it, pray for it, or suffer if it be not so done. Three straight lines meeting will make a triangle, and one of the sides will be shorter than the sum of the other two.

2d. Some years ago Whewell made an argument[1] to show that in any possible universe, where there

---

[1] *Astronomy*, (Bridgewater Treatise), especially B. II.

should be more than one object, and it would not be a *universe* without a good many more than one, these objects must attract each other in a formula or law which we may express by the words "in proportion to their quantity of matter and inversely as the square of their distances." I regarded his argument as a success at the time and have seen no reason to change my view since.

3d. It is pretty well settled now, that if there are to be more than one material object, the objects must be in motion, and all the laws of motion can be determined *a priori* and are in accordance with the formulæ of analytical geometry and the calculus. This results from their nature as inert masses. They must also all revolve around one another and around a common centre, or be kept in motion by some intelligent Power, such as God alone can exert.

4th. The laws of chemical combination, if they are not fixed and determined *a priori* as the laws of motion are, as there seems some reason for supposing them to be, are nevertheless fixed; and so in harmony with the other laws, even the laws of mathematics, that it would seem that there can be but very little that is in any sense of the word arbitrary or that could have been otherwise than it is, or harmonize with another system even if such a thing had been desirable.

Now these four systems of laws make up most of the system of nature in which we have our earthly existence. Could they have been other than they are? Would it have been better if they had been different? Is there anything in these laws that militates against the doctrines of a Providence and a thoroughly righteous Moral Government of the world? If a man conforms to them he is happy and prosperous, so far as their influence can make or mar his happiness or his prosperity. And if he is not in conformity with them whose fault is it, his or theirs?

When, however, we come to consider man we enter a new realm. We have now to deal with spontaneity and to consider actions that cannot be reduced to, or expressed in, the formulæ of mathematics, kinds and modes of action that cannot be foreseen or calculated *a priori*.

Let us now look at this system in which man is placed and of which he is a part, *from man himself*, as our point of observation and see how he stands related to the other things that with him make up the system of which he is part.

Man's body is made of the same chemical elements as the other masses of matter around him and is obedient to the same laws. It is by his mind or soul alone that he differs from them. But by this alone he can understand them, and understanding them and knowing the laws by which they act, he can control them to a great extent; so far, indeed, that the whole face and surface of nature and the course of its events, become changed and totally different in consequence of his presence and agency from what it would be if he were not there. This chapel, these seats, and the waves of air by which I arrest your attention and make you partakers of my thoughts, are all the results of man's presence, and would not be at all but for him.

1st. In the first place, let us remember that man is an *intelligent* being; he can understand the nature of the things around him and the laws by which they act. He can in consequence (1) adapt himself to them or (2), what is perhaps far more important, he can control their operations to a large extent. He cannot, indeed, arrest or suspend the law of gravity, but he can protect himself against a fall. He cannot change the laws of heat and cold, but he can build a fire that will keep him from freezing. He cannot change the laws of chemical combination and analysis; but he can so select and combine the articles of food that he takes into his system that they will digest and be assimilated, instead of producing indigestion, disease and death.

In this way he can exert a "providence" over

affairs, and for his own good, which is analogous to that which God Himself exercises for us, and which is about as far above what the lowest animals can do, as it is necessary that that which He exercises over us should be, in order that it may accomplish all that is claimed for it by Natural Theology.

I wish to emphasize this point somewhat, because I am here speaking not of supernatural interventions by way of miracles. I have said all that I propose to say on this occasion on that subject in a preceding Lecture. What I am speaking of here is the *ordinary* Providence of God in the affairs of Life. This has two branches, (1) the internal, in which He influences the thoughts and wills of men, as in the example of the passenger saved from a steamboat calamity, cited in the last Lecture, and (2) the other in the outward world, exercising there, as I have said, an influence which is analogous in kind, though far above in degree, to that which man is constantly exercising.

On this point I propose to confirm what I have said by citations from two or three authorities, each of which will be recognized as foremost in his kind.

Thus Tyndall, speaking for the men of physical science, says, *Fragments*, p. 468, "The theory that the system of nature is under the control of a Being who changes phenomena in compliance with the prayers of men is, in my opinion, a perfectly legitimate one. It may of course be rendered futile by being associated with conceptions that contradict it; but such conceptions form no necessary part of the theory."

Then, as representing the metaphysicians and logicians, I quote John Stuart Mill, *Theism*, p. 136: "Science contains nothing repugnant to the supposition that every event which takes place results from a specific [note the word 'specific'] volition of the presiding Power, provided that this Power adheres in its particular volitions to general laws laid down by itself."

Here is all that my argument calls for, and all that we can ask. Herbert Spencer, as we have seen several times, admits all this, and more than this. "We are *obliged*," he says (§ 27), "to regard every phenomenon as a manifestation of some Power by which we are acted upon." And again (§ 34), "Every man may properly consider himself as one of the myriad agencies through whom works the Unknown Cause, and when the Unknown Cause produces in him a certain belief," etc.

Here the Divine influence in external nature is spoken of as that which we are "obliged to admit," and the action *in* and *upon* the mind as what we may "properly believe" and act upon.

If Spencer would change his phraseology and call Him the Incomprehensible instead of the Unknown and the Unknowable, we could agree with most of what he says of God, and he would, moreover, be calling Him by a name that indicates all that his premises call for or justify. For surely, as has been well said, He of whom so much may be said cannot be regarded as unknowable or as altogether unknown.

2d. In the next place, man can greatly *change himself* by his own acts. There is hardly anything by way of virtue, moral excellence or good habits, that one may not acquire and make of it a sort of second nature to himself, by the power of will and self-control which he possesses. In this he is totally unlike the masses and molecules of inanimate matter. Nothing that they can devise or do will change their nature or properties, make them better or more adapted to things that surround them in their environments. What they were made to be that they must remain and continue to be to the end.

3d. Then again, man can suffer. And here we reach the central point of our subject. A *thing* falls and breaks, but does not suffer or feel pain. A *man* falls, breaks a limb, and is in pain and suffers disability for a long time. This is a controlling fact, and gives significance to the other three facts in man's constitution and nature just named. (1) He can understand the laws of nature and conform his acts to them. (2) He can control the operation of other things to some extent so as to bring events much more nearly into accordance with his will and judgment as to what is right, than they would otherwise be, and (3) he can so mould and change himself as to bring his own nature, his "second nature," to a large extent, into harmony with whatever there is in "the constitution and course of nature" that he cannot change; and he may thus grow in strength and righteousness of character, to an extent to which we know no limit and to which probably no limit can be prescribed.

Man's relations to these things and his experience with them is under three codes of laws.

1st. In the lower there is no such thing as pardon, favor, or consideration of persons, their character, their worth or worthlessness, their aims whether good or bad, their ignorance of the law, or their knowledge of it, their mistakes or their misfortunes. We say "the burnt child dreads the fire." By that bit of experience he has learned one fact and a law of nature; he has made a beginning of scientific attainment. By a repetition of such experiments he soon learns that the recurrence of the phenomena under the same circumstances is uniform, and that the operation of the laws of nature is inexorable.

But he has acquired a new instinct also. He now *dreads*, and *shrinks from*, the burning taper. He generalizes and applies his conclusion and extends his instinct to the burning coals, the heated iron, and whatever else has the appearance of a burning heat.

Now in this we have the philosophy of a large share of man's education. He studies into and learns the laws of nature and becomes a man of scientific attainments. He learns also to respect and obey those laws as something that are immeasurably his superior, something to which he must submit and conform, or be crushed and killed by them. They will not respect him, and he learns to respect them.

But does he suffer the consequences every time he transgresses nature's laws? This is the law. The mere inanimate objects of nature can make no exceptions, show no favor, exercise no mercy or forbearance. They are not intelligent moral agents; they have no power of choice, no spontaneity of action.

And yet I think it manifest that, for some reason or another, we do not suffer the consequence for "one in a thousand" of our faults of this kind. Hundreds go to sea in ships that are unseaworthy and escape, arriving safely to the haven where they would be. But by and by a ship goes down, and some are lost. All were offenders, though possibly most of them knew it not. And yet most of them escaped. Few suffered, and a few only, what all, from a mere natural point of view, were liable to and perhaps deserved, and what they certainly had exposed themselves to.

Now I think here is evidence of providential interference and of goodness in the exercise of Moral Government.

They, therefore, who would exclude pain from the universe would exclude wrong doing and with it the possibility of the highest excellence and the crowning glory of the universe. It has been suggested that for those whose hearts are evil, the restraint and constraint which would keep them from doing and saying what ought not to be done and said, and compel them always to act and speak right and do what ought to be done whether they feel like it or not, would be the worst of pains, the very $\kappa \acute{o} \lambda \alpha \sigma \iota \nu$ $\grave{\alpha} \iota \acute{\omega} \nu \iota o \nu$ which our Lord threatens as the doom of the finally impenitent. In this view those who complain of the present constitution of the universe would seem to be about as unreasonable as if they were to complain that two and two will not sometimes be five, or that a crooked line will not sometimes be the shortest between two points, when it suits their convenience to have it so.

This form of objection is very old, as old as St. Augustine at least. He said in view of it that there are some things which God cannot do because He is omnipotent. *Quædam non potest quia omnipotens est.* They are not questions of power, whether of *omni*potence or *im*potence, but only of the feasibility of the things themselves. A space enclosed between two straight lines is no space. The intersection of two parallel lines and such like fictions are no questions or tests of wisdom or of power. They are not merely inconceivable; they are simply nothings.

And this is in accordance with the common sense of mankind. We speak of things as easy or as difficult. But when we so speak of them we do it under the idea that they are in themselves feasible, possible or practicable. Hence we speak of those who can do only the easy things as weak, whether in body or in mind, and of those that can do the more difficult as strong, comparatively, and of Him that can do all things that are in themselves feasible or conceivable, we say that He is omnipotent, able to do all things. And it is only when the thing is confessedly possible, and sustains some relation to power, that we so speak of it or of him that can do it. But to make two straight lines enclose a space is no more within the reach of the strongest, whether in mind or in body, than of him who is the weakest or has no power and even no existence.[1]

We have seen that man can intervene and change to some extent the course of events. The forces of nature are indeed wild horses, but man can tame them and make them subservient to his purposes, as well as destructive of his life and happiness. He can guide the fire so that it will burn the gas that lightens his study, or the coal that warms his dwelling, so that it will consume the noisome nuisance of decaying matter or become the conflagration of the city that destroys the homes and lives of thousands of human beings. But he cannot make it consume the granite mountain or burn all the waters of the ocean.

And assuredly God can do more than man in

---

[1] There is much in Mill's line of argument that reminds me of the question said to have been proposed by the bewildered Sunday school boy to his teacher: "Please, sir, can God make a stone so big that He can't lift it"?

I do not know what answer was given to the poor boy's question, but I presume it was answered in some way to save the "infinite power" of God.

I have often heard, however, among the unsophisticated country people, with their strong, practical common sense, the remark that "God cannot make two mountains without a valley between them." The remark, however, was never regarded by them as any impeachment of His attributes, whether His goodness or His power, but it was intended rather as a rebuke to those who were expecting unreasonable things.

controlling and guiding the forces of nature in the production of events. He can "*intervene*" without "*interfering*"—in the offensive sense of the word—to show mercy and exercise loving kindness. He can send the rain in time of need, or avert the coming pestilence, if to Him it seems good to do so. It is idle and vain to say that we know the laws of nature well enough to deny His Providence in such matters. To say that He *cannot* intervene is impertinent and blasphemous. To say that He *does* not is mere assumption. Nothing short of omniscience can assert a universal negative of that kind.

It is well for scientific men to assume, and for the purposes of mere science they must assume, that everything in nature occurs regularly and *as though* there were nothing concerned in its production but the forces and laws of nature—the forces that we can see and handle and the laws that we can learn by observation and generalization. But then we must admit, also, that there is no one fact or event in nature that man knows so well and understands so thoroughly that he can say that God was not concerned as an Agent in its production; that God was not "acting" in it, to use Spencer's expression; that it was not the result of a "specific volition" on His part, to use Mill's expression; or, to use the still stronger one of Tyndall, that it was not a phenomenon that had been "changed" by Him "in compliance with the prayers of men."

In this way, and to this extent, we may all very properly confess to an agnosticism.

It is much more probable, therefore, in view of what we do know that He overrules and guides all things, leaving us to suffer only when, or as, it is for our own good that we should do so.

For man will not learn without suffering. It is only the "burnt" child that dreads the fire. And I think we are fast approaching the conviction that throughout the whole realm of nature, man suffers in this way no more than is good for, perhaps no more than is indispensable to, his progress in knowledge and virtue.

2d. I now reach the second code of laws under which man lives. And here I can be much more brief. In this domain he is to be considered as in relation to his fellow-men. Here we soon learn that certain courses of action produce good-will, and a disposition to respect and favor us; while actions of an opposite character produce quite different results, such as loss of character, of the respect and good-will, and even of the charity and forbearance of others. We see, also, that these courses of action have a relation to moral laws, and that by these laws certain kinds of actions are seen to be right as well as pleasing to others.

But the main feature of the case, now to be considered, is the fact that these agents are not like the mere inert masses around us. They are intelligent moral beings. They can consider our case, make excuses where excuses are deserved. They can show favor and make exceptions to the enforcement of general rules. They can exercise forgiveness and forbearance where none are deserved. With them ignorance of a law is often an excuse—good intentions are accepted for right performances. Mistakes are often corrected so that we get credit for the good which we intended, instead of suffering for the evil we actually, though unintentionally, wrought for fellow-men. Here we experience the interference and exercise of a moral government by our fellow-men, tempered and softened, though not always so by compassion, by sympathy and tenderest love.

3d. But we rise to a higher region than this; to a purely spiritual experience, a world of supernatural life, in which a different law prevails and religion forms the controlling element.

And as I wish to connect with the discussion of it, another principle of a more general character and application, I will turn aside for a few moments to consider it.

It is the use which God in His Providence makes of wicked men and their wicked deeds.

Why sin is in the world I do not know and shall make no attempt to explain. I shall not even offer a conjecture. But it is here; and we can see much good that is accomplished by it, which, so far as we can see, could no more have been accomplished without sin and suffering than man could have been made to study into, learn, respect and use those laws of nature which make up our science and make us masters of the world, subjecting all things in it to our use, without the pain that follows upon the violation.

And I put the two together. I think we are fast approaching the conclusion, even if we have not yet already reached it, that there is no suffering in this world without some previous transgression of some one or more of the laws, moral or physical, of nature or of grace, under which we live. Hence suffering, though it does not always fall upon the offender himself, is nevertheless always a sign and a reminder of a law that has been broken and violated, though quite possibly not yet fully known. It is a hint and a stimulus to inquiry and discovery. It is also a spur and an incitement towards the formation of a new habit, the acquiring of a new element in our second nature, and thus bringing us into a nearer conformity to a higher state of law and of life. We grow by means of it, both in knowledge and in grace, in strength of character and in nearness to our ideal standard of perfection.

Now the way in which, both in history and in individual life, God brings good out of evil and makes even "the wrath of man to praise him," is to me one of the most striking proofs of Providence, working for a purpose in history and in the exercise of Moral Government.

Take a case in history for illustration, the crucifixion of our Lord. And in discussing it I assume nothing as to its dogmatic character or theological bearing. I look at it only as a matter of history.

He was a just and holy man, in whom there was no guile, no cause or justification for His death. Yet His enemies hated Him most bitterly, and put Him to death. One of His own disciples and trusted friends betrayed him. Of course the fault, the mistake, the crime and the guilt, were all their own.

But we risk nothing in saying that if He had not been put to death in some such manner, His religion would never have taken root in the world; and the greatest step in the advancement of humanity to a higher level and a cleaner and holier mode of life, would have proved a failure from the outset.

Who then should put Him to death? Who deliver Him up to be crucified? Surely no friend could do it; no loving disciple could be guilty of such a thing. No one that feared God and loved righteousness above all things else, could have thought of it. No devotee of the doctrine of expediency could ever have persuaded himself that, in this case, the end would justify the means. And yet, betrayers and murderers were found, men who had no conscientious scruples at the time, whatever may have been the case with some of them, as Judas for example, afterwards. God used them for the accomplishment of his purposes. He made them no worse than they were, and if we may presume to judge in such a case, He showed them no mercy on account of the most blessed results, that He, by His providence and grace, brought out of their act.

And the case gains unspeakably in breadth of significance and in the depth of its pathos when we view it in the light of the Christian doctrine of the Atonement and the Redemption of mankind.

Now history is full of such examples, although, of course, on a vastly smaller scale. In fact, it seems sometimes almost as if God could not well get along, govern this world, and work out what are manifestly His purposes in history, without His enemies and the use He makes of them to do His work, His strange work; just as it has been said of the Queen of England, that she could scarcely get along and administer the affairs of her Empire without what has been facetiously called "her majesty's opposition," as well as the assistance and co-operation of her friends and loyal subjects.

But I must hasten to my closing thought, which is, to my mind, the crowning glory of the whole subject. It may be stated as the doctrine, that there is no pain or suffering in this world that we may not, by such means and aids as are always at our command, turn to our own good.

I am willing to admit that this doctrine cannot be fully made out without the recognition of a future life into which the results of discipline, if not the economy of rewards and punishments, must enter, and in which growth in knowledge and in grace are possible. And although I have not made any effort in these Lectures to prove the future life of rewards and punishments, as one of the doctrines of Natural Theology, I think, that in view of what has been said by others in the pursuit of the methods I have been vindicating, I have a right to assume that doctrine, so far at least as my present object requires that it should be regarded as a doctrine of Natural Theology.

I think, indeed, that the argument for a future life which may be derived from the facts and laws I have been considering, is overwhelmingly strong.

If we regard this world and this life as a scene for the highest and the greatest amount of mere *animal* enjoyment for such a being as man, it may indeed well be considered, as Mill has called it, an "ignominious failure."[1] But is it not wiser, more logical and scientific, as well as a safer and more prudent way, to infer from all we know of God and of nature, that this is not the last or the highest state of existence for man? Does not everything, in fact, tend to show that this world and this life for man is only a part of a far more comprehensive plan? a something hereafter that gives a new meaning and importance to all there is here?

And in this connection I am willing, and more than willing, to forego and repudiate what is sometimes offered by way of answer to the objection to the doctrine of a Moral Government growing out of the fact of suffering, namely, the consideration of the insignificance of the individual man, the unspeakable nothingness of his significance and worth in comparison with the general good of the whole. I am quite willing to admit that, in this respect, each man is to himself infinitely valuable. What good to him if the universe flourishes and prospers and he himself is annihilated and become extinct? What to him the happiness of millions, if he is consigned

---

[1] *Theism*, p. 192.

to everlasting woe? to the regions of the lost and the despised and damned? Their happiness is nothing to him. The only thought there can be which, so far as I can imagine, can be of any comfort or alleviation to him, is the thought that he has deserved his doom; that God is just and holy and merciful, though he suffers what no tongue can tell, no heart but that of him who has endured it can conceive. And the being that can entertain such a thought under such circumstances is not far from the kingdom of heaven; and from all the ideas and thoughts that Natural Theology can suggest, it is evident he will soon be there, in the midst of its glories and enjoyments.

I cannot tell, or pretend to, why children die. In some cases we see that from circumstances of disease or deformity life to them could be no scene of happiness if it should be prolonged. In others, we see that they are taken away from the evil to come, and in all, we may hope that they only go before us, and earlier than we do, to that world where we must all be gathered at last.

But to the kindred question, why do the righteous suffer? we can offer a very different answer. This question presents a problem of an entirely different kind.

It is a doctrine now well understood that there is

no coming to a right mind, no growth in grace, no attainment in the higher qualities of intelligence and moral excellence, without a good deal of pain and suffering. This is a doctrine which, although Christ may have first taught it to the world, has now become confirmed by the experience and the philosophy of the last eighteen centuries.

This is true in intellectual growth. The child gets its first lesson in thermotics by the pain in the burnt finger. As we grow old we grow cautious. We learn to regard very slight indications and to take many gentle hints. But the terrible rod of chastisement is always there for the heedless and the careless, for the presumptuous adventurer and the trifler. And in this sphere there is seldom any amends that can be made, or any escape from the penalty once inflicted. The palsied limb, the broken constitution, remain as both proofs and penalties of the transgression.

In the moral sphere we meet with the first instances of the higher administration of a moral government. Here repentance, if it is genuine and sincere, is always respected; amends for the evil done are always accepted; and the offender may be restored to the place in private affection or in public confidence, which, by his fall, he had lost. And here, too, it sometimes happens that one becomes stronger, both in character and in public confidence, after his transgression, by the intensity of his penitence. The thoroughness of his reform and the increased comprehension of, and faith in, the great moral principles that are alike the foundation of character and the source of strength and stability to all that is good and trustworthy in human life, often afford ground for a confidence that would not be otherwise felt.

But in the spiritual sphere we, for the first time, find the possibility of repentance, and amendment with complete recuperation, and full forgiveness. We find more. We find gain. We find the possibility of turning all evil into good, and out of any adversity, misfortune or suffering, that can possibly come upon us, whether it come from our own transgression or from the faults and wickedness of others, we may educe the pure gold, the sparkling gem, the pearl of great price and of priceless value, spiritual worth; though we lose the world, we gain our own souls.

There can be no need of an induction of examples to establish this truth. Enough is to be seen in the experience of every thoughtful person, enough in the life of every holy man or woman, every lofty and noble character that we have known, to suggest and illustrate the doctrine and to satisfy us of its truth.

But here as everywhere, as in each of the other spheres, the conditions are the same: faith and submission to the authority of Him who ordained the laws and still rules to enforce them.

With this experience comes deeper humiliation, more entire self-renunciation, with stronger faith, more earnestness of effort, and somehow, nobody perhaps can tell how, but there comes somehow a strength and a bounding upwards from earth and earthly things towards heaven and the highest and the holiest that we conceive of. The very things that these pessimists complain of come to be the very opportunity and means that are given us to become spiritually great and strong. They make what the world most honors. No man, after such an experience, doubts the goodness of God or the righteousness of His Moral Government. No one doubts His providence over all His works or His presence wherever a humble, penitent, believing soul needs his presence and help.[1]

---

[1] Mill rests his argument chiefly upon the amount of pain and suffering there is in the world. But I doubt very much whether the greatest sufferers are the greatest complainers. Those whom we most respect for their noble qualities, seldom complain or even so much as think that they have had anything to complain of. Nay, we have read of, if we have not seen, more than one who could "glory" in his infirmities and "rejoice" in his "tribulations," knowing that their "afflictions" worked for them a far more exceeding and eternal weight of glory.

It is hard to discover, and still more painful and humiliating to confess, that the remedy and the cure for all the ills of this life is in ourselves or within our reach. True, indeed, this fact does not become entirely clear and satisfactorily demonstrated until we can contemplate it as *Christians* and from the point of view of that reconciliation with God which He has wrought through Christ. In Him is our strength, our help, and our salvation.

But at any rate we can see enough by the light of nature alone, to justify us in the assertion that if we will but make the right use of it, nothing can occur to us that we cannot turn to our spiritual gain and come out the better for it in the end.

Of course this solution will not suit immoral men, worldly minded men and agnostics, who do not want to be anything but immoral or worldly minded. But I know of no way of making the world suit them without first making of them something quite different from what they now are, or intend to become. Evidently this world was not made for such as they wish to be, nor was the universe, of which we all are parts, arranged for such a life as they propose to lead, or for such an end of life as is the most and the best they hope for. But for those who will accept it, God has ordained and provided something better by way of remedy in this world and of reward in the next.

There was a Christian hero once of old who said, "I can do all things through Christ Who strengtheneth me." He, as he assures us, could rejoice even in tribulations. I think that with the same help we can do as much. He knew, and nobody had tested the matter more thoroughly, that "all things work together for the good of them that love God." There is a way by which we can all become "the children of God and heirs of the Kingdom of Heaven," making all the pains and sufferings of this life work out for us an exceeding and eternal weight of glory.[1]

---

[1] Mill is sometimes inclined to take rather a philanthropic view of the existence of evil and suffering. He says, *Theism*, p. 185:

"The imperfections in the attainment of the purposes which the appearances indicate, have not the air of having been designed. They are like the unintended results of accidents insufficiently guarded against."

Again, p. 193, "If man had not the power by the exercise of his own energies for the improvement both of himself and of his outward circumstances, to do for himself and other creatures, vastly more than God had in the first instance done, the Being who called him into existence would deserve something very different from thanks at his hands."

And this idea of working with God and helping Him to overcome the evils and difficulties that were too much for Him at the time of the creation, seems to be rather a favorite thought with Mr. Mill.

But oh, how different the spirit from that of St. Paul, "We, then, as *workers together with Him*, beseech you that ye receive not the grace of God in vain." With Mill, it is "help Him because He needs help"; with St. Paul, "help Him because He has helped us, and given His only begotten Son for us that we, through Him, need not perish, but might have everlasting life."

But the evil complained of is one for which I know no other remedy and for which I seem to see that there is a good reason why there should be no other. In this case Evolution cannot help us. Agnosticism is of no avail; for whatever else we may know or not know, there are evils in this life against which we are weak, helpless and hopeless, except as our help and our strength come from Christ through faith in Him and the ministrations of His Gospel. The terms may not suit our pride of intellect or our pride of heart. The reward that is promised may not be just such as we would choose if we were sure of getting what we choose. But there is a Wisdom and a Power that is above us, that has been at work in the past history of our race and in ten thousand instances in our own lives, "bringing us by ways that we knew not and leading us by paths that we had not known," to results that were far above, and far better than, any that we should have chosen if the choice had been left to ourselves. Cannot we trust Him?

And now, in conclusion, I think I have considered and disposed of all the objections that have been raised in these modern times or that can well be raised against the Methods and the Truths of Natural Theology, whether physical or metaphysical, logical or ontological. These truths, however, are at best of but very little value to us or to mankind at large, if we stop with them. I confess, however, that I have a much higher estimate of them and of their value to mankind than I should have had, had it not been for the testimony which St. Paul has borne in their favor. After speaking of the great truths of Natural Theology that are "manifest" in the works of creation, even "the eternal power and godhead or divinity of God," which makes those that reject Revelation "without excuse," he goes on to speak of the Gentiles who had had no means of knowing the gospel as "doing *by nature* the things that are written in the law," and says of them, if I understand him rightly, that they also, following this light of nature, will be saved, in the day of their final account, both theirs and ours alike, through the merits of Christ's atoning blood. If, then, these truths may be a guide to salvation for those who have had no opportunity to learn more of the Divine Will and of the way of salvation than these Methods can teach, they certainly deserve a higher estimate than we should otherwise be inclined to put upon them.

But for us, my brethren, their value, as I said at the beginning of these Lectures and now repeat in concluding them, consists, as I think, chiefly in the fact that they lead us to the doctrines of Revelation, and remove the objections that might otherwise prove insuperable obstacles to the reception of Him Whom it hath pleased the Father to make unto us " wisdom and righteousness and sanctification and redemption," and Whose Name is " the only Name under heaven given among men whereby we can be saved."

And now, after due thanks to those fathers and brethren by whose favor I have had this opportunity to say these words to you, I desire, if I have been able to say anything that will tend to promote the glory of God and the more effectual setting forward the salvation of men by the extension of the Redeemer's Kingdom, to render all gratitude and praise, all thanksgiving and honor, to Him who was and is and ever shall be, God over all blessed now and forevermore.

THE END.

www.ingramcontent.com/pod-product-compliance
Lightning Source LLC
Chambersburg PA
CBHW030429300426
44112CB00009B/913